SUNDAY

WEEKLY LEADER GUIDE

Sundays, Feast Days & Solemnities

Year A

SUNDAY WEEKLY LEADER GUIDE

Sundays, Feast Days & Solemnities
Year A

In Canada
NOVALIS

In England
T. SHAND PUBLICATIONS, Ltd.

In the United States
T R E E H A U S

TREEHAUS COMMUNICATIONS, INC. P.O. BOX 249, LOVELAND, OHIO 45140

[ ] Text that appears in brackets
    may be omitted by the reader.

United States Publisher
TREEHAUS COMMUNICATIONS, INC.
P.O. Box 249
Loveland, Ohio 45140

Canadian Publisher
NOVALIS
St. Paul University/Ottawa
P.O. Box 990
Outremont, Quebec
H2V 4S7

Great Britain Publisher
T. SHAND PUBLICATIONS, LTD.
The Chapel, St. Mary's Abbey
The Ridgeway
Mill Hill, London
England NW7-4HX

Nihil Obstat:
Rev. Donald Senior, C.P.,
Censor Deputatus.

Imprimatur:
Rev. James P. Roache, Vicar General,
Archdiocese of Chicago
November 6, 1989

The *Sunday Weekly Leader Guide* includes the adapted scripture texts
from *The Sunday Book of Readings Adapted for Children*
which has been endorsed for liturgical use in Canada by
The Episcopal Commission for Liturgy,
Canadian Conference of Catholic Bishops.

Printed and bound in the United States.

ISBN 0-929496-93-0

Contents

Contents

Holy Days, Feasts of the Lord, and Solemnities

PART TWO

* *In keeping with the* Directory For Masses With Children *(Paragraph 43), some of the readings assigned to the day have been changed when they appear "unsuited to the capacity of children." Changes have been made in the following occasions: Easter Sunday, Trinity Sunday, Body and Blood of Christ, All Souls, Dedication of St. John Lateran.*

The Seasons of Advent and Christmas

FIRST SUNDAY OF ADVENT

YEAR A

PRAYER OF THE DAY:

God, you love us so much
you want to be among us
and share your life with us.
Make us ready to welcome you
by following your ways
and living at peace
with one another.
We ask you to do this
through Christ, our Lord.

FOCUS OF THE READINGS:

Culturally, we are accustomed to thinking of all Advent as a preparation for the birth of Jesus. But liturgically, we find quite a different emphasis. Only on the fourth Sunday do we focus on the birth of Jesus, the Messiah. The first Sunday reminds us of the coming of Christ at the end of time. The second and third Sundays focus on the acceptance of Christ in our lives today, through baptism. It is this tension between the present and future that gives meaning to the fourth Sunday and indeed to our celebration of the historical birth at Christmas.

Our first reading speaks of a time when all will live in peace. This will come because one day everyone will know the house of God and everyone will follow God's ways. Given the human condition, we cannot expect this prophecy to be fulfilled in this world. The church wisely combines this hope-filled reading from *Isaiah* with today's Gospel which directs our attention to the last days.

The Gospel exhorts us to "stay awake" and be ready for the return of the Lord. We do not know the time, but we do know it will be a time of

FIRST READING: *Isaiah 2:1-5*

This is a reading from the prophet Isaiah.

After the prophet Isaiah had a vision,
this is what he said to the people of Jerusalem,

"The time is coming
  when everyone will know the house of God.
People of all nations will say,

  'Come, let us go to the house of God
    so that we may learn to follow God's ways.'

"God will decide what is right for the people.
When that day comes,
countries will not fight
against each other anymore.
Instead, people will take their swords
and make them into tools for farming the land.
They will take their spears
and make them into tools for pruning trees.
And there will never be war again.

"O people of God, come!
Let us walk in the light of God."

The Word of the Lord.

RESPONSE: *Psalm 122*

RESPONSE:
In the House of our God, in the House of our God, we give praise to the Lord in the House of our God.

VERSES:
1. I was glad when they said: "Let us go to God's house!" And now with joy we are standing.
2. It is here that we find peace for our families and friends, here that we find justice.

2

GOSPEL ACCLAMATION:

Stay a-wake, be read-y. You do not know the hour when the Lord is com-ing. Stay a-wake, be read-y. The Lord is com-ing soon! Al-le-lu-ia, al-le-lu-ia! "The Lord is com-ing soon."

*After Gospel, repeat Acclamation from here.

GOSPEL: *Matthew 24:42-44*

This is a reading from the Gospel of Matthew.

Jesus said to his disciples,

"Stay awake! Always be ready!
You do not know when your Lord is coming.

"You know that if the owners of a house
knew at what time of night a thief was coming,
they would stay awake
and would not allow the thief
to break into their house.

"Well, in the same way,
you must always be ready
because you do not know the time
when the Lord is coming."

The Gospel of the Lord.

justice and peace, as the first reading tells us. Like the early Christians, we are called by these readings to strive to learn the ways of the Lord and to bring about the peace and justice that will accompany the return of the Lord.

REFLECTING ON THE READINGS WITH CHILDREN:

NOTE: As a basic principle, it is important to have the children express what they heard in the readings. One need not do this by asking "What did you hear?" each time you gather. But once you set up that style of reflection, the children will naturally learn to participate by sharing what they have heard.

Give the children time to share what they have heard. Then help them see that we usually prepare for events because we know when they are expected. For example, we prepare for Christmas now because we know that it is celebrated on December 25th. We prepare for a birthday party because we know the date of the birthday. But Jesus tells us today that we do not know the date when he will return, and so we must always be prepared for that great event. We must be ready to meet him when he comes.

How do you think we can be ready? What does Jesus mean, "be ready"? What would you want to be doing when Jesus comes? Would you want to be at war or fighting someone?

Ask the children what the prophet Isaiah told us about this special time.

Help the children see that we can always be ready by trying to make peace instead of war. Be sure the children understand this in terms of their own lives rather than focusing on world peace. Children are not responsible for international conflicts, but they can relate to making peace in their families, schools, with friends, etc.

The children should leave today believing that we are waiting for a day of joy and peace and that there are things we can do to be ready for it.

3

SECOND SUNDAY OF ADVENT

YEAR A

PRAYER OF THE DAY:

Forgiving God,
help us prepare
for your coming by being sorry
for what we have done wrong.
Fill us with your power
so that we may know you
and love you more and more,
and let all the world
live in peace.
We ask you to do this
through our friend and brother,
Jesus Christ, who lives forever.

FOCUS ON READINGS:

Last Sunday we were urged to watch"for the second coming of Christ. This Sunday, as well as next Sunday, the readings focus our attention on the present and move us toward the theme of the Incarnation on the last Sunday of Advent.

In the first reading, Isaiah presents the qualities hoped for with each new king in the line of David. He tells us of one who is coming to fulfill these ideals. He will bring peace and justice, and he will judge everyone fairly because he will be anointed by the Spirit of God.

John the Baptist speaks of one who is to come who will baptize with the Holy Spirit. He is preparing the people for the ministry of Jesus; the acceptance of Jesus requires that they change their lives.

FIRST READING: *Isaiah 11:1-4a, 6, 9-10*

This is a reading from the prophet Isaiah.

This is what the prophet Isaiah said to the people of Israel about a child who will be born in the family of Jesse.

This child will be filled with the Spirit of God,
the spirit of wisdom and understanding,
the spirit of strength and truth,
the spirit of knowledge and love of God.
The one who is coming
will not judge by what people look like
or by what others say
but will judge the poor with justice and fairness.
Then the wolf will live with the lamb.
The leopard and the goat will rest together.
The calf and the lion will eat together
and be at peace,
and a little child will lead them all.
This child will be a sign for all the world.
Then no one will hurt others anymore
because everyone will know God.

The Word of the Lord.

RESPONSE: *Psalm 72*

RESPONSE:
For all that you do we wor-ship you, we wor-ship you, we wor-ship you. For wor-ship you.

VERSES:
1. You will bring jus-tice and peace. _____ For
2. You save the weak and the poor. _____
3. We praise the good that you do. _____
4. Peo-ple will know of your name. _____

4

GOSPEL ACCLAMATION:

Change your lives, he's com-ing. The one who will baptize with the Ho-ly Spir-it. Change your lives, he's
com-ing. The reign of God is near!
Al-le-lu-ia, al-le-lu-ia! "The reign of God is near."

*After Gospel, repeat Acclamation from here.

GOSPEL: *Matthew 3:1-6, 11*

This is a reading from the Gospel of Matthew.

When John the Baptist
went to the desert to preach,
he always said to the people,

"Change your lives!
The reign of God is near!"

Long ago, Isaiah, the prophet,
was talking about John the Baptist
when he said,

"There is someone in the desert
who is proclaiming,

'Prepare the way for the coming of God!
Make a straight path
for the coming of God!' "

John wore clothes
that were made of camel's hair,
and he wore a leather belt around his waist,
and he ate locusts and wild honey.
Many people went to the desert
to see John and confessed their sins.
John baptized them in the Jordan River
and told them,

"I am baptizing you in water
to change your lives.
But someone is coming after me
who is more powerful than I am.
He will baptize you with the Holy Spirit."

The Gospel of the Lord.

REFLECTING ON THE READINGS WITH CHILDREN:

Isaiah uses images of various animals living together in harmony to depict the peace that will be realized with the coming of the Messiah.

These images will, naturally, appeal to children. You might want to ask them questions such as:

- What happens when you leave a cat alone in a room with a goldfish?
- Would you leave a tiny puppy alone with a wolf?
- What do you think the prophet Isaiah was trying to tell us when he said that a wolf and lamb would get along? Or that a leopard and a goat will eat together and a bear and a lion will be friendly? Do these animals usually get along well together? What do you think Isaiah meant by using these examples? Isaiah tells us that someone is coming to bring this kind of peace. Why will this child be able to bring peace and justice? What special help will he have? (You may want to reread the section from the first reading which describes the Spirit of God.)

Help the children see that Isaiah reminds us that God wants us to live in justice and peace and not to hurt one another. It is with God's Spirit that we are able to bring about justice and peace in the world. Remind the children that because we are baptized, we, too, have the Spirit of God and can make good and right decisions that will help us live in peace. Help the children see that John the Baptist came to encourage people to change their lives—to live more justly—to prepare for the coming of Jesus.

Discuss with them ways that we can truly change our own lives as we prepare to celebrate the coming of Jesus.

5

THIRD SUNDAY OF ADVENT

YEAR A

PRAYER OF THE DAY:

Give us strength,
build up our courage,
mighty God,
because we are sometimes
weak and afraid.
You sent Jesus
to make the sick better
and to be a friend of the poor.
May we believe in him
and be happy
that you always support us.
We pray to you
through Jesus, our Lord.

FOCUS OF THE READINGS:

Today's readings speak of the signs that reveal God's presence among us.

The first reading is a prophecy addressed to the people of God in exile in Babylon. Israel has become a wasteland. The holy city, Jerusalem, is in ruins and is occupied by foreigners. The people feel empty, dry and deserted, but the prophet encourages them to keep hope. With bright images of a land which will rejoice and bloom, Isaiah urges the people to have courage and not to fear.

For most of the year, large parts of Palestine are barren of all vegetation. When Isaiah speaks of the desert blooming with many flowers, he is speaking of a real transformation of nature. Such a transformation would surely reveal the power and glory of God—just so, says Isaiah, when those who are blind can see; those who are deaf can hear; those who are lame can walk, and those who are captive return in joy. This too will reveal the power and glory of our God.

In the Gospel, John the Baptist sends messengers to ask if Jesus is the Messiah, the long-awaited one. Jesus responds with a litany of the signs which were prophesied throughout the Old Testament as the manifestation of God's saving presence. Jesus simply invites the seeker of the Messiah to look at the signs.

As we prepare for the coming of Christ, the Messiah, the liturgy recalls God's promise and its fulfillment in Jesus.

FIRST READING: *Isaiah 35:1-6, 10*

This is a reading from the prophet Isaiah.

This is what the prophet Isaiah said:

"Let the desert be glad,
and the dry lands be filled with flowers.
Let everyone rejoice, singing for joy.
For they will see the glory
and the wonder of our God.

"Say to those who are weak and frightened,

'Be strong!
Have courage!
Do not be afraid.
Your God is coming with justice
to reward and save you.'

"Then those who are blind will be able to see;
those who are deaf will be able to hear;
those who are crippled will jump like deer,
and those who could not talk will sing."

The Word of the Lord.

RESPONSE: *Psalm 72*

RESPONSE: For all that you do we wor-ship you, we wor-ship you, we wor-ship you. For wor-ship you.

VERSES:
1. Glo - ry and praise to your name. _____ For
2. You come like rain to the earth. _____
3. You will bring jus - tice and peace. _____
4. You save the weak and the poor. _____
5. You give us bless - ings and joy. _____

GOSPEL ACCLAMATION

Go back, tell John all that you have heard and have seen me do-ing. Go back, tell John the won-ders that you see! Al-le-lu-ia, al-le-lu-ia! "The won-ders that you see."

*After Gospel, repeat Acclamation from here.

GOSPEL: *Matthew 11:2-6*

This is a reading from the Gospel of Matthew.

While John was in prison,
he heard about the things Christ was doing.
So he sent messengers to ask Jesus,

"Are you the one
we have been waiting for?"

Jesus said to them,

"Go back and tell John
what you see and hear.
People who were blind can see.
Those who were crippled can walk.
Those who had leprosy are cured.
Those who were deaf can hear.
People who were dead are raised to life,
and the Good News
is being preached to the poor.
Blessed is everyone who believes in me!"

The Gospel of the Lord.

REFLECTING ON THE READINGS WITH CHILDREN:

What did you hear? Encourage the children to recall the images of *Isaiah* and the signs of Jesus.

In about two weeks it will be Christmas. We have been waiting for a long time. We are already preparing the manger and gifts. Our streets are decorated with lights. Stores are crowded with shoppers. But where is Jesus? How will we recognize him in all of the activities of Christmas, all the parties, the shopping, the lights, the music?

The people of God had been waiting for a long time too. They waited for the Messiah, the one who would come to save them. And they wondered too: How will we recognize the Messiah? Will the Messiah be a queen, a king, perhaps the leader of an army or a farmer? How were they to know when the Messiah would come? What would be the sign that would tell them?

John the Baptist, while he was in prison, asked these same questions: How are we to know if Jesus is the Messiah for whom we have been waiting, or should we wait for someone else? What signs will show us if Jesus is the Messiah?

John sent his messengers to ask Jesus, "Are you the Messiah?" How did Jesus answer? He reminded them of what the prophet Isaiah had said. Do you remember what Isaiah told us about the Messiah? What signs would we see?

Jesus told the messengers of John, "Go tell John what you see and hear—those who were blind can see; those who were deaf can hear...."

Do we see any signs of God's presence among us today? When we see sick people being healed, sadness being turned into joy, people helping one another, these are signs that Jesus is here.

Who are the people today who are waiting for the Messiah? Who are the blind, the deaf, the crippled, the poor?

Do you know some who help these people? These helpers show us that the Messiah is with us. (Help the children identify people they actually know in their family, parish, community, neighborhood.)

Jesus wants to be their Messiah. He calls us to help these people in his name, to bring the Good News of the Messiah to all the people around us.

FOURTH SUNDAY OF ADVENT

YEAR A

PRAYER OF THE DAY:

God, you chose
ordinary people,
common people,
to make a home for Jesus.
We want to make a home
for him in our hearts.
Give us the love to do this,
and let him be our brother,
forever and ever.

FOCUS OF THE READINGS:

Both of our readings for today speak of the intervention of God in human history and call us to trust in the signs that reveal the power of God.

In our first reading, Isaiah speaks of a sign that will assure King Ahaz that God will intervene on his behalf and save Judah from the threat of Syria and Israel. The sign will be the birth of a baby to a young maiden, and the child will be called Emmanuel. While this most probably referred to the birth of the King's son, Hezekiah, and, therefore, the preservation of the Davidic line of kings, Matthew has interpreted it to refer to the birth of Jesus.

In our Gospel for today, we have the Annunciation to Joseph. God reveals the birth of a son to the virgin, Mary, by the power of the Holy Spirit. Like the first reading, the focus is on the saving intervention of God in human history.

REFLECTING ON THE READINGS WITH CHILDREN:

Ask the children what they heard in the Gospel.

FIRST READING: *Isaiah 7:10-14*

This is a reading from the prophet Isaiah.

Isaiah said to King Ahaz,

"Ask God to give you a sign
(so you will know what to do.)
Ask anything you wish, large or small."

But Ahaz answered,

"No, I won't ask for a sign.
I will not tempt God!"

Then Isaiah said to Ahaz,

"Listen, you have already caused problems
for our people;
must you make God tired as well?
But God will give you a sign anyway!
And this is what the sign will be—
A virgin will give birth to a child,
and she will call him Emmanuel."

The Word of the Lord.

RESPONSE: *Psalm 80*

1st time: Leader; 2nd time: All

God our Shep-herd and Lord, let your face shine on us. face shine on us.

Leader: *Shine on us and we shall be saved.* All: Shine on us and we shall be saved.

GOSPEL ACCLAMATION:

By the pow'r of the Spir-it Ma-ry will give birth to a Son called Je-sus. By the pow'r of the Spir-it Em-man-u-el is near! Al-le-lu-ia, a-le-lu-ia! "Em-man-u-el is near."

*After Gospel, repeat Acclamation from here.

GOSPEL: *Matthew 1:18-24*

This is a reading from the Gospel of Matthew.

This is how the birth of Christ came about.
Mary, his mother,
was engaged to a man called Joseph.
But before they lived together,
they found that she was going to have a child
by the power of the Holy Spirit.
Now Joseph was a good man,
so he decided to break their engagement quietly.
But an angel of God came to Joseph in a dream
and said,

"Joseph, do not be afraid
to take Mary as your wife.
It is by the power of the Holy Spirit
that she is going to have a son.
You are to give him the name Jesus, because
he will save his people from their sins."

All of this happened so that what God said
through the prophet Isaiah
would be made clear—

"A virgin will give birth to a child,
and she will name him Emmanuel.
This name means, 'God is with us.' "

When Joseph woke up,
he did what the angel of God told him.
He took Mary into his home as his wife.

The Gospel of the Lord.

Caution: because we are accustomed to the Annunciation to Mary in the Gospel of Luke, which we will hear next year, we may overlook here what is truly the Annunciation to Joseph. Help the children see the story as Matthew tells it, from Joseph's point of view.

The Infancy Narratives, which include the Annunciation, birth and infancy of Jesus, were written as a sort of a preface to the entire message of the Gospel. They contain profound theological teachings told in story form with concrete imagery. Because of the many rich and beautiful customs that have developed around these stories, the children retain these concrete images and probably assume that the stories, with all their details, are actual accounts of the birth of Jesus. While it is nearly impossible to keep the children from taking these stories literally, we can help them to discover, at least partially, the deeper meaning intended by the evangelists. Children, as we do, will continue to cherish these images while continuing to grow in a deeper understanding of their meaning for our lives. It seems appropriate to encourage the joy children have in these vivid stories, which do, in fact, create images for them of the love of God expressed in the mystery of the Incarnation.

Dealing with "she conceived a child by the power of the Holy Spirit" is not easy for adults, much less children! What is important here is that the children see that God acts in our lives to be with us, sometimes in a surprising and even startling way. Matthew means to highlight here that Jesus is truly "Emmanuel . . . God with us" and that he is our Savior.

Talk about the two names given to Jesus in this story—Emmanuel and Savior. What do they mean? Ask the children why it is important to have God with us today. Ask the children if they think the world needs a Savior now. Do we, each of us personally, need a Savior? What does Jesus save us from? How can our lives be different because of Jesus? How can we help others to see that God is truly with us, and with them?

CHRISTMAS DAY

YEAR A

PRAYER OF THE DAY:

God in heaven,
you never forget we need you,
and that is why
you sent your son, Jesus,
to be born as a baby
like one of us.
We thank you
for such a tremendous gift
and praise Jesus
who is mighty God
and prince of peace,
now and forever.

FOCUS OF THE READINGS:

The Gospel for Christmas Day is taken
from the prologue of John's Gospel
(1:1-18). This magnificent hymn of the
Incarnation is perhaps one of the most
beautiful passages in all of scripture. But,
its language, at once poetic and highly
theological, is scarcely understood by
children. We have, therefore, chosen to
use the nativity story of *Luke* which is
proclaimed at the Mass of Midnight and
Dawn.

While it too is highly theological
(please see "Introduction to the Infancy
Narratives," p. 163), it is written in a
language children can understand and
enjoy. They may miss many of the
theological references, but they will surely
understand the joy and excitement which
accompanies our salvation. They will
understand the great love God has for us
as expressed in this event. And this, we
suggest, is the focus of our readings:
God's great love for the world—God's
great gift to the world. Into a world of
darkness and sin, a child is born, bringing
light and peace. The Gospel proclaims,
"Do not be afraid. I bring you good news.
A Savior has been born for you."

*Rejoice, all people on earth! Today a
Savior is born for you, Christ the Lord!*

FIRST READING: *Isaiah 9:2a-3a, 6-7*

This is a reading from the prophet Isaiah.

The people who were in darkness
have seen a great light.
You, God, have filled them with great joy.

For a child is born to us;
a son is given to us.
He is called:

"Wonderful Counselor,
the Mighty God,
the One Who Lives Forever,
the Prince of Peace."

His kingdom will be great.
He will rule with justice and peace,
now and forever.
The love of our God will make this happen!

The Word of the Lord.

RESPONSE: *Psalm 96*

RESPONSE:
All the peo-ple on_ the earth, re-joice to hear of the Sav-ior's birth.

VERSE:
to Response
Pro-claim sal - va-tion!_ God's won-ders done for the earth. _

GOSPEL ACCLAMATION:

Good news, good news! Al - le - lu - ia!_

To - day our Sav - ior is born._

GOSPEL: *Luke 2:1-20*

This is a reading from the Gospel of Luke.

When Caesar Augustus, the ruler of Rome,
passed a law that everyone in the world
should be enrolled,
all the people went to be registered in the towns
where they were born.
Joseph and Mary went from the town of Nazareth
to the city of David, which is called Bethlehem,
because Joseph was born in the family of David.
While they were there,
the time came for Mary's child to be born,
and she gave birth to her first-born son.
She wrapped him in swaddling clothes
and laid him in a manger
because there was no room for them in the inn.
At that time, there were shepherds in the fields,
watching over their sheep during the night.
An angel of God appeared to them,
and the glory of God surrounded them with a great light.
And they were frightened. The angel said to them,

"Do not be afraid.
I have come to bring you good news—
news of great joy to be shared by all the people.
Today, in the city of Bethlehem,
a Savior has been born for you, Christ the Lord!
And this will be a sign for you—you will find a child
wrapped in swaddling clothes and lying in a manger."

Suddenly, all the angels of heaven
were praising God and singing,

"Glory to God in heaven,
and peace to all people on earth."

The shepherds said to one another,

"Let us go over to Bethlehem
and see this wonderful thing God has told us about."

They hurried to Bethlehem, and found Mary and Joseph,
and saw the baby lying in the manger.
When they saw the child,
they repeated what the angel had said about him.
Everyone who heard it was amazed
at what the shepherds told them.
And Mary thought about all these things
and kept them in her heart.
The shepherds returned to their fields,
thanking and praising God
for all they had heard and seen.

The Gospel of the Lord.

REFLECTING ON THE READINGS WITH CHILDREN:

We offer two possibilities for the children's reflections.

If there has been an opportunity to prepare, the children may enjoy participating in a dramatization of the Christmas story. One example is provided on the following pages. If this is not possible, we suggest reflecting with the children as follows.

Welcome the children in the joy of this holy season. Usually we stand for the Gospel. Today, because this is a story and the children are likely to be excitable, we may want them to sit and listen to the story. It should be read in great story form so the children *hear* every detail.

After the Gospel, ask the children to recall the details of the story:

- What did the ruler of Rome want everyone to do?
- Where did Mary and Joseph go?
- What is the story of the inn and the manger?
- What did the angels tell the shepherds?
- What was the song the angels sang?
- What can you recall about the coming of the shepherds to the manger?
- What do you remember about Mary in the Christmas story?
- What is your favorite part of the Christmas story?

Jesus was born a long time ago in Bethlehem. But we still read the story of his birth.

- Why do we do this?
- What does Jesus want us to learn from this Christmas story today?
- How is Jesus born again today—on Christmas?
- How can we be like the angels?
- How can we be like the shepherds?
- How can we be like Mary?
- How can we be like Jesus?

CREED (If there is time)
- Do you believe God made you and loves you?
- Do you believe God sent Jesus to show us how to live and how to love each other?
- Do you believe that Jesus was born of the Virgin Mary and came to earth as a little baby so that everyone could be saved?
- Do you believe that Jesus wants everyone to know his love and live together in peace?
- Do you believe that the Holy Spirit lives in our hearts to help us live the way Jesus wants us to?

This is the faith of our church. "Amen."

Gospel Drama for Christmas Season

Gospel: *Luke 2:1-20*

Children always enjoy acting the Christmas story. It should be prepared before Christmas. Children will be needed for the roles of:

Mary	Shepherds
Joseph	Youngest child to bring child Jesus
Angels	Narrator (older child)

Props required: A crib or manger.
A candle for each child.
A doll.

Narrator: In those days, Caesar Augustus, the ruler of Rome, passed a law that everyone in the world should be counted, And so, all the people went to the town where they were born to give their names. Joseph and Mary went from Nazareth to the city of David, which is called Bethlehem, because Joseph was born into the family of David.

Action: Mary and Joseph travel to Bethlehem. Under her cloak, Mary hides a doll wrapped in swaddling clothes.
Or: Standing "off-stage," the youngest child holds the doll.

Narrator: While they were there, the time came for Mary's child to be born. She gave birth to her first-born son and wrapped him in swaddling clothes and laid him in a manger because there was no room for them in the inn.

Action: Mary carries the doll under her cloak and places it in the manger.
Or: The youngest child brings the doll and gives it to Mary and remains at her side.

Narrator: At that time, shepherds who lived in the fields were watching over their sheep at night. An angel of God appeared to them, and the glory of the Lord surrounded them like a great light. And they were very much afraid.

Action: An angel approaches the shepherds.

Angel: Do not be afraid, I come to bring you Good News, news of great joy to be shared by all people. Today, in the city of Bethlehem, a Savior has been born for you. This Savior is Christ the Lord! And here is a sign for you: you will find a child wrapped in swaddling clothes and lying in a manger.

Narrator: Suddenly, all the angels of heaven were praising God and singing,

Angels: Glory to God in heaven, and peace to all people on earth. *(A few children join in the singing of the Gloria.)*

Narrator: Let us join our voices to the voices of the angels and sing, "Glory to God in heaven, and peace to all people on earth."

All: (Sing a gloria taken from the Christmas carols repertoire.)

Narrator: The shepherds said to one another:

One Shepherd: Let us go over to Bethlehem and see this wonderful thing God has told us about.

Narrator: They hurried to Bethlehem and found Mary and Joseph and saw the baby lying in the manger. When they saw Jesus, they repeated what the angel had said about him, and they knelt down and adored Jesus, their Lord and Savior.

Action: Three shepherds kneel and sing a song.

All: (Continue singing "Glory to God.")

Action: The shepherds slowly leave.

Narrator: The shepherds returned to their fields, thanking and praising God because of all that they had heard and seen. They told the Good News to many. Everyone who heard what they saw were amazed at what the shepherds told them. And Mary thought about all these things and kept them in her heart.

Today we are happy to hear again the Good News which the shepherds have told to so many. Let us take our lighted candles and bring them to the crib. Today we come to see and worship this child, our Lord and Savior, who was born from Mary in Bethlehem, many years ago.

Action: Lighted lamps or candles are given to everyone. The children form a procession and bring the lights to the crib where they are carefully placed in sandboxes. The leader may invite the children to kneel before the child Jesus. A Christmas song or a gloria acclamation may be sung. After some time all return to their places and the celebration continues with the profession of faith.

HOLY FAMILY

YEAR A

PRAYER OF THE DAY:

God, you care for us
and protect us
like a mother and father.
Teach us to be kind and patient,
honest and gentle,
and, most of all,
at peace with the people
with whom we live.
This is our prayer to you,
through Jesus Christ, our Lord.

FOCUS OF THE READINGS:

Our readings focus on the importance and holiness of family life. By holiness we mean that the family truly reflects and participates in the creative activity of God.

In the first reading, Paul gives us the Christian principles that both animate and characterize the family life of baptized Christians. We are to live in mutuality, each respecting and loving the other. We are to help each other grow by being kind, forgiving, gentle, honest, peacemaking and, most of all, by our love for one another. Christian families live this way because they are chosen and loved by God.

FIRST READING: *Colossians 3:12-21*

*This is a reading
from Paul's letter to the Colossians.*

Brothers and sisters,
you are God's chosen people,
holy and well loved.
Therefore, be kind and patient
with one another.
Be honest and gentle with one another.
Forgive each other as God has forgiven you.
And most of all, love one another.

Let the peace of Christ be in your hearts.
And always be thankful.
Let the word of Christ,
which is so wonderful, live in you.
Help each other to grow and to become better.
Everything you say or do,
do it in the name of the Lord Jesus.
And always give thanks to God through Jesus.

Wives and husbands, love one another,
and take care of each other
because this is what God asks of you.
Children, obey your parents
because this is what God asks of you.
Parents, be patient and gentle
with your children,
so they will be encouraged.

The Word of the Lord.

RESPONSE: *Psalm 96*

RESPONSE:

All the fam-'lies of— the earth, re-joice to hear of the Sav-ior's birth.

VERSE: to Response

Pro-claim   sal - va-tion!__ God's won-ders done for the earth.___

14

GOSPEL ACCLAMATION:

Good news, good news! Al - le - lu - ia!

Our Lord and Sav - ior is born.

GOSPEL: *Matthew 2:13-15*

This is a reading from the Gospel of Matthew.

An angel of God appeared to Joseph in a dream and said,

"Get up, take the child and his mother
and go quickly to Egypt.
Stay there until I tell you to return.
Herod is looking for the child
because he wants to kill him."

Joseph got up and took Jesus
and his mother, Mary,
and left that night for Egypt.
They stayed there until Herod died.
Then the angel of God said to Joseph in a dream,

"Get up, take the child and his mother
and go back to your home.
Those who wanted to kill him have died."

And so what God had said through the prophet came to be:

"I have called my son out of Eygpt."

So Joseph got up,
took Mary and the child Jesus,
and settled in the town of Nazareth.
And so what God said
through the prophet came true,

"He will be called a Nazarene."

The Gospel of the Lord.

The Gospel text, though it involves the holy family, is truly unrelated to the theme of family. Its basic meaning is to present Jesus as the "new Moses" and to relate the entire life of Jesus to the Hebrew people. The principal event for the Jewish people was their exodus from Egypt. Matthew, here, applies the meaning of the exodus event, namely salvation, to the life of Jesus. The purpose for its inclusion in the Christmas season is to show God's intervention in human history for our salvation. Jesus is that saving intervention!

Rejoice, all families of the earth! Our Savior is born and lives among us.

REFLECTING ON THE READINGS WITH CHILDREN:

Ask the children what they heard. Help the children see that it is mutuality that makes for peaceful and loving family life. In this environment everyone can grow, as Jesus did, physically, mentally, and spiritually. One example might be the growth of a plant. It needs sun, rain, good soil, and so forth. Rain alone will not produce growth. Sun or good soil alone will not produce growth. Each one is needed for good growth. Discuss with the children how family members share God-given talents to help bring about a peaceful family life. The children should see their value to the family group which personalizes this feast. Help the children to see that we live this way because God loves us and because we are baptized Christians.

MARY, MOTHER OF GOD

YEAR A

PRAYER OF THE DAY:

Loving God,
through the power
of your Spirit,
you have made
Mary the mother
of your Son, Jesus.
In the name of Mary,
we proclaim your glory.
In the name
of Jesus, our Savior,
we rejoice in the gift
of your Spirit,
and we bless your name
forever and ever.

FOCUS OF THE READINGS:

The focus of both of our readings is the significance of "the name." In the first reading from the book of *Numbers*, we have the well-known blessing of the Jewish people. But the meaning of the blessing comes from the last line: "When they bless . . . . *in my name*, I will bless them." In other words, when we bless in God's name, it is actually God who is blessing. The name stood for the whole person. To say, "in God's name," is to say in or with all that God is and all that God does. To bless in God's name is to make God totally present.

The Gospel reading for today recounts the circumcision and naming of Jesus. It is interesting that in the past this feast has been called both the Feast of the Circumcision and the Feast of the Holy Name. At the presentation, Jesus was given the name foretold by the angel at the Annunciation—Jesus, the name which means "Savior." Because the whole

FIRST READING: *Numbers 6:22-27*

This is a reading from the book of Numbers.

God said to Moses,

"Tell Aaron and all the priests of Israel
 that when they bless the people,
 they must say,

'May God bless you and keep you.
 May God's face shine on you.
 May God be kind to you and give you peace.'

"When they bless the people like this,
 in my name,
 I myself will bless them."

The Word of the Lord.

RESPONSE: *Numbers 6:24-26*

RESPONSE: May God bless and keep you, may God's face shine on you: May God be kind to you and give you peace.

16

GOSPEL ACCLAMATION:

The an-gel said to Ma-ry: "You shall call him Je - sus."
Al - le -lu - ia! "Ma - ry, you shall call him Je - sus."

GOSPEL: *Luke 2:16-21*

This is a reading from the Gospel of Luke.

When the shepherds went to Bethlehem,
where Jesus was born,
they found Joseph and Mary,
and they saw the baby lying in the manger.
When they saw the child,
they repeated what the angel had said about him.

Everyone who heard it
was amazed at what the shepherds told them.
And Mary thought about all these things
and kept them in her heart.
The shepherds went back to their fields,
thanking and praising God
for all they had heard and seen.

When the baby was eight days old,
he was circumcised,
and Mary and Joseph gave him the name Jesus,
which was the name the angel Gabriel
told Mary to call him.

The Gospel of the Lord.

person is represented by the name, scripture tells us that "at the name of Jesus, every knee should bend" and "those who call upon the name of the Lord will be saved." When Mary proclaims in the Magnificat, "Holy is God's name!" she proclaims that all that God is and all that God does is holy! Today's feast celebrates the naming of Jesus. This feast proclaims that Jesus is the Savior!

He is God's blessing and peace! You shall call him Jesus!

REFLECTING ON THE READINGS WITH CHILDREN:

You might ask the children if they know why they received their name or if they know what their name means. It would be interesting to share with them the meaning of some common names. There are several little books available that give brief meanings.

Explain to the children that in the past, people's names often stood for who they were and what they did. For example, people who made bread often had the name Baker; the name Smith comes from families who were blacksmiths, etc. In the Old Testament, people often had names that indicated their mission in life or some significant event in their life. The name Moses means "I drew you out of the water." Moses was saved from drowning when he was a baby and later became the leader of his people.

This introduction to the significance of names will lead naturally to a discussion of today's Gospel which recounts the naming of Jesus. Jesus was given this name because it means "Savior."

EPIPHANY

YEAR A

PRAYER OF THE DAY:

God, you love all people
and want them to know
Jesus, your Son.
Make us know him better,
and, by the way we live,
may others get to know him
through us.
We ask you this through Jesus
who lives with you,
forever and ever.

FOCUS OF THE READINGS:

The birth of Christ is the manifestation (epiphany) of God in the world. In Christ, salvation has come for everyone, Jew and gentile alike.

Our first reading tells us that the light has come, a light to guide us all. In *this* light, the glory of God shines forth. This light is the Epiphany of God. The Gospel tells us that this light shone in the east and brought visitors from afar to see this manifestation of God's love. Christ is the one to whom all people will come, bringing gifts fit for a king. He is the "newborn King of the Jews" and, indeed, of all the earth. He reveals God's unconditional love for all people.

God's love is made known to all the world! Let all the nations rejoice!

FIRST READING: *Isaiah 60:1-6*

This is a reading from the prophet Isaiah.

People of Jerusalem, arise! Stand up!
Your light has come!
The glory of God shines on you!
And the rulers of nations
will come to your shining light.
Look all around you and see;
people are gathering and coming to you.
They will come from far away,
bringing gifts of gold and frankincense
and singing the praises of God.

The Word of the Lord.

RESPONSE: *Psalm 96*

All the nations of the earth, rejoice to hear of the Savior's birth!

Proclaim salvation! God's wonders done for the earth.

GOSPEL ACCLAMATION:

Good news, good news! Alleluia!

The world will know of his love!

GOSPEL: *Matthew 2:1-12*

This is a reading from the Gospel of Matthew.

When Jesus was born in Bethlehem of Judea,
while Herod was king,
some magi came from the east.
When they arrived in Jerusalem,
they asked the people,

"Where is the newborn King of the Jews?
  We have seen his star in the east,
  and we have come to worship him."

When they said this,
Herod and all the people of Jerusalem
became very disturbed.
Herod gathered the leaders of the Jewish people
and asked them
where the Messiah was supposed to be born.
They told him,

"In Bethlehem of Judea."

Then Herod asked the magi to tell him the exact time
they had seen the star in the east.
When they told him, Herod said,

"Go to Bethlehem and find out
  all you can about this child.
  When you have found him,
  come back and tell me
  so that I may go, too, and worship him."

And so they left for Bethlehem.
The star, which they had seen in the east,
went ahead of them,
and it stopped over the place where Jesus was.
When they went in,
they found the child with Mary his mother.
And they were filled with joy.
They knelt down and worshipped Jesus,
and they gave him gifts of gold,
frankincense and myrrh.
That night, God told the magi in a dream
not to go back to Herod.
So they went back to their own country by another way.

The Gospel of the Lord.

REFLECTING ON THE READINGS
WITH CHILDREN:

Children will not grasp the
profound theological signs in these
readings. However, they will
experience the joy and wonder at
such an event.

Again, we offer you a drama in
which the children may participate.
These presentations require a little
preparation but should not become a
major production.

If the children are not participating
in the dramatization, lead them in
reflections on the signs Matthew
presents and on God's love for all
people of every race, nationality and
belief. These reflections could begin
with "What did you hear?"

Gospel Drama for Epiphany

Gospel: *Matthew 2:1-12*

The Story of the Magi

Children will be required for the roles of:

Narrator	Mary
Herod	Joseph
Magi (3)	Jesus
Child holding a star	

Props required: Star
Gifts

Narrator: This is the Good News from the Gospel of Matthew.

Action: Mary, Joseph and the child Jesus take their place on one side. A child holding a star leads the magi to Herod who is seated on the other side.

Narrator: After Jesus was born in Bethlehem of Judea, while Herod was king, magi from the east came one day to Jerusalem. They asked:

Magi: Where is the newborn King of the Jews? We have seen his star in the east, and we have come to worship him.

Action: Herod's friends at the back of the stage murmur to one another: Where is the Messiah? Where was he born?

Narrator: When they said this, King Herod and all the people of Jerusalem became very disturbed. Herod gathered the leaders of the Jewish people and asked them where the Messiah was to be born. They said:

All: In Bethlehem of Judea.

Narrator: Herod asked the magi to tell him the exact time they had seen the star. Then he sent the magi to Bethlehem, and he told them:

Herod: Find out all you can about this child. When you have found him, come back and tell me so that I, too, may go and worship him.

Narrator: And so they set out for Bethlehem. The star, which they had seen in the east, went ahead of them, and it stopped over the place where Jesus was.

Action: The magi kneel before the child and give their gifts. All kneel before the child and sing an epiphany song which is familiar to the children.

BAPTISM OF THE LORD

YEAR A

PRAYER OF THE DAY:

God of heaven and earth,
when Jesus was baptized
in the River Jordan,
you sent the Holy Spirit
upon him to show the world
that he was your Son.
Send us the Holy Spirit also,
that we may be the messengers
of your Good News.
We ask you this
through Christ our Lord.

FOCUS OF THE READINGS:

The first reading describes the mission of the servant who is chosen by God to bring justice and truth to the world and to make God known to the people. At his baptism Jesus is revealed as the Son of God and is anointed with the Spirit. Coupled with our first reading, the Baptism of the Lord also reveals Jesus as the servant described by Isaiah. He is anointed for mission. His mission is to bring justice, to be a light to the nations, to be a healer and a liberator. In this liturgy, the church holds before us the power and the challenge of our own baptism: we are children of God, anointed with the Spirit, and the mission of Jesus is *our* mission.

REFLECTING ON THE READINGS WITH CHILDREN:

In reflecting on the baptism of the Lord with children, we encounter a particular difficulty. The baptism of Jesus was like most experiences in the early church—an adult experience. While the essential truth of gratuitous grace was certainly recognized, baptism was intimately linked with conversion and a life of service.

FIRST READING: *Isaiah 42:1, 6-7*

This is a reading from the prophet Isaiah.

Our God says,

"This is my servant, my chosen one.
 I give him my strength and my spirit
 to bring justice to all the people.
 And I say to him,

 'I, your God, have called you.
 I have taken you by your hand.
 I have sent you as my covenant to the people,
 as a light for the world.
 I have sent you
 to open the eyes of the blind,
 to free those in prison,
 and to give light to those who live in darkness.' "

The Word of the Lord.

RESPONSE: *Psalm 146*

RESPONSE:
I praise you, O God, for your faith-ful love. I praise you, O God, for all that you do.

VERSES: [repeat by singing or clapping rhythm]   to Response
1. You free the op-pressed and save the poor.
2. The hun-gry are fed, the blind can see.
3. Hap-py are all who hope in you.

GOSPEL ACCLAMATION:

A voice from heav-en said,___ "This is my be-lov-ed Son."___ Al-le-lu-ia. Al-le-lu-ia.___ Al-le-lu-ia. Al-le-lu-ia.___ Al-le-lu-ia. Al-le-lu-ia. Al-le-lu-ia.

GOSPEL: *Matthew 3:13-17*

This is a reading from the Gospel of Matthew.

Jesus came to John the Baptist
to be baptized in the Jordan River.
But John said to him,

"No, I should be baptized by you."

Jesus answered,

"But we must do it this way because this is
what God wants us to do."

So John baptized Jesus.
And when Jesus came up out of the water,
he saw the Spirit of God
coming to him in the form of a dove.
Then a voice from heaven said,

"This is my beloved Son
with whom I am very pleased."

This is the Good News of the Lord.

The baptism of Jesus is the inauguration of his public life, a life of service. Our baptism, like that of Jesus, calls us to the service described in our reading from *Isaiah*. This connection is more difficult to see and reflect on in light of infant baptism, which is the case of most of the children with whom we are ministering. And so, we hope in this reflection to plant a seed of this truth which the children will gradually come to understand and live more fully.

After the Gospel, ask the children what they heard. After they have given their reflections, help them to recall especially "water," "Spirit," "You are my Son." Ask them if they have been present for a baptism or if their parents have told them about their own baptism. Help them to recall what happens at a Christian baptism. Draw from them comments about the following:

- Water.
- Spirit ("I baptize you in the name of the Father, and the Son and the Holy Spirit.").
- We receive the Holy Spirit at our baptism, as Jesus did.
- We are sons and daughters of God.

Ask the children to recall what the first reading was about. You may want to read it again. How is this reading like the Gospel story on the baptism of Jesus:

- "Spirit."
- "With whom I am well pleased."

What did God ask the servant to do? (Bring justice, heal people, free people.) Did Jesus do these things after his baptism? Can you recall any stories about that?

God said to the servant: "I have sent you as a light to the people."

Remind the children that we receive a lighted candle when we are baptized. Because we are baptized and receive the Holy Spirit, we are like Jesus. We can be a light for other people. We are like Jesus; we can serve other people.

- How can we be a light for people in our homes, classrooms, neighborhoods?
- How can we help people, as Jesus did, in our homes, classrooms, neighborhoods? (As always, it is important that this reflect their age.)

Conclude by asking the children to ask their parents to share with them pictures and memories of their baptism.

The Season of Lent

FIRST SUNDAY OF LENT

YEAR A

PRAYER OF THE DAY:

Protect us, our God,
from all evil
that would attract us
away from your love.
May we be loyal to you
and worship you
above all things
which you have made.
We ask you to do this,
through Christ, our Lord.

FOCUS OF THE READINGS:

Both of our readings focus on the relationship between human beings and God—the created and the creator. While we cannot know the origins of the human choice to turn away from God, the first reading presents for us in vivid imagery the reality that something has gone wrong in this relationship, and it was humankind, not God, who caused the separation. In this story, God has provided human beings with all they need. But they wanted one thing more—to end the difference between creature and creator, to become gods themselves, to deny the uniqueness of God as God. In the end, they succumbed to this temptation.

In the Gospel for today, Jesus is also tempted by Satan. With appealing rewards, he is tempted to live a life of power and self sufficiency and to acknowledge Satan as a god. But Jesus refuses the temptation and three times proclaims that God and God alone is the Savior. Only God gives real life, real power, real security.

FIRST READING: *Genesis 2:7-9, 3:1-7*

This is a reading from the book of Genesis.

God created the first human beings
out of clay from the ground,
and breathed into them the breath of life,
and they became living people.
And God planted a garden in the east
in a place called Eden,
and God put the first human beings there.
God put many wonderful fruit trees in the garden,
and it was beautiful.
In the middle of the garden, God put the tree of life.
It was a tree that taught what is good and evil.
Now the serpent was the sneakiest
of all the wild creatures that God had made.
And the serpent said to the woman,

"Did God tell you
not to eat the fruit of the trees here in the garden?"

The woman answered,

"We may eat the fruit of all the trees
except the tree in the middle of the garden.
God told us,

'You may not eat the fruit of the tree
in the middle of the garden.
You may not even touch it, or you will die.' "

But the serpent said to the woman,

"No, you won't die.
God knows that if you eat from that tree,
you will be like gods.
Then you will know what is good and what is evil."

So when the woman saw how beautiful the tree was
and how good the fruit looked,
and that it could give her knowledge,
she took some of the fruit and ate it.
And she gave some to her husband, and he ate it, too.
Then they realized that they were naked.
So they made themselves clothes out of fig leaves.

The Word of the Lord.

RESPONSE: *Psalm 51*

RESPONSE:
In your kind-ness, O my God, have mer-cy on me, have mer-cy on me.

VERSES:
to Response

1. I know____ that I have sinned and done what is wrong.
2. O God____ for-give my sins and make my heart true.

GOSPEL ACCLAMATION:

(sing and clap)

If you live by my Word, the Good News of God is for you.

[sing and clap]

After Gospel, repeat Acclamation

GOSPEL: *Matthew 4:1-11*

This is a reading from the Gospel of Matthew.

After Jesus was baptized in the Jordan River,
the Spirit led him into the desert.
Jesus stayed in the desert for forty days and forty nights.
During all that time,
he did not eat, and so he was hungry.
Then the devil came to him and said,

"If you are the Son of God,
tell these stones to become loaves of bread."

But Jesus said,

"It is written in the books of Moses,

'People do not live only by eating bread.
They also live by every word that comes from God.' "

Then the devil took Jesus to the very top
of the temple in Jerusalem and said to him,

"If you are the Son of God, jump down from here,
because it is written in the book of Psalms,

'God will tell the angels to take care of you.
And they will catch you
so that you will not hurt your foot on a rock.' "

But Jesus said,

"It is also written,

'You shall not test your God.' "

Then the devil took Jesus up on a very high mountain
and showed him all the kingdoms of the world.
The devil said to Jesus,

"You can have all these kingdoms.
I will give them all to you if you will worship me."

Jesus said,

"Leave me alone, Satan!
It is written in the books of Moses,

'You must worship only God
and serve no one else.' "

Then the devil left him,
and the angels came and took care of Jesus.

The Gospel of the Lord.

REFLECTING ON THE READINGS WITH CHILDREN:

While reflecting on these readings with the children, we will want to keep two things in mind. First, the security that is found in God often seems abstract and even unrelated to our daily needs. Second, temptations are real, and most of us are faced with them throughout our lives. Our discussions with the children should not minimize these facts.

The point of the two readings is not that God provides all we need, or that we are not responsible for our lives. It is clear to the children that money and power do buy the things we need in order to live, such as, food, shelter, clothes, entertainment. Our emphasis should not be that these things have no value. Jesus said we do not live by bread *alone*. We should never pit God against the necessities of the world as though they are evil. After giving the children time to share their reflections, help them understand these:

- *All things ultimately come from God.* For example, one can work and acquire a home, food, clothes, and enjoy good health— all are gifts of God.

- *It is the exaggeration* of the importance of possessions and dependence on personal money and power *that Jesus warns against.*

- We are sometimes tempted to want more than we need and to care more about what we have than about others. Jesus was also tempted. But like Jesus, *we have the Spirit of God to help us to do what is right.*

During Lent, God asks us to think about the times we are tempted and to try to do what Jesus did—not give in to the temptations. Help the children reflect on temptations which may be problems for them at *their* age and in *their* circumstances. Jesus said to Satan, "Leave me alone!" We can do that, too.

SECOND SUNDAY OF LENT

YEAR A

PRAYER OF THE DAY:

God in heaven,
you gave the apostles courage
by showing them a glimpse
of the victory that would be won
by your Son after his death.
Make us always true to him,
quick to overcome our fear,
and trust in his Resurrection.
We ask you to do this
through Jesus Christ,
who lives with you
and the Holy Spirit,
forever and ever.

FOCUS OF THE READINGS:

While the relationship between the two readings may not be evident, both focus on God's call to participate in salvation history and to do so with trust and confidence.

In our first reading, Abraham is called to leave the security of home and venture forth to share in God's plan. Abraham has only God's word for it: no road map, no travelogue, and no reservations. He has only the promise that God will bless him and all families of the earth because of him.

In the Gospel, Peter, James and John are also called to participate in God's plan. But, true to the New Testament, they are given a glimpse of what their participation will involve. In the Transfiguration of Jesus, the disciples see a preview of their future glory. Like Jesus, we are called to live in light and splendor. Abraham's immediate requirement was "leave your country." Our immediate requirement is "listen to him."

FIRST READING: *Genesis 12:1-5*

This is a reading from the book of Genesis.

This is what God said to Abraham:

"Leave your country and your relatives,
and go to a place that I will show you.
You and your family
are going to become a great nation
because I will bless you.
Everyone will honor your name,
and you will be a blessing to them.
All the families of the earth
will be blessed because of you."

So Abraham went, just as God told him. [Abraham was 75 years old when he left Haran. He took his wife, Sarah; his nephew, Lot; all his servants, and everything he owned and left for the land of Canaan.]

The Word of the Lord.

[ ] *Reader may omit text that appears in brackets.*

RESPONSE: *Psalm 33*

RESPONSE:
Lord, be with us, with your love, be with us, all our hope is in you.

VERSES:
1. For your faith-ful word and all you
2. (♩) We are cho-sen, God, by

to Response
1. do, all your works we trust in you.
2. you. Bless us all, we trust in you.

GOSPEL ACCLAMATION:

"This is Je-sus my Son, lis-ten, his words are for you."

After Gospel, repeat Acclamation

GOSPEL: *Matthew 17:1-9*

This is a reading from the Gospel of Matthew.

One day Jesus took Peter, James, and
James' brother John up on a high mountain,
away from everyone.
While they were there,
his face changed and shone like the sun,
and his clothes became white as light.
Suddenly, the disciples
saw Moses and Elijah there,
talking with Jesus. Peter said,

  "Lord, it's good for us to be here!
    If you want me to, I will make three tents—
    one for you, one for Moses,
    and one for Elijah."

While Peter was still talking,
the shadow of a cloud came over them,
and a voice came from the cloud saying,

  "This is my Son, whom I love very much.
    Listen to him."

When the disciples heard this,
they fell to the ground and covered their faces
because they were afraid.
But Jesus came and touched them and said,

  "Get up. Don't be afraid."

And when they looked up,
they saw only Jesus standing there.
When they were coming down
from the mountain, Jesus told them,

  "Don't tell anyone what you have seen
    until I am raised from the dead."

The Gospel of the Lord.

REFLECTING ON THE READINGS WITH CHILDREN:

Obviously, while God asked Abraham to leave his home and relatives, God does not ask children to leave their homes and families as a sign of faith. To pose this as a possible response to God may even be frightening to children. You can, however, explore with the children how they, at their age, can show their faith in God's call.

In your reflections on the Gospel, ask the children what they heard. After they have had time to share that, you may wish to lead them with questions such as:

- Who did Jesus take with him to the mountain?
- What happened while they were there?
- Who did Peter, James and John see with Jesus?
- What did Peter say? What did Peter, James and John hear God say?

Ask the children if they have ever seen previews of coming attractions on television or in a theater. Help them understand that previews tell us what the coming attraction is going to be and help us look forward to it.

Help them see that, at the Transfiguration, Jesus was giving a preview of what he will be like after the Resurrection. He was also showing us that we will be like him. We will live with him in glory. As Jesus was showing this to Peter, James and John, God told them what we must do to live with Jesus forever.

Do you remember what God said to Peter, James and John? God tells us, too, *"This is my beloved Son; listen to him."*

How do we listen to Jesus today
- in the Bible?
- in our parents and others who teach us?
- in the good thoughts we have that encourage us to do the right thing?

29

THIRD SUNDAY OF LENT

YEAR A

PRAYER OF THE DAY:

God, who knows all things,
you made us your children
in the waters of our baptism.
Keep us faithful to you
by obeying your Son, Jesus,
who lives with you,
forever and ever.

FOCUS OF THE READINGS:

Both readings focus on *water* as a sign of salvation. Wearied from their journey, the Israelites began to complain to Moses, "We are going to die of thirst." They had lost their confidence that God would supply their needs. They are called back to faith by the gift of water: "I will be there with you. . . .Water will flow out for the people to drink."

Our Gospel is the well-known story of Jesus and the woman at the well. The complete reading (*John 4:5-42*) has many different themes running through it—from the initial call of Jesus, "Please give me some water," to the preaching ministry of the woman, "Many Samaritans believed in him because of her words." We have chosen to retain only the *living water* theme in our adaptation.

In the dialogue between Jesus and the woman, they speak first of water from a well. And as in our first reading, the gift of water is a call to faith. Jesus' promise of living water stirs initial faith, and he responds in self-revelation—"I am the Messiah."

FIRST READING: *Exodus 17:3-7*

This is a reading from the book of Exodus.

After the Israelites
had been out in the desert for a long time,
they became very thirsty.
They started complaining to Moses, saying,

"Why did you bring us away from Egypt?
We are going to die of thirst here.
And so will our children and all of our animals."

So Moses cried out to God,

"What am I going to do with these people? They are
ready to kill me!"

God said to Moses,

"Take some of the leaders of the people
and go to the rock of Horeb.
Take the rod that you used at the Nile River.
I will be there with you.
When you hit the rock,
water will flow out for the people to drink."

So Moses did just as God said.
[Then he named the place *Massah*, because it was
the place where the Israelites tested the Lord.
He also called it by another name, *Meribah*, because
that was where they quarreled, saying,
"Is God with us or not?"]

The Word of the Lord.

[ ] *Reader may omit text that appears in brackets.*

RESPONSE: *Psalm 36*

RESPONSE: 1st time: Leader; 2nd time: All

You are the light, the foun-tain of life.

VERSES: Leader

1. Your love is true____ and sets us free. ____
2. You give us light____ that lets us see. ____

All:
to Response

1. Your love is true____ and sets us free. ____
2. You give us light____ that lets us see. ____

GOSPEL ACCLAMATION:

"I am the liv-ing wa-ter,__ you will have life__ in me.

I am the liv-ing wa-ter,__ you will have life__ in me."

After Gospel, repeat Acclamation

GOSPEL: *John 4:5-7, 9-11, 13-19, 25-26*

This is a reading from the Gospel of John.

One day, as Jesus was going through
the country of Samaria,
he stopped at a well called Jacob's well.
He sat down to rest
because he was tired from his journey.
It was about noon. A woman from the town
came to the well to get some water. Jesus said to her,
  "Please give me some water."
The woman said,
  "I am surprised that you are asking me for water.
    You are a Jew and I am a Samaritan."
She said this because, at that time,
Jews and Samaritans were enemies
and did not speak to each other. But Jesus said to her,
  "If you only knew the gift that God offers you and
    who is speaking to you, you would be asking me
    for water. And I would give you living water."
The woman said,
  "But this well is deep, and you don't have a bucket.
    Where will you get this living water?"
Jesus said,
  "Anyone who drinks the water from this well
    will be thirsty again. But anyone who drinks
    the water I give, will never be thirsty again.
    The water I give will be
    like a spring of flowing water inside of them.
    And this water will give them eternal life."
[The woman said to Jesus,
  "Sir, give me this water that you are talking about
    so that I won't be thirsty again.
    Then I won't have to come
    to this well anymore to get water."
Jesus said to the woman,
  "Go and get your husband."
She said,
  "I'm not married."
Jesus said,
  "Yes, that's true. You have been married five times.
    So the man you are now living with
    is not really your husband."
The woman said to Jesus,
  "I can see that you are a prophet.
    I know the Messiah is coming, and, when he comes,
    he will explain everything to us."
Jesus said to the woman,
  "I am the Messiah."]

The Gospel of the Lord.

REFLECTING ON THE READINGS WITH CHILDREN:

Help the children understand the setting of the reading—the dryness of the desert and the land of Palestine. Perhaps you could obtain posters or large pictures to help the children visualize a land almost barren of vegetation. For the Israelites wandering through the desert and living in Palestine, water was a natural sign of life, of salvation.

Ask the children to visualize the Gospel. (Whenever the Gospel presents a visual story, take time to help the children sense the scene.) What might Jesus look like? (Again, perhaps a picture would help.) Imagine Jesus, tired from walking in the hot sun and sitting down to rest. How did the woman collect her water? Ask:

- What did Jesus say to her?
- How did she answer?

Help the children recall the dialogue.

- What kind of water was the woman talking about?
- What did Jesus mean by "living water"?

Help the children to gradually see the relationship between Jesus' promise of living water and baptism. We were baptized in living water, and we will have eternal life. If you have catechumens in your parish, explain to the children that catechumens are people who have been preparing for a long time to be baptized. They have been learning more and more about Jesus, and, during this Lent, they are preparing in a special way to be baptized at Easter. We have already been baptized in water, and, during Lent, we too, are preparing to make new again our baptism at Easter, expressed in the renewal of baptismal promises.

Explain to the children that the holy water at the entrance of the church is a symbol of the water used for baptism. When we sign ourselves with it, we are reminding ourselves that we are baptized Christians.

"I am the Messiah." Jesus gives us living water.

FOURTH SUNDAY OF LENT

YEAR A

PRAYER OF THE DAY:

Saving God,
you sent Jesus
to wash away our sins
and help us to see things
your way.
Do not let our hearts go blind
so that we do not love
other people
as much as we love ourselves.
We make this prayer to you
through Jesus, your Son.

FOCUS OF THE READINGS:

Today's readings focus on conversion
from darkness to light. We have chosen
the New Testament reading instead of the
one from the Old Testament because
Paul's letter relates more directly to the
Gospel theme. In our first reading, Paul
reminds his community that before they
knew Christ, they lived in the darkness of
sin. But now that they are baptized, they
must live as children of the light, doing
what is good and right and honest. Paul
believes baptism should make a radical
difference in our lives.

The Gospel story begins with the
healing of a blind man. But the dialogue
which follows leads us to focus on spiritual
sight. The blind man accepts the free gift
of Jesus and receives both physical and
spiritual sight. Those who reject the
power of Jesus remain spiritually blind.
In their blindness, they refuse to "see"
who Jesus is. ("We know he is not a man
of God.")

In contrast, the blind man, now healed
by Jesus, insists simply, "I do know one
thing; I was blind and now I can see." The
story's climax comes with the statement of
faith, "Yes, Lord, I do believe."

*"I am the light of the world." Jesus
gives us sight.*

FIRST READING: *Ephesians 5:8-14*

*This is a reading from Paul's letter
to the Christians living in Ephesus.*

Brothers and sisters,
there was a time when you were darkness,
but now you are light in the Lord.
Live as children of the light.
When we live in the light,
we do what is good and right and honest.
Try to learn what pleases the Lord.
Never take part in things
that are evil or done in secret.
Instead, let everything be seen in the open.
Everything done in the light is seen as it really is.
That is why it is said,

"Wake up, you who sleep;
rise up from the dead,
and Christ will give you light."

The Word of the Lord.

RESPONSE: *Psalm 36*

RESPONSE: 1st time: Leader; 2nd time: All

You are the light, the foun - tain of life.

VERSES: Leader

1. Your love is true___ and sets us free.___
2. You give us life___ that makes us rise.___

All: to Response

1. Your love is true___ and sets us free.___
2. You give us life___ that makes us rise.___

GOSPEL ACCLAMATION:

"I am the light in dark-ness,_ you will have life__ in me.

I am the light in dark-ness,_ you will have life__ in me."

After Gospel, repeat Acclamation

GOSPEL: *John 9:1, 6-9, 13-17, 34-38*

This is a reading from the Gospel of John.

NARRATOR: As Jesus was walking along, he saw a man who had been born blind. And he said to his disciples:

SPEAKER 1: While it is day, I must do the work of the One who sent me. When night comes, no one can work. While I am here, I am the light of the world.

NARRATOR: Jesus spat on the ground, made mud, and put the mud on the man's eyes. Then Jesus told him:

SPEAKER 1: Go wash in the pool of Siloam.

NARRATOR: So the man went and washed his eyes and came back able to see. His neighbors and the people who had always seen him begging began to ask:

SPEAKER 2: Isn't this the man who used to sit and beg?

NARRATOR: Some said it was. Others said it was not he, but someone who looked like him. The man himself said:

SPEAKER 3: Yes, I am the same man.

NARRATOR: Next some of the people took the man who had been blind to the Pharisees because it was on the Sabbath that Jesus had healed him. The Pharisees asked the man how he was now able to see. He told them:

SPEAKER 3: A man called Jesus put mud on my eyes. I washed it off, and now I can see.

SPEAKER 4: The one who did this cannot be a man of God, because he works on the Sabbath.

SPEAKER 2: But if one is a sinner, how can he do these miracles?

SPEAKER 3: I don't know if he's a sinner or not. But I do know one thing—I was blind, and now I can see.

[*NARRATOR:* And they began to argue about it. Then they asked the blind man again:

SPEAKER 4: Since it was your eyes he healed, what do you have to say about him?

SPEAKER 3: He is a prophet.

NARRATOR: Because the man said, "He is a prophet," they threw him out of the temple. Jesus went and found the man and asked him:

SPEAKER 1: Do you believe in the One sent by God?

SPEAKER 3: Tell me who he is so that I can believe in him.

SPEAKER 1: I am the One sent by God.

SPEAKER 3: Yes, Lord, I do believe!

NARRATOR: And he knelt down to worship him.]

The Gospel of the Lord.

[] *Reader may omit text that appears in brackets.*

REFLECTING ON THE READINGS WITH CHILDREN:

What did you hear? Allow the children to retell the story or to state simply what they heard, without discussion.

Begin on the level of human sight and gradually move to spiritual sight. Help the children reflect on their own experiences with sight. This may be done by asking questions like:

- What is your favorite color?
- What is your favorite book or story?
- When did you learn to read?
- What is your favorite place to visit? What does it look like?

Children come easily to a sense of gratitude for the gift of sight because they experience it every day.

Help the children reflect on the blindness of the man in the story. He had never seen colors, or places or books. Imagine his joy and gratitude when he was healed and could see. He was so grateful that he even gave praise to Jesus when the Pharisees were angry with him and tried to make him say that Jesus didn't really heal him. And when he said that Jesus was a prophet, they threw him out of the temple.

The Pharisees, even though they could see things with their eyes, were blind to the power of Jesus. They didn't believe, even when Jesus had given such a powerful sign; that is a kind of blindness. We have two ways of seeing: with the eyes of our body and with the eyes of faith.

The man in the story received a wonderful gift to be able to see with the eyes of his body. He also received the wonderful gift of faith. So he was grateful for the gift of seeing in both ways and said, "Yes, Lord, I do believe."

When we were born, we had the gift of seeing with the eyes of our body. When we are baptized, we celebrate the gift of faith, of seeing things in a new way. This new way of seeing helps us to live as Jesus lived and as Jesus wants us to live as children of light. For example, sometimes when we find it hard to love someone, our faith helps us. Jesus, the Light of the world, lives in us and helps us to see others the way he sees them, and to love them the way he loves them.

When we come together with other Christians at mass, we thank Jesus for all the wonderful gifts he has given us. We thank him for the gift of faith that helps us live as children of the light. And we can say, with the man in the story, "Yes, Lord, I do believe!"

FIFTH SUNDAY OF LENT
YEAR A

PRAYER OF THE DAY:

God, who made us
and gives us life,
your Son, Jesus,
came among us
to raise the dead
from their graves and give us
all a life that will never end.
We love you for this
and pray to you
that we will have that life,
and so live with you, and Jesus,
and the Holy Spirit,
forever and ever.

FOCUS OF THE READINGS:

Our readings today focus on resurrection to new life. The reading from *Ezekiel* speaks to new life on two levels. The people will experience new life when they have been brought home to Israel after their exile. But the reading also speaks of God opening graves and raising those inside to life. Both of these will reveal the person and power of God. Although this passage does not refer to individual resurrection, it is one of the early hints in the Old Testament of a belief that there is life after death. This belief, inconsistent in the Old Testament, is more developed in its later books.

Our Gospel also reveals the person and power of God. The significance of the story is in the apparent irreversibility of the situation. Martha has already expressed a belief in a general resurrection at the end of time. But Lazarus had been dead four days. At Jesus' word, Lazarus is raised to life and "many of the people. . . believed in him."

"I am the resurrection. I am life."
Jesus gives us life.

FIRST READING: *Ezekiel 37:12-14*

This is a reading from the prophet Ezekiel.

This is what God says,

"O my people, I am going to open your graves
and raise you from death.
I am going to bring you home to Israel.
Then you will know that you are my people,
and I am your God.
And I will put my Spirit in you so you will live.
Then you will know that I, your God,
will do what I said I would do."

The Word of the Lord.

RESPONSE: *Psalm 36*

RESPONSE: 1st time: Leader; 2nd time: All

You are the light, the foun-tain of life.

VERSES: Leader

1. Your love is true____ and sets us free. ____
2. You give us wa-ter that lets us live. ____

All: to Response

1. Your love is true____ and sets us free. ____
2. You give us wa-ter that lets us live. ____

GOSPEL ACCLAMATION:

"I am the Res-ur-rec-tion,__ you will have life__ in me.

I am the Res-ur-rec-tion,__ you will have life__ in me."

After Gospel, repeat Acclamation

GOSPEL: *John 11:1-45*

This is a reading from the Gospel of John.

Martha, Mary, and their brother, Lazarus,
lived in the village of Bethany. They were friends of Jesus.
So when Lazarus was very sick, his two sisters
sent a message to Jesus saying,

"Lord, your friend, Lazarus, is very sick."

Jesus was with the disciples when he got this message,
and he said to them,

"This sickness is not going to end in death.
No, this has happened to Lazarus
so that you will believe in me."

Jesus loved Martha and Mary and Lazarus very much,
yet he stayed where he was for two more days.
Then he said to his disciples,

"Now, let's go to Bethany."

By the time Jesus got there, Lazarus was already dead and
had been buried in a tomb for four days. Martha said to Jesus,

"Lord, if you had been here before,
my brother would not have died."

Jesus said to Martha,

"Your brother will rise again."

Martha said,

"Yes, I know he will rise again at the end of time
in the resurrection of all people."

Jesus said to Martha,

"I am the resurrection. I am life.
Anyone who believes in me will live forever.
Even though they die, they will live forever.
Do you believe this?"

Martha answered,

"Yes, Lord, I believe you are the Christ."

Then Martha went to get her sister, Mary. She said,

"Lord, if you had been here,
my brother would not have died."

When Jesus saw her crying, he was filled with pity,
and he began to cry. When the others saw Jesus crying,
they said,

"See how much he loved Lazarus."

Then Jesus asked,

"Where is Lazarus buried?"

They said,

"Come and see."

Lazarus was buried in a cave, and there was a large stone in
front of it. When Jesus came to the tomb,
his heart was again filled with pity, and he said,

"Roll the stone away from the cave."

So they took the stone away.
Then Jesus looked up to heaven and said,

"Father, I thank you for hearing my prayers.
I know that you always hear me,
but I am praying especially now
so that these people will believe that you sent me."

Then he shouted,

"Lazarus, come out of the tomb!"

Lazarus came out. His hands and feet and face
were wrapped in pieces of white cloth. So Jesus said,

"Untie him, and let him go."

Many of the people who came to be
with Martha and Mary were Jews.
And when they saw what Jesus did, they believed in him.

The Gospel of the Lord.

REFLECTING ON THE READINGS
WITH CHILDREN:

Ask the children what the Gospel
said to them. Invite the children to
imagine the characters. Martha and
Mary and Lazarus were good friends
of Jesus. He went to their home for
dinner and to visit (*Luke* 10:38). The
two sisters sent a message to Jesus
that his friend, Lazarus, was sick.

When Jesus arrived, Lazarus was
already dead. How do you think
Martha felt when she saw Jesus
coming? What did she say? How did
Jesus answer her?

Lead the children in a recollection
of the dialogue between Jesus and
Martha, and Jesus and Mary.

Remind the children that Jesus
was filled with pity when he saw how
sad Martha and Mary were, and he
cried. It is important that the
children see the humanity of Jesus.

What did Jesus do before he
called Lazarus out of the tomb?

The significance of the story rests
on the seemingly impossible task
ahead of Jesus. It is on the basis of
his power that "many who came to be
with Martha and Mary. . .believed in
him."

Jesus can do all things.

*Jesus will raise us up after we die.
He asks us, as he asked Martha and
Mary, to believe that even now.*

PASSION SUNDAY

YEAR A

PRAYER OF THE DAY:

Dearest God, through Jesus
you show us that to love you
we must be humble, as he was,
and put up with tough times.
When we are proud
of what we have done,
may we thank you
for your gifts to us.
When we are tempted
not to follow Jesus,
may we pray to you
to be strong,
through Jesus, your Son,
who lives with you,
forever and ever.

FOCUS OF THE READINGS:

Jesus, eternal God, humbled himself to
be identified with humankind. Those who
sought their own importance humiliated
Jesus and denied his identity: Messiah,
King of the Jews, builder of the temple.
They put him to death, but God raised
him up and proclaimed his true identity—
Jesus Christ is Lord!

Jesus suffers and dies.

Note on reading the Passion in parts:

1. Each leader will need to determine
how many children will do each part,
according to the number in the group. The
goal is to involve as many children as possible.

2. It is very important that the role of
those yelling "crucify him" be assigned to
a small group (2-3 children) rather than
asking all the children to take this part as
we have traditionally done in the adult
community. To have the entire community
take that part suggests that the ordinary
people of the congregation are the sinners
who willingly, even eagerly, call for the
death of Jesus. While this practice is
widespread, it is not really appropriate for
the adult congregation. It is even less
appropriate—and may even be
harmful—with children.

THE PROCESSION WITH PALMS:

Sing ho-san-na, sing ho-san-na, to the King, sing ho-san-na!

GOSPEL: *Matthew 21:1-11*

This is a reading from the Gospel of Matthew.

When Jesus and his disciples
were on their way to Jerusalem,
they stopped on the Mount of Olives.
Jesus said to two of his disciples,

"Go into the next village,
and you will find a young donkey tied there.
Untie it and bring it to me.
If anyone asks you why you are doing that, just say,

'The Lord needs it,
but he will send it right back.' "

This happened to make clear
what the prophet meant a long time ago
when he said,

"Your king is coming to you.
He is humble and is riding on a donkey."

The two disciples went
and did everything Jesus had told them.
When they brought the donkey to Jesus,
they put their coats on its back,
and Jesus got onto the donkey.
Many of the people spread their coats
on the road in front of him,
and others cut branches
and laid them on the road.
The crowd of people that were with him shouted,

"Hosanna to the Son of David.
Blessed is the one
who comes in the name of the Lord.
Hosanna in the highest."

And when he came into Jerusalem,
everyone was excited and asked,

"Who is this?"

The people said,

"He is Jesus, the prophet from Galilee."

The Gospel of the Lord.

"Bless-ings on the King who comes in the name of the Lord!"____ They came run-ning down the streets so ex-cit-ed were the chil-dren as he came, sing-ing:

FIRST READING: *Philippians 2:5-11*

*This is a reading
from Paul's letter to the Philippians.*

Brothers and sisters,
you must think and live like Christ.
Even though he was always God,
Jesus did not try to hold onto that.
Instead, he became a human being just like us.
As a human being, he lived a humble life.
Jesus obeyed God in everything,
even though it meant he would die on a cross.
Because he obeyed God in everything,
God raised Jesus up and gave him the name
which is above every other name,
so that at the name of Jesus
everyone should kneel and worship.
Everyone in heaven and earth and everywhere,
should give glory to God by proclaiming,

"Jesus Christ is Lord!"

The Word of the Lord.

RESPONSE: *Psalm 34*

Glo-ri-fy God, glo-ri-fy God, glo-ri-fy God with me. Let us praise God's ho-ly name. Glo-ri-fy God glo-ri-fy God's ho-ly name!

GOSPEL ACCLAMATION:

Je-sus____ has giv-en his life for us.____
Je-sus____ has giv-en his life for us.

REFLECTING ON THE READINGS WITH CHILDREN:

We suggest that the Passion be read in parts as has become customary in many parish communities.

The experience of Holy Week is more of a meditation than a theological study. These reflections should allow the children to enter into the drama of the Passion in a way that touches them personally.

After the Passion, ask the children to recall the scene:

- Who was there? (Jesus, chief priests and other leaders, Pilate, a crowd of people, soldiers, Simon, the two criminals crucified with him.)
- Why did the people take Jesus to Pilate? Why did they want Jesus crucified?
- How do you think Jesus felt when they made fun of him as a king?
- Who was the man Pilate wanted to let out of prison?
- How do you think Jesus felt when his own people kept shouting, "Crucify him, crucify him"?
- Why were the people making fun of him on the cross? What did they say? How do you think Jesus felt when they said these things?
- After Jesus died, what did one of the soldiers say? How do you think that soldier felt?

If some of the older children have done the reading, you might ask those who read:

- How did you feel being Jesus?
- How did you feel being Pilate?
- How did you feel being the chief priests and leaders?
- How did you feel when you were shouting "crucify him"?
- How did you feel being the soldier at the end?

Gospel Drama for Passion Sunday

Gospel: *Matthew 27:11-54*

Children will be required for the roles of:

Narrator 1	Pilate	Pilate's Wife	Soldier	Robbers (2)
Narrator 2	Jesus	Crowd (2 or 3	Simon	Chief Priests &
Narrator 3		Children)		Leaders (3 or 4)

Props required: Purple robe, crown of thorns, stick, large cross, sign reading: "This is Jesus, King of the Jews."

Narrator 1: The story of the suffering and death of Jesus, from the Gospel of Matthew. Jesus stood in front of Pilate, the governor of Jerusalem. Pilate asked Jesus,

Pilate: Are you the king of the Jews?

Jesus: You have said so.

Narrator 1: The chief priests and leaders started accusing Jesus, but he didn't answer them. So Pilate said,

Pilate: You hear all these things they are saying against you. Don't you have anything to say?

Narrator 1: Still Jesus did not say anything, and Pilate wondered why. Now every year at the feast of Passover, the governor would free one person from the prison, anyone the people wanted. At that time, there was a man in prison named Barabbas, and everyone knew who he was. So Pilate asked the people,

Pilate: Who do you want me to set free, Barabbas or Jesus?

Narrator 1: Pilate did this because his wife sent a message to him saying,

Pilate's wife: Do not do anything to hurt Jesus. He is a good man. I had a dream about him today, and it worries me.

Narrator 1: But the chief priests and leaders told the people to ask for Barabbas and have Jesus killed. So when Pilate asked them again, they said,

Crowd (2 or 3 children): Free Barabbas!

Pilate: Then what should I do with Jesus, who is called "the Christ"?

Crowd: Kill him! Crucify him!

Pilate: Why? What has he done wrong?

Crowd: Crucify him! Crucify him!

38

Narrator 2: So Pilate set Barabbas free. He told the soldiers to whip Jesus, and then he gave him to the people so they could crucify him. The soldiers put a purple robe on Jesus and made a crown out of thorns and put it on his head. And they put a stick in his hand. They knelt in front of Jesus and made fun of him, saying,

Crowd: Hail, king of the Jews!

Narrator 2: They took the stick away from Jesus and started hitting him on the head with it and spitting at him. After they had made fun of him and laughed at him, they took the purple robe off and led Jesus away to crucify him. As they were taking him away, they saw a man from Cyrene, named Simon, and they made him carry Jesus' cross.

Narrator 3: When they came to a place called Golgotha, which means "the skull," they crucified Jesus. They put a sign over his head which said, "This is Jesus, the King of the Jews."

Narrator 2: Two robbers were crucified with him, one on his right and one on his left. And while they were hanging there, they made fun of Jesus. And the people who were going by laughed at Jesus and said,

Crowd: If you are the Son of God, come down off that cross!

Narrator 2: And the chief priests and leaders also made fun of him, saying,

Crowd: He saved other people, but he can't save himself. If he is the King of the Jews, let's see him come down from that cross. Then we will believe in him! He trusts in God and even said, "I am the Son of God." Well, let's see if God wants to save him now!

Narrator 3: About noon, everything became dark and stayed dark until about three o'clock in the afternoon. Jesus cried out in a loud voice,

Jesus: My God, my God, why have you left me alone?

Crowd: He is calling for help. Let's see if God comes to help him.

Narrator 3: Then Jesus cried out again, and he died.

    PAUSE

The people who were there were terrified. One of the Roman soldiers said,

Soldier: This man really was the Son of God.

Narrator 1: This is the Passion of our Lord, Jesus Christ.

PASSION (PALM) SUNDAY

PASSION: *Matthew 27:11-54*

REFRAIN:
Leader: Jesus has given his life for us.
All: Jesus has given his life for us.

The story of the suffering and death of Jesus,
from the Gospel of Matthew.

Jesus stood in front of Pilate, the governor of Jerusalem.
Pilate asked Jesus,

> "Are you the king of the Jews?"

Jesus answered,

> "You have said so."

The chief priests and leaders started accusing Jesus,
but he didn't answer them. So Pilate said,

> "You hear all these things they are saying against you.
>   Don't you have anything to say?"

Still Jesus did not say anything, and Pilate wondered why.

Now every year at the feast of Passover,
the governor would free one person from the prison—
anyone the people wanted.
At that time, there was a man in prison named Barabbas,
and everyone knew who he was.

So Pilate asked the people,

> "Who do you want me to set free, Barabbas or Jesus?

Pilate did this because his wife sent a message to him saying,

> "Do not do anything to harm Jesus. He is a good man.
>   I had a dream about him today, and it worries me."

But the chief priests and leaders told the people
to ask for Barabbas and have Jesus killed.
So when Pilate asked them again, they said,

> "Free Barabbas!"

Pilate said to them,

"Then what should I do with Jesus, who is called *the Christ*?"

They all shouted,

"Kill him! Crucify him!"

REFRAIN:
Leader: Jesus has given his life for us.
All: Jesus has given his life for us.

But Pilate said,

"Why? What has he done wrong?"

But the people kept on shouting,

"Crucify him!"

[When Pilate saw that the people were starting a riot,
he knew that he could not change their minds.
So he took a bowl of water
and washed his hands in front of the crowd and said,

"I don't want to be guilty of killing this man.
I don't want anything to do with it.
Kill him yourselves."

All the people said,

"We will take the blame for killing him,
we and all our children."]

So Pilate set Barabbas free.
He told the soldiers to whip Jesus,
and then he gave him to the people so they could crucify him.
The soldiers put a purple robe on Jesus
and made a crown out of thorns and put it on his head.
And they put a stick in his hand.
Then they knelt in front of Jesus and made fun of him saying,

"Hail, King of the Jews!"

They took the stick away from Jesus
and started hitting him on the head with it and spitting at him.
After they had made fun of him and laughed at him,
they took the purple robe off and led Jesus away to crucify him.

As they were taking him away,
they saw a man from Cyrene, named Simon,
and they made him carry Jesus' cross.

When they came to a place called Golgotha,
which means "the skull," they crucified Jesus.

[They tried to give him some bitter wine to drink, but he wouldn't drink it.
After they crucified Jesus, they divided his clothes among themselves
by rolling dice for them.]

They put a sign over his head which said,

"This is Jesus, King of the Jews."

REFRAIN:
Leader: Jesus has given his life for us.
All: Jesus has given his life for us.

Two robbers were crucified with him, one on his right and one on his left.
And while they were hanging there, they made fun of Jesus.
And the people who were going by laughed at Jesus and said,

["If you are the Son of God, come down off that cross!"

And the chief priests and leaders also made fun of him, saying,]

"He saved other people, but he can't save himself.
If he is the King of the Jews,
let's see him come down from that cross.
Then we will believe in him!
He trusts in God and even said, 'I am the Son of God.'
Well, let's see if God wants to save him now!"

About noon, everything became dark
and stayed dark until about three o'clock in the afternoon.
Jesus cried out in a loud voice,

"My God, my God, why have you left me alone?"

Some of the people said,

"He is calling for help. Let's see if God comes to help him."

Then Jesus cried out again, and he died.

REFRAIN:
Leader: Jesus has given his life for us.
All: Jesus has given his life for us.

The people who were there were terrified. One of the Roman soldiers said,

"This man really was the Son of God."

This is the Passion of our Lord, Jesus Christ.

Easter Sunday
and
The Season of Easter

EASTER SUNDAY

YEAR A

PRAYER OF THE DAY:

God of us all,
you gather us here today
and help us see
that Jesus lives among us.
Send us your Holy Spirit
to open our hearts
and our minds
to believe your Son
is really risen from the dead
and also lives with you
and the Holy Spirit,
forever and ever.

Note: In keeping with the Directory for Masses With Children *(Paragraph 43), the authors have elected to use the first reading from Easter Day Mass and the Gospel from Easter Night Mass because they seem best suited "to the capacity of children."*

FOCUS OF THE READINGS:

The first reading is a proclamation of the Good News that Jesus is risen from the dead! Peter gives witness to those who killed Jesus, and his witness is based on experience—"we have seen him." It is based on the command of Jesus—"to preach to the people." And what they are to preach is that Jesus has overcome death, and his Resurrection brings forgiveness and salvation to all who believe.

FIRST READING: *Acts 10:34a, 37-43*

This is a reading from the Acts of the Apostles.

Peter said to the people:

"I am sure that you know what has been told
   all over Judea about Jesus of Nazareth—
   that it all began in Galilee
   when John was preaching about baptism,
   and God anointed Jesus
   with the Holy Spirit and with power;
   that Jesus went from place to place
   doing good works
   and healing people from evil,
   for God was with him.

"We ourselves saw all that he did
   in the land of the Jews and in Jerusalem.
   They killed him by hanging him on a cross.
   But God raised him up on the third day.
   And we have seen him.
   We ate and drank with him
   after he rose from the dead.
   He told us to preach to the people
   and to tell them that he is the one
   chosen by God to be the judge of all people,
   both living and dead.
   All the prophets tell us
   that everyone who believes in Jesus
   will have their sins forgiven in his name."

The Word of the Lord.

RESPONSE: *Psalm 118*

RESPONSE: This day was made by the Lord, let us re-joice, let us be glad! let us re-joice in sal-va-tion!

VERSE: Leader You o-pened the gates of heav-en,___ you have giv-en me life. You have giv-en me life.

All: (clap) I will pro-claim the won-ders you do! (to Response)

44

GOSPEL ACCLAMATION:

"Christ is ris-en from the dead," Al - le - lu - ia!

"He is ris-en as he said," Al - le - lu - ia!

GOSPEL: *Matthew 28:1-10*

This is a reading from the Gospel of Matthew.

On the first day of the week, very early in the morning,
Mary Magdalene and another woman named Mary
went to the tomb where Jesus was buried.
Suddenly, there was a big earthquake,
and an angel of God came down from heaven.
The angel rolled the stone away
from in front of the tomb and sat on it.
The angel was wearing bright white clothes
that were shining like lightning.
The soldiers who were guarding the tomb
were very frightened,
and they fell down like they were dead!
Then the angel said to the women,

"Don't be afraid.
   I know you are looking for Jesus who was crucified.
   But he isn't here.
   He has been raised from the dead,
   just as he said he would.
   Come and see the place where his body was laid.
   Now, hurry and tell his disciples about this.
   Say to them,
      'Jesus has risen from the dead.
       He is going to Galilee where you will see him.'"

So the women hurried away.
They were filled with joy,
but they were also a little afraid.
Suddenly, Jesus was standing right in front of them.
He said,

"Peace!"

The women fell down and hugged his feet
and worshipped him.
Then Jesus said,

"Don't be afraid.
   Go and tell my disciples
   that they must go to Galilee where they will see me."

The Gospel of the Lord.

In the Gospel, the women are the first disciples to return to the tomb; there they find not the body of Jesus, but an empty tomb. They are filled with uncertainty. Yet even in their fear and confusion, they are greeted with the Good News: He is alive! If you are looking for Jesus, the One who was crucified, he is not here—in a tomb. He has risen! And they hastened to tell the apostles and the others. So our readings focus on the central message of our faith: *Christ has died, Christ has risen, Christ lives among us.*

REFLECTING ON THE READINGS WITH CHILDREN:

We are a symbolic people! And often it is in the rich symbols of our ordinary lives that God's self-revelation is available to us. We are accustomed to certain symbols that surround Easter, and they are not without meaning, for they generally have to do with newness.

You might explore these symbols with the children:

- Why do we wear new Easter clothes?
- Why do we see bunnies and chicks on cards?
- Why do we have Easter eggs?

All of these are signs of new life. We see signs of new life even in nature—new grass, flowers, buds on trees. Everything is beginning to grow new life! Perhaps some will visit relatives or friends today—perhaps a grandparent, an elderly person, someone who is alone.

How can we bring new life to those we visit? Help the children see that all of these signs remind us that Jesus rose from the dead to new life. We celebrate today that Jesus is alive and that he is with us. He will live forever, and because of him, we, too, will live forever! Today is a joyous celebration of new life!

45

SECOND SUNDAY OF EASTER

YEAR A

PRAYER OF THE DAY:

O God,
you want the whole world
to believe in you
and in Jesus, who you sent
to save us.
Show us how to believe,
and teach us
what we should believe.
Though people may laugh
at us for believing,
give us courage
to stand up for you
and to live as we should.
We ask this through
Jesus Christ, our Lord.

FOCUS OF THE READINGS:

Both of our readings focus on the presence of the risen Lord. In the first reading, this presence is witnessed in the actions of the disciples—their life together in community, their miracles, their teaching, and their belief in the Resurrection. This witness led more and more men and women to believe.

Jesus' first words to his disciples are of peace and forgiveness. "Peace be with you; . . . if you forgive the sins of anyone, they are forgiven." Thomas represents those of us who find it hard to believe that Christ is truly present among us and that living in peace and unity is possible. To him, Jesus says, "Do not doubt, but believe." The Gospel focuses on the faith of those who have not seen the body of Jesus. Christ is "Lord and God" for those who see, not physically, but with faith!

FIRST READING: *Acts 2:42-47*

This is a reading from the Acts of the Apostles.

All the people who believed in Jesus
lived together in a community
and shared everything they had.
They listened to the teaching of the apostles,
broke bread together, and prayed together.
And they were filled with wonder
because of the many signs and miracles
that the apostles did.
Every day they went to the temple to pray,
and in their homes they broke bread
and ate together
with joy and thanksgiving in their hearts.
All the people liked the way the disciples lived,
and many others came to believe in Jesus
and be saved.

The Word of the Lord.

RESPONSE: *Psalm 118*

RESPONSE:
This day was made by the Lord, let us re-joice,
let us be glad! let us re-joice in sal-va-tion!

VERSE: Leader
You are my strength and my Sav-ior.____ You have giv-en me

(clap)
All:
life. You have giv-en me life. I will pro-claim the won-ders you do!

GOSPEL ACCLAMATION:

"We have seen the ris-en Lord!" Al-le-lu-ia!

"I be-lieve my Lord and my God!" Al-le-lu-ia!

GOSPEL: *John 20:19-29*

This is a reading from the Gospel of John.

On Sunday evening (the same day the women
had been to the tomb of Jesus),
the disciples were gathered in a room upstairs.
They had locked the doors
because they were afraid of the people
who had crucified Jesus.
Then Jesus came and stood in the room and said,

"Peace be with you!"

Then he showed them his hands and his side.
The disciples were filled with joy
when they saw the Lord. Jesus said again,

"Peace be with you! As God has sent me to you,
now I am sending you to others."

Then he breathed on the disciples and said to them,

"Receive the Holy Spirit.
If you forgive the sins of anyone, they are forgiven.
If you do not forgive them, they are not forgiven."

Now one of the apostles, Thomas, was not there
when Jesus came. So, later, the other disciples told him,

"We have seen the Lord!"

But Thomas said,

"I'll never believe it until I see the marks
made by the nails in his hands
and touch the wound in his side."

One week later,
the disciples were in the same room again.
This time, Thomas was with them.
Even though the doors were locked,
Jesus came in and stood among them. He said,

"Peace be with you."

Then he said to Thomas,

"Here, touch the marks on my hands
and feel the wound in my side.
Stop doubting, and believe."

Thomas said to Jesus,

"My Lord and my God!"

Then Jesus said to Thomas,

"You believe now because you see me.
How blessed are people who have not seen me
and still believe!"

The Gospel of the Lord.

REFLECTING ON THE READINGS
WITH CHILDREN:

Like the Passion, the theology of
the Resurrection is difficult to discuss
with children. Let the text speak for
itself.

After the first reading, ask the
children to recall how the first
Christians lived and what they did.
Ask them why the Christians lived
that way. How did it show they
believed in Jesus?

After the Gospel, ask the children
what they heard:

- Where were the apostles? Why?
- Wasn't it normal that they
  should be there?
- What did Jesus say when he
  came in? Why?
- Which disciple was not there?
- What did he say when the others
  told him about Jesus?
- Wasn't that a normal way to
  react?
- What happened one week later?
- What did Jesus say again to the
  disciples?
- What did he say to Thomas?
- What did Thomas call Jesus?

Help the children to understand
that when Jesus said, "those who
have not seen," he meant, "seen my
body." Help them understand, also,
that it is truly difficult to believe in
things we haven't seen. Often we
come to believe because someone in
whom we trust tells us. For example,
we believe some food is good for us
because our parents tell us so. (You
might provide other examples.) In
the same way, people come to believe
in Jesus by what we say and do; they
see Jesus in our lives.

THIRD SUNDAY OF EASTER

YEAR A

PRAYER OF THE DAY:

God always true,
after you raised Jesus
from death,
you still let him work for us
though we cannot see him.
Let us hear his voice
as he speaks to us
secretly in our prayers.
Let us feel him near us
when we gather together
in the church.
Never leave us,
but keep close to us
through Jesus, who lives
with you, forever and ever.

FOCUS OF THE READINGS:

The first reading for the Third Sunday of Easter is always a statement on the death and Resurrection of Jesus. In every cycle we read, "You killed him, . . . but God raised him." This is the heart of the preaching of the early church. It is the core of our faith, and that is why at every mass we proclaim the mystery of faith—"Christ has died, Christ has risen, Christ will come again."

The Gospel reading for today is the wonderful story of the road to Emmaus. It tells us how the early church saw and worshipped Christ in their liturgy. The liturgy is made up of two main parts, Word and Sacrament, and Christ is present in both. *The focus here is Christ's presence in the Word* (he explained everything the scriptures said about him) *and in the Sacrament* (they recognized him in the breaking of the bread).

FIRST READING: *Acts 2:14, 22-28*

This is a reading from the Acts of the Apostles.

After they received the Holy Spirit,
the apostles stood in front of the people,
and Peter said,

"People of Judaea,
and all of you who live here in Jerusalem,
listen to what I have to say.
Jesus of Nazareth
gave many wonderful miracles and signs
right here where you could see him.
So you knew that it was God
who was acting through him
and still you crucified him.
You killed him,
but God freed him from death
and raised him up
because Jesus is more powerful than death."

The Word of the Lord.

RESPONSE: *Psalm 118*

RESPONSE: This day was made by the Lord, let us re-joice, let us be glad! let us re-joice in sal-va-tion!

VERSE: Leader
You have shown mer-cy and pow-er. You have giv-en me

All: (clap)
life. You have giv-en me life. I will pro-claim the won-ders you do!

GOSPEL ACCLAMATION:

We have seen the ris-en Lord, Al-le-lu-ia, in the break-ing of the bread, Al-le-lu-ia!

GOSPEL: *Luke 24:13-35*

This is a reading from the Gospel of Luke.

*(It was the first day of the week
when Mary Magdalene and the other women
went to the tomb of Jesus and found it empty.)*

That same day, two of the other disciples
were on their way to a little village called Emmaus.
They were talking about all that had happened to Jesus.
While they were walking,
Jesus himself came along and walked with them,
but the two disciples didn't recognize him.
Jesus asked them,

"What have you been talking about?"

They looked very sad, and one of them, Cleophas, said,

"You must be the only visitor in Jerusalem
who hasn't heard about the things that have happened."

"What things?" Jesus asked.

They said,

"Jesus of Nazareth was a great prophet
who did and said many powerful things in front of all the people.
We were hoping that he was the One who would save us,
but our chief priests and ruler put him to death.
They crucified him three days ago.
And early this morning,
some of the women from our group went to the tomb,
but they couldn't find his body.
They ran back saying some angels told them Jesus is alive.
Then some of the men went to the tomb
and found it exactly as the women had said.
And they didn't see Jesus either."

Then Jesus said,

"You are so foolish!
Why don't you believe what the prophets said?
They told you that the Christ would have to suffer and die
before coming into glory."

Then Jesus explained everything
that Moses and the prophets had said about him.
When they got close to Emmaus, the two disciples said to Jesus,

"It's almost evening. Stay with us."

So he stayed with them.
And while they were at the table, Jesus took the bread,
blessed and broke it, and gave it to them.
Then they understood, and they recognized him.
But Jesus disappeared from their sight.
The two disciples said to each other,

"Remember how excited we were
when he talked to us on the road, explaining the scriptures!"

Then the two ran to Jerusalem to tell the others
everything Jesus had told them,
and how they recognized him in the breaking of the bread.

The Gospel of the Lord.

REFLECTING ON THE READINGS
WITH CHILDREN:

Luke gives a story that is easily imagined. Invite the children to imagine the two disciples walking along a road on their way to Emmaus. Help them with a little description—it is not a busy street in town with lights and stores, and so forth.

- Why were they there?
- What were they discussing?

When Jesus joined them, they didn't recognize him. (It might be helpful to explain that such was usually the case when Jesus appeared after the Resurrection, *perhaps* because people didn't expect Jesus to be present.)

You may wish to refer to the type of questions suggested in the *Handbook* on page 14 under "Reflecting on the Readings with Children," to help facilitate the discussion.

The children should leave with two main ideas:
1. Jesus walks with us in our daily journey.
2. Jesus is still present in the scriptures and the breaking of bread (communion) at mass.

FOURTH SUNDAY OF EASTER

YEAR A

PRAYER OF THE DAY:

Loving Lord,
you sent Jesus to give us
real life—your life.
Because we belong to you,
help us live as your children
and follow Jesus
by loving others and caring
for those who need help.
As his sisters and brothers,
may we always recognize
his voice when he calls us
and leads us to you.
We ask you to do this
through that very same Jesus,
who lives with you,
forever and ever.

FOCUS OF THE READINGS:

Both readings focus on hearing and following the call of God in Jesus.

The first reading is the end of Peter's speech which proclaims the death and resurrection of Jesus. The heart of the story is the response to Peter's message, "What should we do now?" As always, the repentant sinner finds forgiveness and salvation awaiting his or her acceptance of Christ.

The Gospel parable of the Good Shepherd focuses on hearing and recognizing the voice of God. Those who seek honestly will recognize in Jesus the voice of God and will follow because Jesus, the Good Shepherd, will lead them to "a full and happy life."

REFLECTING ON THE READINGS WITH CHILDREN:

The imagery of "shepherd and sheep" may not be familiar to all children. Because this image is so profound in scripture, it will be worth taking time to

FIRST READING: *Acts 2:14, 36-41*

This is a reading from the Acts of the Apostles.

After they received the Holy Spirit,
the apostles stood in front of the people,
and Peter said,

"All the people of Israel must now be told,
and must know for sure,
that God has raised Jesus up
and made him Lord and Christ.
This is the same Jesus whom you killed."

When the people heard this,
they were very upset
and asked Peter and the other apostles,

"What should we do now?"

Peter said to them,

"Show that you are sorry
by changing your lives.
Be baptized in the name of Jesus Christ.
He will forgive your sins,
and you will receive the Holy Spirit.
The promise he made is for you
and for your children,
and for all people everywhere."

About 3,000 people believed in what Peter said and were baptized that day.

The Word of the Lord.

RESPONSE: *Psalm 118*

RESPONSE:
This day was made by the Lord, let us re-joice,
let us be glad! let us re-joice in sal-va-tion!

VERSE: Leader
The stone which the build-ers re-ject-ed __ is the Cor-ner-stone,

All: (clap)
to Response
__ is the Cor-ner-stone. __ I will pro-claim the won-ders you do!

GOSPEL ACCLAMATION:

"I am the Good Shep-herd. _____ I know my
sheep and my sheep know me." Al - le - lu - ia!"

GOSPEL: *John 10:1-5, 10*

This is a reading from the Gospel of John.

One day Jesus said,

"I tell you the truth,
the one who comes into the sheepfold
through the door is the shepherd.
But anyone who tries to climb
in some other way,
must be a thief and a robber.
The sheep hear the shepherd's voice
when he calls each one by name.
He leads them out, and they follow him
because they know his voice.
The sheep will not follow
the voice of a stranger but will run away.
The thief comes only to steal and kill.
But I came so that you will have life—
a full and happy life."

The Gospel of the Lord.

introduce the children to it. In this instance, it may be useful to have pictures of shepherds and sheep today so that children become acquainted with this pastoral scene outside the context of the scriptures. Introduce the children to the meaning of words such as sheepfold, pasture, and so forth.

Even today, it is the shepherd who walks in front of the sheep, leading them from pasture to pasture. As he calls to them, they follow him. When the children see this as part of ordinary, real life, the power of this Gospel—that Jesus is the Good Shepherd—will be real enough to touch their hearts. But for children who are outside of a rural or pastoral setting, the images related to shepherding need to be visual in order to avoid remaining abstract.

Ask the children to identify what the shepherd does and what the sheep do. This may be done as follows:

Shepherd	Sheep
calls	hear
leads	follow
gives life	live happily (in safety)

The life of the sheep is dependent on the shepherd who leads them from pasture to pasture where they will find sufficient food and who leads them home to the sheepfold in the evening so that they will be protected and safe. So it is the Good Shepherd who gives life to the sheep.

Ask the children how we can hear the voice of Jesus today. Help them remember the first reading. Help them see that it was Peter who spoke to the people and who called them to become followers of Jesus.

Ask the children who tells them about Jesus: parents, teachers, priests and other ministers. Help the children see that these people are shepherds in the church today, as were Jesus and Peter. Jesus continues to be our Good Shepherd through others.

Today is Vocation Day. Explain to the children that the word "vocation" means "a calling." The church throughout the world prays together today—on Good Shepherd Sunday—that we will have many women and men who want to become shepherds for us in the church today—people who will be good teachers, parents, ordained ministers and religious. Just as a shepherd leads the sheep, Jesus calls people today to lead his people. When we follow his voice, we are promised a full and happy life.

51

FIFTH SUNDAY OF EASTER

YEAR A

PRAYER OF THE DAY:

God our Father,
you want more
than anything else
to share with us
all the good things of your life.
That is why you sent Jesus
to tell us about it
and show us the way.
So when we get tired
of doing good deeds,
make us strong
and determined again,
and help us to believe in you
more and more.
We pray this prayer
through Christ our Lord.

FOCUS OF THE READINGS:

There is not a direct relationship between the two readings for today. The first reading recounts the appointment of seven men to take care of the daily, physical needs of the community. In fact they (Philip and Stephen) also preach the Word. The most probable focus of the reading is the easing of the tension between the Greek and Jewish Christians. The apostles try to solve this by appointing Greek leaders.

The Gospel, part of the last discourse of Jesus, focuses on Jesus as the revelation of God. We, like Thomas and Philip, long to "see" God. We cannot easily relate to a faceless, voiceless God. Jesus is the face and voice of God. In Jesus, and all he says and does, we see and know God.

FIRST READING: *Acts 6:1-7*

This is a reading from the Acts of the Apostles.

Every day more and more people
were becoming disciples.
Soon some of them, those who spoke Greek,
complained to the apostles
that some of the widows were not being taken care of
and were not getting enough to eat.
The apostles gathered
the group of disciples together and said,

"Our main work is to preach the Word of God,
and we can't stop doing that to hand out food.
So choose seven people from your group,
and we will ask them to take care of the food
and see that it is given to those who need it.
These seven people must be very wise
and must be filled with the Holy Spirit.
They must be people
who are respected by the others.
While they are doing their work,
we will spend our time in prayer
and in the ministry of the Word."

All the disciples liked this idea,
and so they chose seven people.

[Their names were Stephen (a man
who had strong faith and was filled
with the Holy Spirit), Philip, Prochorus,
Nicanor, Timon, Parmenas and Nicolaus.]

When they took these seven to the apostles,
the apostles put their hands on them
and prayed over them.

The Word of the Lord.

RESPONSE: *Psalm 33*

RESPONSE:

Lord, be with us, with your love, be with us, all our hope is in you.

VERSES:

1. For your faith-ful word and all you
2. (♩) We are cho-sen, God, by
   to Response

1. do, for your love we trust in you.
2. you. Bless us God, we trust in you.

GOSPEL ACCLAMATION:

"I am the way. I am the truth. I am the life." Al-le-lu-ia! -lu-ia!

GOSPEL: *John 14:1-12*

This is a reading from the Gospel of John.

Jesus said to his disciples,

"Don't let your hearts be worried and upset.
You already believe in God; believe in me, too.
There are many rooms in my Father's house.
I am going now to prepare a place for you.
But I will come back,
and I will take you to be with me where I am.
And you know the way to the place
where I am going."

Thomas said to Jesus,

"Lord, we don't even know where you are going,
so how can we know the way?"

Jesus said,

"I am the way, I am the truth, and I am the life.
Anyone who wants to come to the Father
must come through me."

[Then Philip said,

"Lord, show us the Father."

Jesus said,

"Philip, anyone who has seen me,
has seen the Father.
I am in the Father and the Father is in me.
You can believe me
because you see the things that I do.
And I tell you the truth, anyone who believes in me
will be able to do the things that I do
and even greater things than I do
because I am going to the Father."]

The Gospel of the Lord.

[ ] *Reader may omit text that appears in brackets.*

REFLECTING ON THE READINGS WITH CHILDREN:

What did you hear?

That the Father and Jesus are one will not be a concept grasped by children. Today's Gospel provides us with the possibility of concentrating on Jesus as the way, rather than the oneness. You might use an example such as the following:

- Has your family ever taken a trip to a part of the country you have never seen before?
- Before a family begins such a journey, they must make many plans:
  1. They must decide where they want to go.
  2. They must know something about the journey so they will be prepared with the right things. (Wouldn't it be foolish to take only shorts and swim suits to Alaska?)
  3. They must pack up all the things they will need.
  4. And they must have a good map and follow it carefully to avoid becoming lost. If they follow the map and are well prepared, they can expect to enjoy their stay when they arrive.

We want to go to heaven to be with God where we will have life forever. But we have never been to heaven, and we have never seen God. Thomas and Philip had the same problem. When Jesus said he was going back to heaven and that he would come for us, they wanted to know the way to heaven, and they wanted to see God. Jesus said, "I am the way, I am the truth, and I am the life." Jesus tells us what we need for our journey, and we know that he tells us the truth. Jesus shows us the way, and we will have a life of joy when we get to heaven.

What does Jesus mean when he says, "I am the way"? Help the children see that Jesus came to show us who God is. When we live the way Jesus lived because we believe in him, we are on the right way. Jesus tells us that we will be able to do even greater things than he has done because he will send us his Holy Spirit.

How can we live the way Jesus lived?

53

SIXTH SUNDAY OF EASTER

YEAR A

PRAYER OF THE DAY:

Lord God,
we can do nothing good
without the help of your Spirit.
Send that Spirit to us now
so that we may be quick
to forgive those who hurt us,
ready to spread the Good News
about Jesus,
and to love our neighbor
as ourself.
We ask you this
through Jesus, your Son,
who lives with you,
forever and ever.

FOCUS OF THE READINGS:

Our readings focus on God's universal love. In the first reading Philip goes to preach the Good News to the people of Samaria, a foreign country, outside of Judaism. For the Jews of Palestine, this represents an enormous sign of God's universal love. The reading also focuses our attention on the coming of the Holy Spirit, the fruit of the death and Resurrection of Jesus.

The Gospel gives us the heart of the Christian message: love. This is not an option for Christians, but a commandment. It is the proof of our discipleship. This love is made possible by the power of the Holy Spirit living in us.

FIRST READING: *Acts 8:5-8, 14-17*

This is a reading from the Acts of the Apostles.

Philip went to a city in Samaria
to proclaim the Good News of Christ.
The people there believed
what Philip told them
because of the way he preached
and the wonderful signs he gave them.
He freed people who had evil spirits in them,
and he healed many people.
All the people were filled with joy
because of what Philip said and did.

When the apostles in Jerusalem
heard that the people in Samaria
believed in Jesus,
they sent Peter and John there to pray
that they would also receive the Holy Spirit.
The people already had been baptized
in the name of the Lord Jesus,
but when Peter and John
laid hands on them and prayed,
they received the Holy Spirit.

The Word of the Lord.

RESPONSE: *Psalm 96*

RESPONSE: All the na-tions will praise you, and know that you are God.

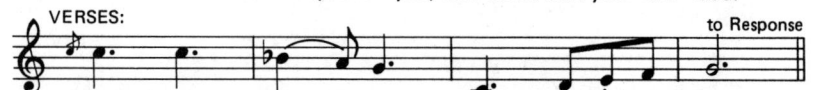

VERSES:
1. Give God glo - ry. Give hon- or and praise.
2. Pro-claim sal - va - tion day af - ter day.
3. Tell the na - tions God's won-der-ful deeds.

54

GOSPEL ACCLAMATION:

Je - sus said: "If you love me, keep my com-mand-ments."

Al - le - lu - ia. __ "Keep my com-mand-ments." Al - le - lu - ia! __

GOSPEL: *John 14:15-21*

This is a reading from the Gospel of John.

Jesus said to his disciples,

"If you truly love me,
you will keep my commandments.
And I will pray to the Father
to send the spirit of truth
to be with you forever.
I will not leave you alone.
I will come back to you.
Yes, I am going back to the Father now,
but you will see me because I am alive.
And because I live, you will live, too.
Anyone who loves me
keeps my commandments.
My Father loves everyone who loves me.
And if you love me,
I will show myself to you."

The Gospel of the Lord.

REFLECTING ON THE READINGS WITH CHILDREN:

Jesus said we should love one another so that we will be happy. Ask the children if that is their experience. Are people happier when they love one another? Perhaps they could share some examples.

- Jesus tells us how he wants us to love others. What did he say?
- What do you think Jesus meant when he said, "Love one another as I have loved you"?

Note: this is a crucial point in our Christian faith. Christian life is based on love of God and neighbor. But children can easily misunderstand this. The love Jesus shares is God's very own divine love. God *is* love. We are not able to love with the fullness of God's divine love as Jesus did. We are, however, commanded to love in the *way* Jesus loved. This commandment is first given in an earlier part of this last discourse of Jesus, just after he has washed the feet of his disciples in an attitude of service. And so we are commanded to love one another in the *way* Jesus loved, that is, by serving one another. The greatest love is shown by giving our lives for others—in service. By doing this in the name of Jesus, we share God's own love with one another. What a wonderful gift to receive and to share. Remind the children that Jesus said, "there is no greater love than to give your life for your friends."

Jesus gave his life for us when he died. But he also gave his life for others by healing them, helping them, and caring for them. How can we give our lives for others now? Help children see and express ways they can give their lives for others. Here are some examples:

- Including all children in games.
- Talking to a child who feels alone.
- Helping someone with a task.
- Taking time, perhaps from play, to help someone.
- Accepting people just as they are. (*We want to catechize, not moralize.*)

Jesus asks us to love this way because he loves us so much. Jesus loves everyone and wants us to love everyone, too. That's what a Christian is—someone who believes Jesus is living and who lives like him.

ASCENSION OF THE LORD

YEAR A

PRAYER OF THE DAY:

Lord, just as when
the disciples were happy
when Jesus returned to you
and then prayed together
for your Spirit to come to them,
listen to our prayer today:
send your Spirit upon us
to carry on the work
you gave Jesus to do.
With your help,
may everyone who sees
the way we live and behave
come to know and love Jesus,
who ascended to you
and now lives with you,
forever and ever.

FOCUS OF THE READINGS:

The mission of the church is to evangelize.

Our Gospel reading tells us that before Christ left his disciples physically, he commissioned them to "go to every part of the world, and tell everyone the Good News." The Lord was with them, and they accomplished much good in his name.

The passage from *Acts* tells us how they were able to do this. Jesus reminds the disciples of his promise to send his Spirit. Baptized in the Holy Spirit, they have the power to preach in the name of Jesus. Like love, evangelization is not an option for the church. We are commanded in today's readings, "Go; . . . you will be my witnesses. . . ."

FIRST READING: *Acts 1:3-5, 8-11*

This is a reading from the Acts of the Apostles.

After Jesus died and rose,
he appeared to his apostles many times
to show them that he was really alive.
They saw him,
and he talked to them about the reign of God.
He told them not to leave Jerusalem
but to wait for the gift of the Holy Spirit.
Jesus said,

"I have told you about this promise.
John baptized with water, but in a few days,
you will be baptized with the Holy Spirit.
The Holy Spirit will give you power
to be my witnesses in Jerusalem, in Judaea,
in Samaria, and all over the world."

After he said this, Jesus was taken up to heaven.
And even though they couldn't see him any more,
the disciples stayed there staring into the sky.
Two men, dressed in white robes,
appeared to them and said,

"Jesus has been taken up to heaven,
but he will come back to you."

The Word of the Lord.

RESPONSE: *Psalm 47*

1. Praise God with trumpets, praise God with songs. Proclaim Good News to all of the earth!
2. Sing praise to Jesus our Lord and God. Proclaim Good News to all of the earth!

GOSPEL ACCLAMATION:

Round ① ② ③

Sing al - le - lu - ia, sing al - le - lu - ia! Sing

④

al - le - lu - ia, sing al - le - lu - ia!

GOSPEL: *Matthew 28:16-20*

This is a reading from the Gospel of Matthew.

The eleven disciples
went to the mountain in Galilee
where Jesus told them to meet him.
Jesus came to them there and said,

"God has given me
  all the power and authority
  of heaven and earth.
Now I am sending you out
  to preach to all the nations.
I want you to make disciples
  and baptize them in the name of the Father,
  and of the Son, and of the Holy Spirit.
Teach them to keep my commandments
  and do all that I have taught you.
And I promise you that I am with you always,
  even to the very end of the world."

The Gospel of the Lord.

REFLECTING ON THE READINGS WITH CHILDREN:

After the Gospel, ask the children what they heard. Ask them to listen to the Gospel again, this time listening for the word they think is very important. Hopefully, they will give a variety of words such as:

- sending,
- preach,
- disciples,
- baptize,
- teach,
- promise.

You may wish to write on newsprint the words the children say. Help them reconstruct Jesus' directions to evangelize—to tell the Good News and baptize.

Ask the children how the disciples were able to do this. Remind them of the first reading that tells us that the disciples were baptized in the Holy Spirit. With that power they were able to do many things—especially be witnesses for Jesus.

We also received the Holy Spirit when we were baptized: "In the name of the Father, and of the Son, and of the Holy Spirit."

And so we too have the power of the Holy Spirit to be witnesses for Jesus. How can we do this?

Jesus said he wants everyone to hear the Good News that he is risen and loves them and wants them to live forever with him.

Jesus said, "Go to every part of the world and tell everyone the Good News." How can we help do that?

(As always it is important to keep the children focused on ideas truly possible for them at their ages.)

SEVENTH SUNDAY OF EASTER

YEAR A

PRAYER OF THE DAY:

O God, we belong to you
and to Jesus, your Son.
Help us to pray to you,
and as we pray,
may we get to know you
more and more each day.
We ask you this through Jesus,
who lives with you,
forever and ever.

FOCUS OF THE READINGS:

Both readings are concerned with prayer and the future of the church.

In our first reading, we see the apostles along with Mary the mother of Jesus, the brothers of Jesus, and other people gathered in the upper room. They have been promised the Holy Spirit, and they wait in prayer. The Holy Spirit will empower them to carry on the work of Jesus. Notice that not only the apostles but also other believers are empowered, for it is together that they constitute *church*.

All of Chapter 17 of John's Gospel is Jesus' prayer for the church. A portion of this prayer, sometimes called the "priestly prayer of Christ," is read on the Seventh Sunday of Easter in each cycle. The focus of the portion in today's Gospel is the gift of eternal life made possible by the death and resurrection of Jesus. While the other three Gospels use parables to describe the reign of God or the reign of heaven, only here does an evangelist attempt a definition of eternal life. Our salvation—eternal life—is knowing God and Jesus Christ. Knowing, in the biblical sense, does not mean simply having an intellectual grasp of God, but rather being one with God and Jesus Christ. Throughout the prayer, Jesus prays that we will have that oneness.

FIRST READING: *Acts 1:12-14*

This is a reading from the Acts of the Apostles.

After Jesus was taken up to heaven
from Mt. Olivet,
the apostles went back to Jerusalem
where they were staying.
All of the apostles—Peter and Andrew,
James and John, Philip, Thomas,
Bartholomew and Matthew, James,
Simon and Jude—
spent their time in the upper room praying.
They prayed with some of the women
and with Mary, the mother of Jesus,
who stayed there with them.

The Word of the Lord.

RESPONSE: *Psalm 130*

RESPONSE:

Lis-ten to my prayer, I trust in you my God. God.

VERSES:
to Response

1. In my heart I pray to you. Hear my voice and come to me.
2. My soul hopes in you my God. You have saved me by your love.
3. My soul waits for you my God like the night that waits for day.

GOSPEL ACCLAMATION:

"E - ter - nal life is know-ing you, the on - ly true God; and Je - sus Christ, the one you sent." Al - le - lu - ia!

GOSPEL: *John 17:1-11*

This is a reading from the Gospel of John.

As Jesus was teaching his disciples,
he said this prayer:

"Father, the time is now here.
Glorify me
so that you will be glorified, too.
You have given me power
to give eternal life to everyone.
And this is what eternal life is:
to know you, the only true God;
and to know Jesus Christ, the one you sent.

"I did everything you sent me on earth to do.
I told the people about you.
And now they know that I came from you
and that you sent me.
And so I pray for them
because they are yours,
and they are mine."

The Gospel of the Lord.

REFLECTING ON THE READINGS WITH CHILDREN:

After the first reading, ask the children, "What did you hear? Who can remember who was gathered in the upper room?"

Children enjoy memorizing, and while this is not the focus, it will be helpful for them to know the names of the apostles. But be sure they realize that others were there as well, especially Mary, the mother of Jesus.

Mary appears very infrequently in the New Testament, but over the course of the three-year cycle, the children should see that when she is mentioned, it is because she has an important role to play in the church. It is through this biblical view that the children will grow into a deep and rich understanding of Mary.

Before the Gospel, explain to the children that Jesus made this prayer just before he died. He is talking to God about his mission on earth. Invite them to listen to his prayer.

After the Gospel, ask the children:

- What did you hear?
- What did Jesus say in his prayer?
- What did Jesus say eternal life is?
- What does it mean to "know God" and to "know Jesus"?

Help the children see the difference between knowing *about* someone and *knowing* someone. To know someone also involves entering into a relationship of love.

God is often an abstraction to children. They will understand better what it means to know and love Jesus. We love Jesus because we know all the wonderful things he does for us. And most of all we love Jesus because he loves us so much and was willing to suffer and die for us. Through all of Easter we have been hearing that Jesus is always with us. And because we love him, we will live with him forever.

PENTECOST SUNDAY

YEAR A

PRAYER OF THE DAY:

God of all people,
thank you for your gift
of the Holy Spirit to us
and the whole church.
Through the power
of your Spirit,
may we tell the whole world
about Jesus;
forgive those who have hurt us,
as we have been forgiven;
and live a happy life,
doing all that you want us to do.
We pray this prayer
through Jesus, your Son,
who lives with you
and the Holy Spirit.

FOCUS OF THE READINGS:

The mission of the church is to do the work of the Holy Spirit.

Jesus breathed into his disciples his own life, the Holy Spirit. By the power of that Spirit, the church is born. The followers of Jesus are now to do what his death and Resurrection was all about—forgive. Peace is the greeting of the risen Lord, and peace is his continued presence in the church.

This Spirit comes upon the disciples with power. In the name of Jesus, in every language, they are empowered to preach about "the great things God has done."

REFLECTING ON THE READINGS WITH CHILDREN:

Before the first reading, remind the children of the first reading for Ascension. Reread to them the center part of the reading. Begin with, "One day when Jesus was with the disciples. . ." And end with, ". . . and you will be my witnesses in Jerusalem, in Judea and Samaria, and all over the world."

Now invite the children to listen to today's first reading.

FIRST READING: *Acts 2:1-8, 11b*

This is a reading from the Acts of the Apostles.

On the day of Pentecost,
the believers were gathered together
in one room.
All of a sudden they heard a sound
like a strong wind
that seemed to fill the whole house.
Then they saw what looked like tongues of fire
coming and resting on each one of them.
They were all filled with the Holy Spirit,
and immediately they started to speak
in other languages.

At that time, there were visitors in Jerusalem
who had come from all over the world.
They were amazed
because they heard the believers
speaking in so many languages.
They said,

"How are they able to speak like this?
Aren't all of these people from Galilee?
Yet we can all hear them
telling in our own languages
about the great things God has done."

The Word of the Lord.

RESPONSE: *Psalm 104*

RESPONSE: Send us your Spir-it, O Lord, and re-new the face of the earth!

VERSE: May your glo-ry last for-ev-er. May you re-joice in all we do!

60

GOSPEL ACCLAMATION:

"Peace— be with you! Re - ceive the Ho - ly Spir - it."
Al - le - lu - ia!

GOSPEL: *John 20:19-23*

This is a reading from the Gospel of John.

In the evening,
the disciples were gathered in a room.
They had locked the doors
because they were afraid of the people
who had crucified Jesus.
Jesus came and stood in the room
and said,

"Peace be with you!"

Then he showed them
his hands and his side.
The disciples were filled with joy
when they saw the Lord.
Jesus said again,

"Peace be with you!"

Then he breathed on the disciples
and said to them,

"I give you the Holy Spirit.
If you forgive the sins of anyone,
they are forgiven.
If you do not forgive them,
they are not forgiven."

The Gospel of the Lord.

After the first reading, ask the children how Jesus kept the promise that he had made. Ask them what it seemed like to the disciples when they received the Holy Spirit. It is important to help them understand that the Holy Spirit is not "strong wind" and "tongues of fire." These are images used to describe an event which cannot really be put into words. We often do this. We say things such as, "She is like a cute little kitten." Or we say, "She is as strong as a rock." We are using metaphors to help us express more a feeling or a quality than a physical presence.

The disciples were able to preach with clarity, and so, later, when writing this account, they described the event as receiving "tongues of fire." We don't know what the event was like. We know only that they received the power of the Holy Spirit to do Christ's work, especially of preaching and healing.

Ask the children (as we have before) what words are said at the Christian baptism—"I baptize you in the name of the Father, and of the Son, and of the Holy Spirit."

Help them to understand that we, too, have received the Holy Spirit. Ask them what the disciples did when they received the Holy Spirit. The stress here should not be on speaking other languages but on telling about the great things God has done.

Ask the children how we can do this today, because we, too, have the Holy Spirit. Ask them to give some examples of how they can tell about the great things God has done:

- What great things today?
- Whom can we tell?

After the Gospel, ask the children what else Jesus gave us the power to do besides telling the great things God has done. Explore ways in which they can forgive others. Help them to see that if we truly forgive someone, that person "feels" the power of the freedom of being forgiven. If we refuse this, that person "feels" the burden of not being forgiven. We have the power of the Holy Spirit to free people by being forgiving. Help them to see that when we live this way, as we pray in the Psalm refrain, "the face of the earth will be like new."

Feasts of the Lord
and
Sundays in Ordinary Time

TRINITY SUNDAY
YEAR A

PRAYER OF THE DAY:

God of all creation,
you embrace us
with the love
of a mother and father.
You send your own Son,
Jesus, to save us.
Through the power
of your Holy Spirit,
you raise us
to life everlasting.
Your life is a mystery
that we will celebrate
and proclaim
forever and ever.

Note: In keeping with the Directory for Masses
With Children *(Paragraph 43), the authors
have elected to use both readings from Year B
instead of Year A because they seem best suited
"to the capacity of children."*

FOCUS OF THE READINGS:

The focus of our readings is the
experience of God acting in our lives in
various ways. We have no adequate
language for God, because God is beyond
any single image we may have. We
experience God in Jesus Christ who
shares with us his experience of God—as
creator, as redeemer, and as a person of
intimate relationship. Our experience of
this relationship is the Spirit of God living
in us.

In the first reading, Paul tells us that
because we live in the Holy Spirit, and
because we are brothers and sisters of
Christ, we are children of God. We too can
enjoy the intimate relationship that Jesus
called "Abba."

In the Gospel, Jesus tells his disciples
to preach, baptize and teach in the name
of God—the God who is intimate like a
parent (Father), who comes as Savior
(Son), and who lives within us (Holy
Spirit).

FIRST READING: *Romans 8:14-17*

*This is a reading
from Paul's letter to the Romans.*

Brothers and sisters,

Everyone who is guided by the Holy Spirit
is a child of God.
We have been adopted by God,
and when we pray, "Abba, Father,"
it is the Holy Spirit and our own spirit
telling us that we truly are God's children.
And if we are God's children,
we will have eternal life like Jesus
who is God's Son.

The Word of the Lord.

RESPONSE: *Psalm 104*

VERSES:

1. Chil-dren ev-'ry-where sing your song of love:
2. Moon and stars you made, in the heav'ns to shine:
3. Mak-ing birds of air, fish-es in the sea:
4. Lit-tle though we are, yet you care for us:
5. You, our lov-ing God, bring us close to you:

REFRAIN:

Won-der-ful, won-der-ful, won-der-ful your name!

GOSPEL ACCLAMATION:

"Make dis-ci-ples and bap-tize them, in the name of the Fa-ther, the name of the Son, the name of the Spir-it." Al - le - lu - ia!

GOSPEL: *Matthew 28:16-20*

This is a reading from the Gospel of Matthew.

The eleven disciples
went to the mountain in Galilee,
just as Jesus had said.
When Jesus met them there, he said,

"God has given me all the power
and authority of heaven and earth.
Now I am sending you out
to preach to all the nations.
I want you to make disciples
and baptize them
in the name of the Father,
and of the Son,
and of the Holy Spirit.
Teach them to keep my commandments
and do all that I have taught you.
And I promise you that I am with you always,
yes, to the very end of the world."

The Gospel of the Lord.

REFLECTING ON THE READINGS WITH CHILDREN:

As noted previously, Trinitarian language poses difficulties for children (as well as adults!), and even well-intentioned analogies may serve only to confuse them more. We suggest that with the children we not concern ourselves with doctrinal language for Trinity, but rather with the experience of God in our lives.

Ask the children what Jesus asked the disciples to do (preach, baptize and teach). Are the disciples of Jesus still doing those things today?

Jesus said, "preach to all nations." This might be a good time to tell the children a little about missionary work. Besides preaching in our own parishes, some people are called to go to other parts of the world.

Jesus said, "teach them to keep my commandments." Help the children discuss the many ways the church teaches (religious education classes for children and adults, special classes on the Bible, informal teaching by parents, teachers, friends, and so forth). Draw attention especially to teaching activities in your own parish.

Jesus said, "baptize them in the name of the Father and of the Son and of the Holy Spirit." Ask the children if they remember being at a baptism. What words does the priest or deacon say? Remind them that we proclaim that we are baptized Christians every time we make the sign of the cross and say those words.

If time permits, you may wish to reflect on the first reading as well. Remind the children that Jesus often used the name "Father" or even "Abba" which is like our word "Daddy." What is important here is not the masculine image of God, but rather the intimate relationship that Jesus experienced with God. St. Paul tells us that because Jesus chose us to be his brothers and sisters and gave us his Holy Spirit, we too are children of God and can call God "Abba!" The children should leave today's Liturgy of the Word knowing that God loves them and wants to be close to them.

BODY AND BLOOD OF CHRIST

YEAR A

PRAYER OF THE DAY:

God of life, help us to know
that when we share our food,
as you do,
with all who are in need,
we satisfy our hunger;
when we share our drink,
as you do,
with all who are in need,
we satisfy our thirst.
We offer this prayer
as we gather
to eat the bread
and drink the wine
of your Son, Jesus,
who lives with us
now and forever.

Note: In keeping with the Directory for Masses
With Children *(Paragraph 43), the authors
have elected to use the first reading from Year
C because it seems best suited "to the capacity
of children."*

FOCUS OF THE READINGS:

Our readings for today focus on the
presence of Christ in the Eucharist. In the
first reading, Paul presents what he was
taught concerning the actions and words
of Jesus at the Last Supper. While the
words may vary in the four accounts
(*Matthew, Mark, Luke* and *1 Corinthians*),
what remains consistent is the belief that
in the sharing of bread and wine Christ is
present.

The Gospel proclaims that Christ
himself is our life. It is he who satisfies
our hunger and thirst. He chose to make
this concept reality in bread and wine.
Jesus invites us to share his body and
blood, which in Hebrew are symbols of
person and life. In these symbols we
encounter the living Lord, ever present to
us. To share in his life, to be one with him,
is to live forever.

FIRST READING: *1 Corinthians 11:23-26*

*This is a reading
from Paul's first letter to the Corinthians.*

Brothers and sisters,

This is what Jesus did at supper
the night before he died.
He took bread, and after he gave thanks,
he broke the bread and said,

"This is my body, which I am giving for you.
When you eat this bread, remember me."

After supper, he took a cup of wine and said,

"This cup is the new covenant in my blood.
When you drink from this cup,
remember me."

For when you eat this bread
and drink from this cup,
you are proclaiming the death of the Lord
until he comes again.

The Word of the Lord.

RESPONSE: *Psalm 104*

You are the one who feeds us, giv-ing us food from your hand.
You are the one who feeds us, giv-ing us all we need.

GOSPEL ACCLAMATION:

1. "I am the Bread of Life," says the Lord.
2. Al - le - lu - ia, al - le - lu - ia!

1.-2. "All who eat this Bread will live for - ev - er."

GOSPEL: *John 6:35, 51-56*

This is a reading from the Gospel of John.

Jesus said to the people,

"I am the bread of life.
Anyone who comes to me
will never be hungry,
and anyone who believes in me
will never be thirsty.
I am the living bread
that came down from heaven.
Anyone who eats this bread,
which is my life, will live forever.
This bread gives life to the world.
Unless you eat this bread
and drink from this cup,
you do not have real life in you.
For I am real food and real drink for you.
Everyone who eats this bread
and drinks from this cup
lives in me and I live in each of them.
Those who eat this bread
and drink from this cup
have eternal life
and I will raise them up on the last day."

The Gospel of the Lord.

REFLECTING ON THE READINGS WITH CHILDREN:

What did you hear?

Discuss with the children the many times we celebrate our unity by sharing in a special meal: Christmas, Easter, Thanksgiving, birthdays, and so forth. Are there other times? Ask the children what their family eats on these special occasions. Help them see that certain foods have become symbols of what we are celebrating. When we see and eat certain food, it makes the event real and even brings to our memory past celebrations. For example, many families have turkey for dinner every year on Christmas. It has become symbolic for the celebration of this important event. And sharing in that special dinner brings members of the family closer together.

Jesus celebrated a special meal with his disciples the night before he died. They shared bread and wine. Jesus told them that from now on, whenever his disciples share that bread and wine and remember him, he is there in a special way. When we come together for mass, we remember what Jesus said and did. We too share that bread and wine which is the very life of Jesus, and it brings us all closer together. When we eat this bread and drink from this cup, we say that we believe in Jesus, and we believe that he gives us life and that he will give us life forever.

SECOND SUNDAY IN ORDINARY TIME

YEAR A

PRAYER OF THE DAY:

Loving God,
you told the world
about the coming of your Son,
Jesus, not through thunder,
lightning, or earthquake,
but through people
such as John the Baptist.
Now it is our turn
to pass on the Good News.
May we forgive those
who hurt us
just as Jesus forgives them
and now lives with you,
forever and ever.

FOCUS OF THE READINGS:

Our readings continue the theme of last week, the baptism of the Lord, focusing on the call of God and, specifically, on the call to mission. The first reading is again the call of the servant of God to bring back the lost and to seek out the stranger (light to the nations). This servant is empowered for this mission by the honor and strength which God gives.

Jesus, too, was called and anointed to be the Lamb who will take away the sin of the world. He, too, is empowered for his mission by the strength of God, given to Jesus in his baptism when the Spirit came to rest on him.

FIRST READING: *Isaiah 49:3, 5-6*

This is a reading from the prophet Isaiah.

God created me in my mother's body
and called me to be a special servant.
I have been honored, and now,
God is my strength.
For God said to me,

"You are my servant, Israel,
and I will show my glory
to the people through you.
You will bring my people back to me.
But more than that, I want you
to be a light to all the nations
so that everyone will be saved."

The Word of the Lord.

RESPONSE: *Psalm 40*

RESPONSE:
"Here I am, O my God, I come to do your will."

VERSES: to Response
1. I pro-claim sal - va - tion. I will say to all, "The Lord is great."
2. All will see your kind-ness. They will trust in you and want to say:

GOSPEL ACCLAMATION:

"There is the Lamb of God, _____ who takes a-way the sins of the world." _ " Al-le-lu-ia, al-le-lu-ia!

GOSPEL: *John 1:29-34*

This is a reading from the Gospel of John.

When John the Baptist
saw Jesus walking toward him,
he said to those who were with him,

"Look, there is the Lamb of God!
He is the one who takes away
the sin of the world.
I told you
that someone was coming after me
who is greater than I am.
He was living before I was born.
I did not know who he was,
even though God sent me
to tell everyone about him
and to baptize in water.
God said to me,

'When you see the Spirit
coming from heaven like a dove
and staying with him,
you will know that he is the one
who will baptize with the Holy Spirit.' "

Then John said,

"Now I have seen all of this happen,
and I tell you that he is the Son of God."

The Gospel of the Lord.

REFLECTING ON THE READINGS WITH CHILDREN:

Ask the children if they recall last week's readings. Perhaps some will recall the discussion on baptism. Review with them the main points.

This week it may be helpful to reflect on the images used in the readings.

Discuss with the children their understanding of the word "servant." Our acceptance of the *role* of servant is dependent on our notion of its meaning.

What does a servant do? What does it mean to be a "servant" of God? How can we serve God? The children should realize that we serve God by serving God's people.

John called Jesus the "Lamb of God." Again, the power of this image rests on an understanding of the word. Explain to them the gentleness and innocence of a lamb. In the Old Testament, the people often sacrificed a lamb to show their sorrow for sin and their love for God.

Why is Jesus called the Lamb of God? How can we give ourselves lovingly for others?

If time permits, you may wish to explain to the children that a dove is a symbol of peace. This image is used at Jesus' baptism because he came to bring peace.

69

THIRD SUNDAY
IN ORDINARY TIME

YEAR A

PRAYER OF THE DAY:

God, you are Father
and Mother to us all,
bringing us together
into one family with Jesus.
Gather more and more people
into that family
so that the whole world
may love and praise you.
We ask you to do this
through Jesus Christ,
our Lord.

FOCUS OF THE READINGS:

Our Gospel reading for today
focuses on the call of the disciples.
Their mission—"fishing" for people—
is explained in the actions of Jesus:
preaching the Good News and
healing people of their diseases.

*Note on the adaptation of the
Gospel: The first half of this
Sunday's Gospel is rather difficult,
with its names of locations, and
seems to serve as an introduction to
the mission of Jesus. We have
chosen, therefore, not to include the
opening verses and have started with
the call of the disciples.*

FIRST READING: *1 Corinthians 1:10-13*

*This is a reading
from Paul's first letter to the Corinthians.*

Brothers and sisters,
I beg you in the name of Jesus
to get along with each other and be united
in everything you think and do.
Some of Chloe's friends told me
that you are arguing with each other.
Some of you are saying,
"I belong to Paul!" or "I belong to Peter!"
or "I belong to Apollos!"
or "I belong to Christ!"
But Christ can't be divided up like that.
Was I the one who died for you?
Or were you baptized in my name?
No, we all belong to Christ.

The Word of the Lord.

RESPONSE: *Psalm 71*

RESPONSE:
I have been yours since the day of my birth, and
you have been my God. been my God.

GOSPEL ACCLAMATION:

1. Je - sus said: "From now on you will be
2. Al - le - lu - ia! "You will be

1.-2. gath - er - ing peo - ple in."   peo - ple in."

GOSPEL: *Matthew 4:18-23, 17*

This is a reading from the Gospel of Matthew.

One day, as Jesus was walking
by the sea of Galilee,
he saw two brothers, Peter and Andrew.
They were fishing, and Jesus called to them,

"Come, follow me.
From now on you will be gathering people
instead of fish."

Peter and Andrew
left their fishing nets right away
and followed Jesus.
A little while later,
Jesus saw two other brothers, James and John.
They were also fishermen.
They were in their boat
with their father, Zebedee,
when Jesus called to them.
Right away they left their boat
and followed him.
Jesus went all around Galilee,
teaching in the synagogues,
preaching the Good News,
and healing people of their diseases.

The Gospel of the Lord.

REFLECTING ON THE READINGS
WITH CHILDREN:

Lead the children to recall the
Gospel scene:

- Where did it take place?
- Who was there? What were
  they doing? What did Jesus say
  to them? What did they do?
- What did Jesus mean when he
  said, "From now on, you will be
  fishing for people instead of
  fish?"

Explore this further with the
children. Jesus came so that all
people will know and love God. Jesus
helped people know and love God by
preaching the Good News and by
healing them. He called other
people—disciples—to help him do
this. The disciples also preached and
healed people. We are disciples of
Jesus, and he wants us to "fish for
people." How can we do that?

FOURTH SUNDAY IN ORDINARY TIME

YEAR A

PRAYER OF THE DAY:

Great and glorious God,
all we have and all we are
comes from you.
Look after us always;
keep us from doing
what is wrong,
and let us never forget
how much we need you.
We pray to you
through Jesus, your Son.

FOCUS OF THE READINGS:

Both of our readings focus on the poor and humble. Both praise those who express simplicity and humility in justice and peace. In the first reading, the poor are urged to turn to God for help and they will find peace. The beatitudes present the ultimate paradox of Christian life and can be seen as worthwhile only by the believer whose source of grace is Christ. Those who accept their poverty and humility and who express their need for God in justice and peace are blessed.

FIRST READING: *Zephaniah 2:3, 3:11-13*

This is a reading from the prophet Zephaniah.

Our God says,

"Stay close to me, all you who are poor
and who keep my commandments.
Try to be humble,
and treat people with justice.
Then, when I come,
you will not be punished.
I will take away the people who are proud,
but I will leave a small group of people
who are humble and simple.
They will turn to me for help.
They will not do evil things,
or lie, or be dishonest.
They will have food and rest.
And no one will make them afraid."

The Word of the Lord.

RESPONSE: *Psalm 113*

RESPONSE:

1. You love the poor, you love the need-y.
2. Teach us to love the poor and need-y,

1. You give them help, you care for them.
2. to give them help, to care for them.

72

GOSPEL ACCLAMATION:

"Bless-ed are peo-ple who know they need God. The king-dom of heav-en be-longs_ to them." Al-le-lu-ia, al-le-lu-ia! "The king-dom of heav-en be-longs_ to them."

GOSPEL: *Matthew 5:1-12a*

This is a reading from the Gospel of Matthew.

Jesus went up on a mountain
with his disciples, and he taught them, saying:

"Blessed are people who know they need God,
   for the kingdom of heaven belongs to them.
Blessed are people who are sad now,
   for later, God will comfort them.
Blessed are people who are humble,
   for God will give them everything.
Blessed are people who work for justice,
   for God will give them all they need.
Blessed are people who show mercy to others,
   for God will have mercy on them.
Blessed are people who have hearts
   that are pure, for they will see God.
Blessed are people who make peace,
   for they will be called children of God.
Blessed are people
   who suffer for doing what is right,
   for the kingdom of heaven belongs to them.

["And you are blessed when people hurt you
   and say bad things about you
because you believe in me.
   Be happy and glad,
   for God will reward you in heaven."]

The Gospel of the Lord.

[ ] *Reader may omit text that appears in brackets.*

REFLECTING ON THE READINGS WITH CHILDREN:

   Reflecting on the beatitudes will not be easy with children, for the beatitudes present the opposite of all that seems reasonable. Poverty, sorrow, hunger and mistreatment will hardly seem like blessings. But two things may be hoped for with the children:

   1) To provide familiarity with the beatitudes, the heart of the Christian way of life. Here again, we are planting seeds that, with life's experience and God's constant grace, will grow to maturity. It is enriching for children to hear and be familiar with the truths of our faith, even if, as yet, they do not fully understand them.

   2) To help the children understand that, whatever our condition in life, God asks for our trust. If we are poor or hungry, or sad or mistreated, God can and will make things right. This may, of course, only be realized in heaven. Likewise, if we have more than we need, we must trust that when we share what we have, God will continue to take care of us and bless us. Sorrow comes when we don't trust God and, therefore, live selfishly rather than for others.

FIFTH SUNDAY IN ORDINARY TIME

YEAR A

PRAYER OF THE DAY:

Make us be
like clear windows, God,
so that our family and friends
may see the light of your love
shining through us.
Keep us from being afraid
to show that we love you,
and, instead, let all we say
and all we do
please you in every way.
We ask you to do this
through Jesus Christ,
our Lord.

FOCUS OF THE READINGS:

Both readings focus on "living for others." Jesus uses two metaphors to describe his disciples: salt and light. In this portion of the Sermon on the Mount, Jesus does not instruct his disciples to *become* salt of the earth or light for the world. He tells them that they already *are* so, because of their relationship with him. Just as Christ is the revelation (light) of God, so the Christian is to be the revelation of Christ (light) for the world. The light of the Christian (our relationship with Christ) is shown to the world by the good works that will draw others to God.

FIRST READING: *Isaiah 58:7-10*

This is a reading from the prophet Isaiah.

Our God says,

"Share your bread
with those who are hungry.
And when you see people
who have no home,
give them a place to live.
Give clothes to anyone who needs them
and be kind to your own family.
Then you will be like the morning light
that comes after the darkness of night,
and your sins will be forgiven.

["You will call upon God to help you,
and God will say, 'Here I am!']

"Don't hurt people by lying about them
or by saying unkind things about them.
Give bread to the hungry
and help those who suffer.
When you do these things,
your gloom will be changed into joy,
and you will shine
with the brightness of God's light."

The Word of the Lord.

[ ] *Reader may omit text that appears in brackets.*

RESPONSE: *Psalm 112*

RESPONSE:
Leader: (finger snap)

You are the light that shines in our lives.

All:

You are the light that shines in our lives.

VERSES: Leader:

1. We are blessed when we live by your Word. You are the
2. We are blessed when we give to the poor.
3. We are blessed when we help those in need.
4. We are blessed when we do what is just.

74

GOSPEL ACCLAMATION:

"You are the salt of the earth.__ You are the light__ of the world," says Je - sus. world." Al - le - lu - ia, al - le - lu - ia,__ "You are the light__ of the world."

GOSPEL: *Matthew 5:13-16*

This is a reading from the Gospel of Matthew.

Jesus said to his disciples,

"You are the salt of the earth.
But what happens
when salt loses its taste?
It becomes useless
and must be thrown away.
You are the light of the world.
People don't light a lamp
and then put it under a basket.
No, instead they put it up on a stand
so it will shine everywhere in the house.
In the same way,
you must let your light shine for others
so that people can see
the good things you do,
and give praise to your God
who is in heaven."

The Gospel of the Lord.

REFLECTING ON THE READINGS WITH CHILDREN:

What did you hear in the readings today? When they have had time to share this, ask the children questions about their experiences. For example:

- What kinds of food do you put salt on? Popcorn? French fries? Why do we put salt on certain foods?
- Do you have a night light in your home? Why?
- Do you have lamps in your home? Why?
- Did you ever use a flashlight?
- Have you ever experienced the light going out during a storm?
- Would you ever think of putting boxes over lamps in your home?
- Would you cover a flashlight in a forest?

Jesus tells us that we are the salt of the earth. We are the light of the world. He tells us that we must let our light shine for others to see. Help the children see that the light we received at baptism is the life of Christ within us. This is the light that others must see—that Christ lives in us. This was symbolized by the baptismal candle. We received the light of Christ in our baptism, and now we can be light for others. Others will see our light shining when they see the good works we do.

Isaiah, the prophet, tells us what good works we should do. Ask the children if they remember what Isaiah told us. (You may need to read the text again.) Isaiah tells us that good works are: feeding the hungry, clothing the naked, being fair to others, and so forth.

SIXTH SUNDAY IN ORDINARY TIME

YEAR A

PRAYER OF THE DAY:

Lord, it is so hard
to love everyone
as you love us through Jesus.
We are sorry
for our bad tempers,
for upsetting those
who care for us,
and not helping those
who need our care.
Forgive us,
and show your love
to us again
so that we may truly love
our family and all our friends.
We ask you to do this
through Jesus Christ,
who lives with you
forever and ever.

FOCUS OF THE READINGS:

Both readings focus on fidelity to
God's laws. The first reading tells us
that God is not responsible for the
evil in this world. We are free to
accept God's ways or not. The
Gospel also insists on God's law, but
takes it even further. Jesus insists
on fidelity, not only to the external
law, but the spirit of the law. Both
call for a well-developed conscience.

*Note on the adaptation of the
Gospel: Because of the extreme length
of this Gospel and its complexity, we
have chosen to use a shorter form. We
have included what we feel to be both
the heart of the message and that
which is most easily understood by
small children.*

FIRST READING: *Sirach 15:15-20*

This is a reading from the book of Sirach.

The prophet said to the people,

"It is up to you whether or not
  you will be faithful to God.
You are the ones who must choose.
If you want to,
  you are able to keep the commandments.
You can have either life or death.
Whichever you choose will be given to you.
God doesn't tell anyone to do bad things,
  and God doesn't give anyone
  permission to sin."

The Word of the Lord.

RESPONSE: *Psalm 119*

RESPONSE: With all my heart I turn to you. Teach me your ways, I'll fol-low you.

VERSE: Your word, O God, is good and true. Help us all to fol-low you.

GOSPEL ACCLAMATION:

"Make peace with your broth-ers. ____ Make peace with your sis-ters. ____ Then go ____ and wor-ship God." ____ Al-le-lu-ia, ____ al-le-lu-ia. ____ "Then go ____ and wor-ship God."

GOSPEL: *Matthew 5:17, 20, 21-22a, 23-24*

This is a reading from the Gospel of Matthew.

Jesus said to his disciples,

"Don't think that I came to destroy
what the law and the prophets taught.
No, I came to show you what they meant.
I tell you the truth,
if you want to go to heaven,
you must behave better than
the scribes and Pharisees.
For example, the law said,

'You shall not kill anyone.'

"But I say to you,

'Don't even stay angry with anyone.'

"Whoever insults another person
or says bad things to them will be judged.
So, if you are making an offering
or praying at the altar,
and you remember that your brother or sister
is upset or angry with you about anything,
leave your gifts there at the altar.
First, go and make peace
with your brother or sister,
and then come back and worship God."

The Gospel of the Lord.

REFLECTING ON THE READINGS
WITH CHILDREN:

Two points should be emphasized.

1. Jesus wants us to do what is right—not only on the outside, but also in our hearts. The Ten Commandments say, "You shall not kill anyone." But Jesus says, "Don't stay angry; don't make fun of people; don't say bad things about people." Jesus wants us to do more than avoid murder; he wants us to live in peace with our brothers and sisters.

- Who are our brothers and sisters?
- What does Jesus say about offering our gifts at the altar?

Help the children relate these ideas to mass.

- Do we sometimes come to mass when we are angry with someone, or when someone is angry with us? Jesus asks us to forgive one another.

Explain to the children that our greeting of peace at mass is an expression of peace—but we also must *live* in peace.

While we certainly do not want to lead the children into being overly scrupulous, we do want to help them develop a conscience in accord with Jesus' teachings. The teaching is not that we do not deserve to be at mass; rather, it is there that we are nourished by Word and sacrament to live the commandments of Jesus. The teaching is that what we are nourished to do, we must do!

2. While we are nourished by the grace of God to follow Jesus, we must, in fact, choose to do that or not. God neither forces nor prevents us.

SEVENTH SUNDAY IN ORDINARY TIME

YEAR A

PRAYER OF THE DAY:

God, our Protector,
it is so much easier
to love only those
who love us in return.
Teach us to be like your Son,
who loved and forgave those
who nailed him to the cross.
We pray this prayer
through that same Jesus,
who lives with you,
forever and ever.

FOCUS OF THE READINGS:

The focus of our readings is to love as God loves. Because our society tends to trivialize the word "love," we are apt to miss the profound nature of this teaching in our two readings. The motivation for this commandment in *Leviticus* is the holiness of God. Precisely because God is holy, God's people must be holy, and that holiness is reflected in love of neighbor. Jesus takes the commandment further and adds a positive requirement to it—"Love your enemies and pray for them." But the motivation and conclusion are the same—we must be loving and kind because God is loving and kind.

Note on the adaptation of the Gospel: We have shortened and simplified the text so that children can more easily take its message to heart—to love those whom you don't like, even those who hurt you.

FIRST READING: *Leviticus 19:1-2, 17-18*

This is a reading from the book of Leviticus.

God said to Moses,

"Gather the whole community of Israel
together and say to them,

'You must be holy,
because I am your God,
and I am holy.
You must not hate your brothers
and sisters in your heart.
Tell them when they do something wrong,
but don't try to get even with people,
and don't stay angry with them.
You must love your neighbor
as you love yourself.' "

The Word of the Lord.

RESPONSE: *Psalm 73*

RESPONSE:

I will stay close to you, close to you my God.

VERSES:

1. When I'm feel - ing _____ an - gry.
2. When I'm feel - ing _____ hurt.
3. When I don't un - der - stand you.
4. When I can't go _____ on. _____
5. You are al - ways _____ with me.
6. As you guide my _____ way. _____
7. Hold me, keep me _____ safe. _____

GOSPEL ACCLAMATION:

GOSPEL: *Matthew 5:43-48*

This is a reading from the Gospel of Matthew.

Jesus said to his disciples,

 "You have heard people say,

  'Love your neighbor and hate your enemy.'

 "But I say to you,
 love your enemies and pray for people
 who are unkind to you
 and who say bad things about you.
 Then you will be true children of God,
 for God lets the sun shine
 on both good and bad people.
 If you love only people who love you,
 why should you be rewarded?
 Even sinners do that!
 If you are friendly only to people you like,
 you are no better than anyone else.
 Even people who don't know God do that.
 You must be kind and loving just like God."

The Gospel of the Lord.

REFLECTING ON THE READINGS WITH CHILDREN:

We are accustomed to reflecting on love of neighbor. But today's Gospel calls us to reflect on loving our enemies. Children often have a keen sense of fairness. That quality, positive enough, will also make it difficult to speak about loving those who hurt us. Gently lead the children to see that this is precisely what Jesus asks. It is easy to love those who love us, to be friendly to people who like us. But God accepts everyone and wants us to do the same.

Encourage the children to discuss the difficulties of loving people they don't like. They will likely be able to provide many examples. We can help children develop a biblical conscience in their early years. They should see commandments such as, *"You must be holy,* because I, your God, am holy"; and "You must be kind and loving *just like God,"* as ideals. It is always a delicate ministry to challenge children with the truth of the Gospel while avoiding moralizing or instilling guilt. Every day we *try* to be more like Jesus.

Our holiness consists in being *like* God in the sense that we are striving to live God's commandment because that is *God's way* of living.

EIGHTH SUNDAY IN ORDINARY TIME

YEAR A

PRAYER OF THE DAY:

God of all tenderness,
all you want is for us
to be truly happy
and to enjoy your good gifts.
In trust and confidence,
we put ourselves
into your hands,
knowing that you will guard
and protect us,
forever and ever.

FOCUS OF THE READINGS:

Our readings focus on God's constant care for us. The first reading tells us that God is like a mother who will always care for her child. The Gospel tells us that God is the creator of all and will care for all. When we trust that God, like the mother in the first reading, will take care of us, we are not filled with anxiety or worry. Notice that Matthew does not say we do not have basic needs, but that with trust in God our needs will be served. Our faith is not in the things we need, or in our own ability, but in the one who provides. We are like children in the care of our mother, our creator.

FIRST READING: *Isaiah 49:14-15*

This is a reading from the prophet Isaiah.

The people of Jerusalem were saying,

"God has forgotten all about us
and has left us alone."

But God said to them,

"A mother always loves her own child.
A mother cannot forget her own baby.
But even if a mother could do that,
I will never forget you."

The Word of the Lord.

RESPONSE: *Psalm 131*

REFRAIN:
Like a child rests in its moth-er's arms, so will I rest in you. Like a child rests in its moth-er's arms, so will I rest in you.

VERSES 1-3: *to Refrain*

1. My God, ___ I am not proud. I do not look for things too great.
2. My God, ___ I trust in you. You care for me, you give me peace.
3. O Is-ra-el, ___ trust in God, ___ now and al-ways trust in God.

GOSPEL ACCLAMATION:

"Look for God's king - dom." Al - le - lu - ia. "You will have all that you need." "Look for God's king - dom." Al - le - lu - ia. "You will have all that you need."

GOSPEL: *Matthew 6:24-33*

This is a reading from the Gospel of Matthew.

Jesus said to his disciples,

"You cannot serve God and money
at the same time.
So don't worry about things.
Don't worry about what you will eat,
or drink, or what clothes you will wear.
Life is worth more
than what we eat or drink or wear.
Look at the birds in the air;
they don't plant seeds or save food in barns.
But God feeds them.
Aren't you worth more to God than birds?
And why worry
about what you are going to wear.
Look at the wild flowers in the fields.
They don't make clothes for themselves.
But they are more beautiful
than a king all dressed up in rich clothes.
If God takes such good care
of wild flowers, you can be sure
that God will take good care of you.
So don't worry about food or clothes.
God knows that you need all those things.
Have faith.
Look first for God's kingdom
and being right with God.
Then you will have all you need."

The Gospel of the Lord.

REFLECTING ON THE READINGS WITH CHILDREN:

After the first reading, explore the image of God as "mother" with the children. For some, this may come as a delicate issue. Many children come from single parent families. Just as the "father" image will be difficult for some children, so the "mother" image will be for others. Children should never be pressed to relate to any one image of God. God is not literally a father or a mother. Both are images that may help us relate to God.

- How is God like a mother?
- What does God want us to feel and to know?
- What is the most important line in the reading for *you?*
- *After the Gospel,* explore the images used in the text.
- What two things does Jesus ask us to see in nature?
- What does he say about the birds, about the wild flowers? Have you ever seen wild flowers?
- What do you think about the images Jesus used?

Be sure the children understand that Jesus is not saying that we do not need food, clothing, and so forth. Nor is he saying that we need not work for these things. The comparison with the birds and wild flowers is based not on need, but on worry. We can never stress enough with children how much God loves and cares for us. Our failure to believe this in a practical sense may be an indication that we still need to develop trust in God. Points to remember:

- "I will never forget you. I will always love you."
- "Look first for the reign of God, and all the other things will be given to you."

NINTH SUNDAY IN ORDINARY TIME

YEAR A

PRAYER OF THE DAY:

God, you are always
faithful and true,
and you look after those
who trust in you.
Today,
we put our hands in yours.
Help us to love you
in what we do
as well as in what we say.
We pray to you
through Jesus Christ,
our Lord.

FOCUS OF THE READINGS:

Again this week the readings
focus on the commandments of God.
In the first reading from *Deuteronomy*,
Moses assures the people of God's
blessing if they obey the commandments, keeping them in their hearts
and souls. The notion of choice is
clear from the concluding promise of
punishment if they choose to follow
the ways of false gods. In the Gospel,
Jesus insists that lip service is not
sufficient. Heaven is for those who
do the will of God.

FIRST READING: *Deuteronomy 11:18, 26-28*

This is a reading from the book of Deuteronomy.

Moses said to the people,

"Everything I am telling you,
you must keep in your heart
and in your soul.
Always remember these words!
Today I offer you a choice
between a blessing and a punishment.
You will be blessed
if you obey the commandments of God
which I am giving you today.
But you will be punished
if you follow the ways of false gods
and do not obey
the commandments of God."

The Word of the Lord.

RESPONSE: *Psalm 19*

RESPONSE: Your law, O God, gives us hap-pi-ness, gives us hap-pi-ness and new life.

VERSES:
1. Your law, O God is good and just.— You help us all to fol-low your ways.
2. Your words teach us what is right.— Your word, O God gives joy to my life.

82

GOSPEL ACCLAMATION:

(Musical notation)

Lis-ten to Je-sus. Al-le-lu-ia. Lis-ten and
do what he says. _____ Lis-ten to Je-sus.
Al-le-lu-ia. Lis-ten and do what he says.

GOSPEL: *Matthew 7:21, 24-27*

This is a reading from the Gospel of Matthew.

Jesus said to his disciples,

"It isn't enough just to call me the Lord
without doing what God says.
The people who will enter heaven
are the ones
who do what God wants them to do."

Then Jesus gave them this example:

"Anyone who hears my words
and does what I say
is like a wise person
who builds a house on solid ground.
When it rains and the wind
blows very hard or a flood comes,
the house will not fall down
because it is built on rock.
But anyone who hears my words
but doesn't do what I say
is like a foolish person
who builds a house on sand.
When it rains hard or there is a flood
or the wind is too strong,
the house will fall down
because it was only built on sand."

The Gospel of the Lord.

REFLECTING ON THE READINGS
WITH CHILDREN:

After the Gospel, ask the children
if they remember what examples
Jesus gave. The imagery used here
is clear and simple and should easily
be grasped by children. They can
easily visualize that a house built on
sand will not last when rains and
winds come. Perhaps they have been
in a car or trailer or tent during a
storm. They will know the difference
between that experience and being in
a strong house.

Help the children see the
connection between a "house built
on rock" and "doing what God
wants." When we stay with God and
God's ways, we are strong and
nothing can destroy us. For a child,
this can be likened to being solidly in
a family and knowing that security.
Nothing can shake us or hurt us. We
have the protection of our family.
Jesus tells us that we have that same
security and protection (heaven)
when we stay with God and don't just
say we believe in God.

What can we do to help build our
house on rock? Remember, a strong
house isn't built in a day—and
neither is obedience to God's
commandments. It's something we
strive for and work at with God's help.

TENTH SUNDAY IN ORDINARY TIME

YEAR A

PRAYER OF THE DAY:

Lord, you are calling us
to love you
and to be your friends.
Open our eyes
to the things we are doing
which do not please you.
Make us happy
to follow you
and, through our happiness,
attract others to you.
We make this prayer
through Christ, our Lord.

FOCUS OF THE READINGS:

The readings focus on God's desire for our love and mercy rather than our sacrifices. Though God's ways (the ways of love) shine like the light of day, the people turned to ritual and exterior observances instead. In the Gospel we see how far these externals went. Even to eat with someone outside the law (a sinner) was forbidden. Jesus, the total expression of love and mercy of God, eats with sinners. We are not saved by ritual; we are saved by the one who is love. Without love, ritual is nothing.

FIRST READING: *Hosea 6:3-6*

This is a reading from the prophet Hosea.

[The prophet Hosea said to the people,

"Let us try to know God.
God will come to us
as sure as morning comes after night.
And God's way shines like the light of day.
God will come to us like the gentle rain
that comes in spring to water the earth."]

Then God said to the people,

"My people, what can I do with you?
Your love for me
is like dew on grass in the early morning.
It soon dries up.
That is why I punished you
and spoke harshly to you
through the prophets.
I don't want your sacrifices.
I want your love."

The Word of the Lord.

[ ] *Reader may omit text that appears in brackets.*

RESPONSE: *Psalm 51*

RESPONSE: In your kind-ness, O my God, have mer-cy on me, have mer-cy on me.

VERSES:
1. I know___ that I have sinned and done what is wrong.
2. O God___ for-give my sins and make my heart true.

GOSPEL ACCLAMATION:

Leader: / All: (sing and clap)

1. You call us, Lord, to fol-low you: Al-le-lu-ia, al-le-lu-ia!
2. To love____ peo-ple as you do. Al-le-lu-ia, al-le-lu-ia!

GOSPEL: *Matthew 9:9-13*

This is a reading from the Gospel of Matthew.

As Jesus was walking along,
he saw a man named Matthew
who was working in the tax office.
Jesus said to him,

"Come, follow me."

Matthew got up, left the tax office
and followed Jesus.
Soon after that, Jesus and his disciples
were at Matthew's house having dinner
with many tax collectors and other people.
When the Pharisees saw this,
they asked the disciples,

"Why does Jesus eat with people
like tax collectors and other sinners?"

But Jesus heard them ask this question,
so he said,

"People who are healthy don't need a doctor.
It's the people who are sick who need a doctor.
Now go and try to learn what these words mean:

'I don't want your sacrifices;
I want you to love and show mercy
to other people.'

"I didn't come for people who think they are holy.
I came to help sinners.
I care more about love and mercy
than about your sacrifices."

The Gospel of the Lord.

REFLECTING ON THE READINGS WITH CHILDREN:

After the Gospel ask the children:

- What did you hear?
- Who did Jesus call?
- What was he doing?
- Did Jesus and Matthew ever see each other again?
- Why did it surprise the Pharisee that Jesus had dinner at Matthew's house?
- Why was Matthew considered a sinner?

NOTE: Explain to the children that tax collectors were Jews who worked for the Romans. Their job was to collect the taxes from their Jewish people and give it to the Romans. They often collected more than the people owed and kept it themselves.

- Can you think of other times when Jesus ate with "sinners"?
- What did Jesus say when the Pharisee complained?
- What do you think of Jesus' example?

That's the good news: Jesus came for sinners. And he wants us to love all people too. We show we really believe in Jesus when we show love and mercy to others.

Perhaps the children can give some examples.

What do you think Jesus wants us to remember from today's Gospel?

ELEVENTH SUNDAY IN ORDINARY TIME

YEAR A

PRAYER OF THE DAY:

Everloving God,
you care for all people
but especially those
who suffer.
We give ourselves to you
that you may work through us
for all who are sick or sad
in our families
and our schools.
We ask you to do this
through Christ, our Lord.

FOCUS OF THE READINGS:

There is not a single focus that unites the first reading and the Gospel.

The first reading establishes the notion of a chosen people. The people of Israel are a holy nation, God's own priests, because of the covenant God has made with them. The saving act of God in the exodus is motivation for fidelity.

The Gospel focuses on the mission of the church to the people of Israel. The disciples are called and sent (apostle means "one who is sent") to seek out the lost and care for them as a shepherd cares for sheep.

FIRST READING: *Exodus 19:2-6*

This is a reading from the book of Exodus.

When the people of Israel
were camping in the desert,
Moses went up on the mountain to talk to God.
God called to Moses and said,

   "This is what I want you to say to my people,

      'You have seen for yourselves
      what I have done for you.
      I saved you from the Egyptians,
      and I brought you here safely
      just as an eagle
      carries her young one on her wings.
      If you listen to my voice
      and keep my covenant,
      you will be more precious to me
      than all other people.
      You will be my own priests.
      You will have a holy nation.' "

The Word of the Lord.

RESPONSE: *Psalm 100*

RESPONSE:
Leader: All:

1. God, we come to   wor-ship you:
2. God, you made us, we are yours:
3. God, your love is al-ways true: O-pen our hearts_ to
4. Faith-ful God, we trust in you:

lis-ten to you._   O-pen our hearts_ to lis-ten to you._

GOSPEL ACCLAMATION:

Al - le - lu - ia!   We hear the Good News_ that

God is love,   God cares for us; so al - le - lu - ia!

We hear the Good News_ that God is love.

GOSPEL: *Matthew 9:35-10:8*

This is a reading from the Gospel of Matthew.

Jesus traveled
through many towns and villages
telling the people the Good News
and healing those who were sick.
When he saw how many people needed help,
he felt sorry for them
because they were like sheep
who didn't have a shepherd.
So he said to his disciples,

"There is a big harvest to bring in,
  but there are not enough people to do the work.
  Pray that God, who is in charge of the harvest,
  will send more workers to help."

[Then Jesus called the twelve apostles together.
Their names are Simon Peter and his brother,
Andrew; James and John; Philip and
Bartholomew; Thomas and Matthew, the tax
collector; Simon; Jude and James;
and Judas, the one who turned against Jesus.
Jesus gave the apostles power to heal people
who were sick or who had evil spirits in them.]

When Jesus sent the apostles out,
he said to them,

"Go to the people of Israel
  who are like lost sheep.
  Tell them,

    'The kingdom of heaven is near!'

  Heal people who are sick
  or who have evil spirits,
  cure lepers, and raise people from the dead.
  You were given the power
  to do these things freely,
  so do them without asking to be paid."

The Gospel of the Lord.

[ ] *Reader may omit text that appears in brackets.*

REFLECTING ON THE READINGS
WITH CHILDREN:

What did you hear? Encourage
the children to recall lines, thoughts
or images from the Gospel.

Why did Jesus feel sorry for the
people? Explain that image.

Read the words of Jesus again,
"There is a big harvest to bring in,
but there are not enough people to do
the work. Pray that God, who is in
charge of the harvest, will send more
workers to help." What did he mean
by "harvest"?

Jesus sent his apostles out. What
did he ask them to do?

Do you remember the names of
the apostles? If you have included
this section in the reading, this is not
of primary importance, but children
often enjoy lists and memorizing. It
will also familiarize them with some
of the great leaders of the early
church.

Jesus said, "There is a big harvest
to bring in, but there are not enough
people to do the work." Is that true
of the church today? Who are some
people who are working in the
harvest today in the church?

Help the children focus on
ministers in your own parish: people
who collect food and clothing for the
poor, music ministers, priests,
teachers, sisters, people who visit
shut-ins, the St. Vincent de Paul
Society, doctors, youth ministers, and
so forth.

87

TWELFTH SUNDAY IN ORDINARY TIME

YEAR A

PRAYER OF THE DAY:

God in heaven,
we are more precious to you
than any other creature
you have made.
When we feel ashamed
to say we love you,
make us proud.
When we are frightened
to follow you, give us courage.
We make this prayer to you
through Christ, our Lord.

FOCUS OF THE READINGS:

Both readings focus on the two-fold reality that while the prophet/preacher will surely suffer persecution, God is always there to care for and protect those who remain faithful to the task.

In the first reading, Jeremiah confesses his fear of persecution, even by friends, and then reminds himself that God is with him. So even in the face of persecution, Jeremiah can praise God.

Our Gospel is a continuation of last week's "sending" of the apostles. This section focuses on the inevitable persecution of the apostles with the promise of protection.

God does not remove the suffering but is always there to comfort, protect and see the task to its fruition.

REFLECTING ON THE READINGS WITH CHILDREN:

This theme is not easy to contemplate with children. In the first place, severe persecution and martyrdom are not within their experience.

FIRST READING: *Jeremiah 20:10-13*

This is a reading from the prophet Jeremiah.

Jeremiah said to God,

"People are whispering
terrible things about me,
and I am afraid. They are saying,

'Ignore him! Reject him!'

Even people who used to be my friends
are waiting for me to make a mistake.
They are saying,

'Maybe God will reject him, and he will fall.
Then we can get even with him.' "

Then Jeremiah said to God,

"But I know that you are with me,
like a mighty hero.
Those who hate me
will not be able to hurt me.
They will be ashamed and dishonored.
You see everything,
and you understand every heart.
I know you will stop my enemies
because I have put my trust in you.
You save the lives of the poor
from the power of evil people.
I will sing praise to you, my God;
I will sing praise!"

The Word of the Lord.

RESPONSE: *Psalm 92*

RESPONSE:
1. I will sing praise to you. I will sing to you, my God.
2. I will sing praise to you. I will sing for all you do.

VERSE:
We proclaim you are great. We proclaim your faithful love.
to Response

GOSPEL ACCLAMATION:

1. "If you show you believe in me, I will
2. Al - le - lu - ia. "Be - lieve in me." Al - le -

1. tell God you be - long to me."___
2. lu - ia. "You be - long to me."___

GOSPEL: *Matthew 10:26-33*

This is a reading from the Gospel of Matthew.

Jesus said to his disciples,

"Don't be afraid of anyone.
Everything that I am telling you in secret,
I want you to proclaim out loud to everyone.
Don't be afraid of people
who can kill only your body.
They can't kill your soul.
Think more about God
who has power over both your body
and your soul.
You know that two little sparrows
can be sold for only a penny.
Yet, not even one sparrow dies
unless God allows it to happen.
You are much more valuable to God
than many sparrows.
So don't be afraid.

"If you stand up for me
in front of other people,
I will tell God in heaven
that you belong to me.
If you don't stand up for me
in front of other people,
I will tell God in heaven
that you do not belong to me."

The Gospel of the Lord.

Secondly, the possibility of suffering will hardly appeal as a value! Still children will have the experience of "persecution" in the form of ridicule or exclusion.

Reflection on readings such as these may serve to instill in them a sense of trust in God's presence and protection. Jeremiah and the prophets are role models for courage.

This may be a Sunday for reversing the normal procedure of the reflections following the readings.

Before the first reading, ask the children if they have ever been in a game when someone was either excluded or treated unfairly by others. Or have they ever seen someone punished for something he or she didn't do?

Did anyone speak up for the child who was excluded, treated unfairly, or punished? Allow the children time to share some examples.

What happens when someone takes sides with a child the others don't like? Why are we sometimes afraid to do that?

We shouldn't pretend with children that speaking up for justice, doing things God's way, or speaking the truth are easy. The scriptures are clear, as is the evidence all around us, that suffering for truth and justice is not unusual. Children are naturally afraid of this—so was Jeremiah! Children will naturally be confused by this reality—so were the disciples!

After the discussion, read the first reading. Then point out to the children that Jeremiah too was afraid but he knew God would take care of him.

Read the Gospel. What did you hear? Point out that Jesus promised the disciples that he would protect them. Remind them of Jesus' example of the sparrows.

89

THIRTEENTH SUNDAY IN ORDINARY TIME

YEAR A

PRAYER OF THE DAY:

God,
through your Son, Jesus,
you reached out to people
in every kind of need.
Use us in the same way,
so that by our words
and actions,
others may feel
the power of your love.
We ask you this
through Christ, our Lord.

FOCUS OF THE READINGS:

The focus of our readings is the welcome given to the person who brings God's Word.

In the first reading, we have a delightful story about a woman who goes to great efforts to offer hospitality to the prophet Elisha, a holy man of God. Everything was done to make the prophet welcome in their home.

In the Gospel, Jesus says, "Anyone who welcomes you welcomes me." He praises those who welcome the prophets and holy people.

FIRST READING: *2 Kings 4:8-11, 14-16*

This is a reading from the second book of Kings.

When the prophet Elisha
went to the town of Shunem,
a wealthy woman who lived there
invited him to eat in her home.
After that, whenever Elisha was in that town,
he would stop at her home to eat.
One day the woman said to her husband,

"I can tell that Elisha is a holy man of God.
Let's prepare a room upstairs for him.
We will put in it a bed, a table, a chair
and a lamp. Then, whenever he comes,
he can stay there."

The next time Elisha came, he stayed
in the room they had prepared for him.
He was very grateful for all the kindness
the woman had shown him,
so he said to his servant Gehazi,

"Is there anything I can do for her?"

Gehazi answered,

"Well, she doesn't have any children,
and her husband is getting old now."

Elisha said,

"Call her and ask her to come here."

When the woman came, Elisha said to her,

"I promise you that by this time next year,
you will have a child."

The Word of the Lord.

RESPONSE: *Psalm 118*

RESPONSE:
All: Leader:

Bless - ed is the one who comes____ in the

All: (Fine)

name of the Lord,____ in the name of the Lord.____

1st time: Leader; 2nd time: All

1. I will re-joice
2. I will give thanks
3. I will give praise   } in the name of the Lord.____   name of the Lord.____
4. I will have life
5. For I am saved

GOSPEL ACCLAMATION:

ACCLAMATION:

Blessed is the one who comes ___ in the name of the Lord, ___ in the name of the Lord. ___

1st time: Leader; 2nd time: All | 1 to Verse | 2 to Response

Al-le-lu-ia! in the name of the Lord. ___ name of the Lord. ___

GOSPEL: *Matthew 10:37-42*

This is a reading from the Gospel of Matthew.

Jesus said to his disciples,

["If you want to belong to me,
you must love me more than anyone.
You must be willing to carry your cross
and follow me.
If you are willing to give your life
because you believe in me,
you will live forever.]

"Anyone who makes you feel welcome,
makes me feel welcome.
And anyone who welcomes me,
welcomes the one who sent me.
Anyone who accepts a prophet
will be rewarded like a prophet.
Anyone who welcomes a holy person
will get the same reward as a holy person.
And anyone who gives
even a cup of cold water
to someone who belongs to me,
will be rewarded."

The Gospel of the Lord.

[ ] *Reader may omit text that appears in brackets.*

REFLECTING ON THE READINGS WITH CHILDREN:

The reflections should focus on the various ministers of the Word in the church. Gradually, the children should be led to see that these ministers do the work of Jesus and that when we accept their ministry we are accepting Jesus.

You might begin by suggesting some necessary ministers:
- catechists,
- ministers of the Word with children,
- priests,
- those who teach scripture.

How do these people bring God's Word to us? Who are these people in our parish?

Because they bring God's Word to us, we should welcome them. How can we welcome or accept these people who bring God's Word to us? What does Jesus tell us about welcoming these people?

You will also want to encourage the children to reflect on ways in which *they, too*, are "ministers of the Word." It is our responsibility to be "ministers of the Word" in the way we live. All of the other "ministers" (catechists, priests, and so forth) are there to nourish the community, which is the primary "minister of the Word" in the world. That includes all of us: to serve the poor; to stand up for what is right.

FOURTEENTH SUNDAY IN ORDINARY TIME

YEAR A

PRAYER OF THE DAY:

Lord,
we are filled
with your wonder—
at all you have told us
about yourself
through Jesus, your Son.
May we listen
to what he has to say to us,
place all our trust in him,
and be at peace
in doing his work
because he lives with you,
forever and ever.

FOCUS OF THE READINGS:

Our readings focus on the virtue of humility as the true witness to truth.

The first reading speaks of a king who is powerful yet rides on a donkey, a symbol of lowliness or humility. This king will not be a war lord but a bringer of peace. That is cause for rejoicing.

In the Gospel reading, Jesus rejoices that God, creator of heaven and earth, has chosen to reveal divine truths to the humble. Jesus tells us he reveals God—invites us to imitate him in his humility and gentleness. He, like the humble king of our first reading, is the bringer of peace.

FIRST READING: *Zechariah 9:9-10*

This is a reading from the prophet Zechariah.

Our God says,

"Rejoice and be glad!
Shout for joy, daughter of Jerusalem!
Look, your king is coming!
He is powerful and just,
and yet he is riding on a donkey.
He will take away all weapons of war,
for this king will proclaim peace to all nations.
And his kingdom will go
to the very ends of the earth."

The Word of the Lord.

RESPONSE: *Psalm 118*

RESPONSE:

All: Bless - ed is the one who comes in the name of the Lord, in the name of the Lord. (Fine)

1st time: Leader; 2nd time: All
1. I will be glad
2. I will re-joice
3. I will give thanks
4. For I am saved
in the name of the Lord. name of the Lord.

GOSPEL ACCLAMATION:

1. "I am gentle. I am humble. Learn from me and your soul will find peace."
2. Alleluia, alleluia. "Learn from me and your soul will find peace."

GOSPEL: *Matthew 11:25-30*

This is a reading from the Gospel of Matthew.

One day, after Jesus had been teaching his disciples, he prayed,

"I thank you, God of heaven and earth.
I thank you because you show your ways
to people who are like little children.
They understand your ways better than people
who think they are clever and wise."

Then Jesus said to his disciples,

"God has given me everything.
No one really knows God except God's Son.
And the Son can show God
to anyone he chooses.
Come to me, all of you
who are tired or worried,
and I will give you rest.
Learn from me, for I am gentle,
and my heart is humble.
And when you are with me,
your soul will be at peace
because the things I ask you to do
are not too hard,
and I help you do them."

The Gospel of the Lord.

REFLECTING ON THE READINGS WITH CHILDREN:

Humility and gentleness are sometimes taken for weakness in our society. The scriptures tell us they are the way of God. But we must be sure the children have a proper understanding of humility. It is not silence, timidity, or the self-abasement often found in some books on spirituality. Biblical humility means simply to know oneself and to accept oneself as one is. Humility is the truth about oneself—not pretending to be better or worse.

After the first reading, ask the children, "What did you hear?" When the children have shared this, you might ask why they think the prophet Zechariah talked about a king riding on a donkey? What else does the prophet say about this king? Who do you think the prophet was talking about? Remind the children that this is what Jesus did on Palm Sunday.

After the Gospel, ask the children why they think Jesus likes the ways of people who are like little children?

Help the children see that, in fact, most children are open to truth and goodness. Children tend to trust those who teach them. Children tend to accept others and to be happy with simple things. Most children try to be good and to please others. Help them to see that this is what Jesus calls humility and gentleness and that he wants us always to live that way.

Jesus also tells us that when we are worried or find the way difficult, we can go to him; he will help us. When we are with him, we can have peace, and he will help us do whatever we have to do.

We have many images of Jesus in scripture: teacher, shepherd, king, Lord, and so forth. Our image today is Jesus as our friend. Help the children realize that Jesus is their friend, and they, too, can go to him.

FIFTEENTH SUNDAY IN ORDINARY TIME

YEAR A

PRAYER OF THE DAY:

God of all that exists,
plant your Word
in our hearts,
and may it take root
and grow there.
We want to be
your good soil,
producing a harvest
of kindness and love,
so leading others
to find you
and give themselves to you.
We make this prayer to you
through Christ, our Lord.

FOCUS OF THE READINGS:

The focus of the readings is the eventual success of God's will. The first reading tells us that God's Word will succeed just as surely as rain waters the earth. The Gospel says that even though many seeds seem to be lost, the harvest, in the end, is great. God's Word will triumph. The eventual success of God's Word is not dependent on us, but each of us can personally provide the "soil" for its growth in us.

FIRST READING: *Isaiah 55:10-11*

This is a reading from the prophet Isaiah.

Our God says,

"When the rain and snow
come down from heaven,
they water the earth
so that things will grow
and people will have bread.
My word is like that.
When I speak,
my word goes out from me,
and it does what I send it to do."

The Word of the Lord.

RESPONSE: *Psalm 119*

RESPONSE:
Leader: / All:

1. God, your Word is sent by you:
2. God, your Word is al-ways true:
3. God, your Word will bring us joy:
4. God, your Word shows us the way:

O-pen our hearts__ to lis-ten to you.__ O-pen our hearts__ to lis-ten to you.__

GOSPEL ACCLAMATION:

Lis - ten with your heart. Lis - ten to the Good News.—

Hear what God is say - ing — to you and me. So . . .

GOSPEL: *Matthew 13:1-9*

This is a reading from the Gospel of Matthew.

One day Jesus was sitting by the sea,
and a large crowd of people
gathered around him.
He used parables to teach them many things.
This is one of the parables he told them:

  "There once was a person
   who went out to plant some seeds.
   Some of the seeds fell beside the path,
   and the birds came and ate them.
   Some seeds fell on ground
   where there were lots of rocks.
   The seeds grew up fast,
   but since there wasn't
   much dirt around them,
   the roots didn't grow very deep.
   And when the sun got too hot,
   the seeds dried up and died.
   And some seeds fell into a patch of thorns.
   The thorns grew around them,
   and the seeds didn't have
   enough room to grow so they also died.
   But some of the seeds fell on good soil.
   And when the grain grew up,
   it was 30 or 60 or 100 times
   as much as the farmer had planted.
   Anyone who has ears,
   listen to what I am really saying!"

The Gospel of the Lord.

REFLECTING ON THE READINGS
WITH CHILDREN:

After the Gospel, give the children
an opportunity to share what they
heard in the story.

What happened to some of the
seeds?

Explore those images with the
children.

You will notice that we have
chosen the short form of the reading.
The long form includes an allegorical
interpretation (verses 18-23). Since
these verses are not included, allow
the children to suggest their own
allegories. Ask them what *they* think
Jesus meant by "beside the path,"
"lots of rocks," "patch of thorns."

Some of the seed fell on good soil
and when the grain grew up there
was 30 or 60 or 100 times as much as
the farmer planted. How can we be
sure we are that "good soil" where
the Word of God can grow?

Take time with this. We cannot
always assume the children
understand this kind of imagery.
What is important is that they realize
they can be open to God's Word, they
can help themselves be ready to hear
it and think about it.

95

SIXTEENTH SUNDAY IN ORDINARY TIME

YEAR A

PRAYER OF THE DAY:

God of gentleness and power,
to build the reign of heaven
you work through ordinary,
simple people.
Use us as your helpers.
Though we are young
and weak,
you can fill us
with your strength.
Though we sometimes
do wrong,
you forgive us
when we turn back to you.
Listen to our prayer
which we make to you
through Christ, our Lord.

FOCUS OF THE READINGS:

We have chosen to use only the center portion of today's Gospel. It is a continuation of Matthew's parables on the reign of heaven. In today's reading, Jesus compares the kingdom to a mustard seed and yeast. Both result in a surprise, and that's the point of the parables. The kingdom, here and now, may seem small and hardly noticeable—but like the mustard seed and the yeast, it is more than it seems. We don't always see the results of our small, sometimes hidden efforts. The world situation could lead to discouragement. Today's parables encourage us to see beyond the present and to know that what can and will be is already here in small, hidden ways. The reign of God is already among us.

FIRST READING: *Wisdom 12:13, 16-19*

This is a reading from the book of Wisdom.

You are the only God,
and you love all people.
You are strong,
and you treat everyone with justice.
You are the one who created us,
and so you are gentle and forgiving with us.
By your example, you showed us
that to do your will,
we must be kind to everyone.
We are your children,
and you give us hope
because you forgive our sins.

The Word of the Lord.

RESPONSE: *Psalm 103*

RESPONSE:
My God, my God, have mer-cy on me, for all my hope is in you, my God, all my hope is in you.

VERSES: to Response
1. You teach us how to live,__ and show us how to love.__
2. O God you give us hope,__ you take a-way our sins.__
3. As par-ents love their chil-dren, you love your faith-ful peo-ple.

GOSPEL ACCLAMATION:

Al - le - lu - ia, al - le - lu - ia. Al - le - lu - ia, al - le - lu - ia!

*VERSE:

Plant your Word_ in our hearts._ Let it bear_ fruit in us!_

*Keep singing Alleluia line. Add the verse with a solo or small group.

GOSPEL: *Matthew 13:24-30*

This is a reading from the Gospel of Matthew.

One day, when Jesus was teaching his disciples, he said to them,

"Let me give you an example
of what the reign of heaven is like.
The reign of heaven
is like a mustard seed.
Now, a mustard seed is the smallest
of all the seeds in the world.
But when it is planted in the ground,
it grows into the biggest bush
and becomes a tree.
Then the birds come
and make their nests in its branches.

"And here is another example.
The reign of heaven is like yeast,
which a woman puts in her flour
when she makes bread.
The yeast seems to be hidden in the flour
until the dough rises.

"Anyone who has ears,
listen to what I am really saying."

The Gospel of the Lord.

REFLECTING ON THE READINGS WITH CHILDREN:

Begin with examples with which the children will be familiar. Perhaps you could bring a picture of yourself as a baby. Show it to the children and ask who it is. They will have seen pictures of themselves as infants. Explain to them that they are the same but more developed. When they were babies, everything was there—ready and waiting to become what they are! Also inside them, perhaps hidden, are all their talents, gifts, and so forth—these too are developing. They are getting better and better at many things and that will continue. When we look at a newborn baby—so small—we don't see all of that, but it's there.

Help them see the reference to the reign of God in Jesus' parables. You may need to explain that "reign" is the dominion of a king or queen. This reality is already here. We don't see it all, but it's there. Jesus said it's like yeast! Explain that to the children. Flour and yeast become bread.

- What do you think the reign of God is meant to be?

- What does the woman do to make the ingredients become bread?

- What can we do to bring about the reign of God?

It is important that the children see the cooperation between ourselves and God. The woman measures the ingredients, kneads, and so forth. But for the "rising" she must wait. The same sort of discussion might follow using the mustard seed.

We have approximately four months until the end of the liturgical year and the celebration of Christ the King—the last days. Perhaps today you might plant a seed and watch it grow during this time.

97

SEVENTEENTH SUNDAY IN ORDINARY TIME

YEAR A

PRAYER OF THE DAY:

Lord and Maker
of all the world,
give us these gifts,
we beg you:
a mind to know you,
hands to serve you,
and a heart to love you.
Teach us to understand
that doing your will
is the greatest treasure of all.
This we ask you
through Christ, our Lord.

FOCUS OF THE READINGS:

Our readings focus on seeking the things that are of value.

King Solomon is praised for seeking wisdom rather than riches or personal gain. And he desires wisdom in order to better serve his kingdom.

The Gospel gives us two examples of doing everything possible to attain the reign of God. The person who truly wants the reign of God will sell everything in order to remain faithful to the kingdom. That is true wisdom.

FIRST READING: *1 Kings 3:5, 7-12*

This is a reading from the first book of Kings.

One night, as King Solomon was sleeping,
God appeared to him in a dream and said,
  "Ask me for whatever you want."
Solomon answered,
  "Dear God, you made me king
    when my father, David, died.
  I am only a child, and I don't know
    how to lead your chosen people.
  There are so many of them,
    they can hardly be counted!
  Please give me the gift of wisdom
    so that I will know
    what is good and what is evil.
  Then I will be a good king."
God was pleased
that Solomon asked for wisdom.
So God said,
  "You did not ask to live a long life or to be rich,
    and you did not ask me
    to destroy your enemies.
  Instead, you have asked
    for the wisdom you need
    to know what is good and bad.
  Because you have not asked
    for things for yourself,
  I will give you the wisdom you asked for.
  You will be wiser than anyone
    who ever lived before you
    and anyone who will ever live after you."

The Word of the Lord.

RESPONSE: *Psalm 90*

RESPONSE:
Fill us with your gift of love. Help us find our joy in you. joy in you.

VERSES:
to Response
1. God, our God, ev-er-last - ing, give us wis-dom to know your ways.
2. God, our God, ev-er-last - ing, bless the work that we do to-day.

GOSPEL ACCLAMATION:

Al - le - lu - ia, "The reign of God is near." Al - le -
lu - ia, "The reign of God is near." "When you find a treas-ure —
hid-den in the ground you'll be so hap-py, — so hap-py." Al - le -
reign of God is near." "The reign of God is near." "The

GOSPEL: *Matthew 13:44-46*

This is a reading from the Gospel of Matthew.

One day Jesus told the people
these two parables.

"The reign of God is like a treasure
buried in a field.
When someone finds it,
they are so happy that they go home
and sell everything they have
and come back and buy the whole field.

"And here is another example
of what the reign of God is like.
Suppose someone is searching for fine pearls.
When they find one that is more valuable
than all the others,
they will sell everything they have
in order to buy that special pearl."

The Gospel of the Lord.

REFLECTING ON THE READINGS WITH CHILDREN:

Ask the children to share things they would really like to have (treasure, pearl). Put their wishes into parables.

The reign of heaven is like a little girl who wanted very much to have a stuffed bear that was as big as she was. When she saw one in her friend's home, she traded *every single toy* she had to get it.

The reign of heaven is like a ten-year-old boy who wanted
_____. When he found it, he sold his bike, his skateboard, his TV, his. . . .

Use examples that come from, and suit, your group. Remind the children that Jesus used examples like that to tell us how special the reign of God is. When we know how special it is, we will do anything for it.

Be sure the children understand the notion of parable. Attaining the reign has nothing to do with literally selling everything we have. It is the very expansiveness of the parable that points to its meaning.

EIGHTEENTH SUNDAY IN ORDINARY TIME

YEAR A

PRAYER OF THE DAY:

God of never-ending goodness,
your greatest wish
is to make us happy.
Feed us with your love
so that we may become strong
and grow to be more
like your Son, Jesus,
who lives with you,
forever and ever.

FOCUS OF THE READINGS:

Our readings focus on the Eucharist as a sign of the heavenly banquet.

The first reading speaks of the lasting covenant which provides, gratuitously, the food which satisfies. One might see in this reading the invitation to baptism and eucharist.

The Gospel, Matthew's account of the multiplication of loaves for 5,000, uses the liturgical language of the early church: bread taken, blessed, broken and given. This story, which is found more often in the New Testament than any other incident (six times), probably represents the early church's understanding of eucharist—nourishment now and the promise of future feeding (twelve baskets left over.)

FIRST READING: *Isaiah 55:1-3*

This is a reading from the prophet Isaiah.

Our God says,

"All you who are thirsty, come to the water.
Even if you have no money, come.
Come and have good wine and milk.
It's yours free.
Why spend money on things
that don't really satisfy you?
Come, instead, and eat good bread.
Listen; come to me so that you may live.
I will make a covenant with you,
and my covenant will last forever."

The Word of the Lord.

RESPONSE: *Psalm 104*

You are the one who feeds us, giving us food from your hand. You are the one who feeds us, giving us all we need.

GOSPEL ACCLAMATION:

Jesus blessed the bread, and broke the bread and gave it to his friends. Alleluia! Jesus lu-ia!

GOSPEL: *Matthew 14:13-21*

This is a reading from the Gospel of Matthew.

When Jesus heard
that John the Baptist had been killed,
he went away in a boat to be alone.
But the people went to find him.
When Jesus came back to the shore,
he saw how many people were looking for him.
He felt sorry for them,
and he stayed with them,
healing the people who were sick.
When it was evening,
the disciples came to Jesus and said,

"These people are a long way from home,
    and it's getting late.
    Send them into the village
    so they can buy some food."

But Jesus said,

"They don't have to leave.
    You give them food."

The disciples said,

"But we have only five loaves of bread
    and two fish."

Jesus said,

"Bring them to me."

Then he told all the people
to sit down on the grass.
Over 5,000 people were there.
Jesus took the bread and the fish
and looked up to heaven.
Then he blessed the bread, broke it,
and gave it to the disciples to give to the people.
When everyone had enough to eat,
they collected the bread that was left over,
and it filled 12 baskets.

The Gospel of the Lord.

REFLECTING ON THE READINGS
WITH CHILDREN:

What did you hear in the Gospel today? Ask the children to recall:

- Where did it take place?
- Who was there?
- What did Jesus do first? (healed the sick.) Why?
- What does this tell us about Jesus? It is helpful for children to repeat lines such as, "he felt sorry for them." Jesus is not merely a worker of miracles; he is a compassionate human being.
- What did the disciples say to Jesus?
- How much food did the disciples have?
- What did Jesus do?

Help the children recall the words as they appear: *took* the bread, *blessed* it, *broke* it and *gave* it to the disciples. . . .

- After everyone had eaten, how much bread was left over?
- What does this story tell us about Jesus?

Help the children see both the power and the caring in this event.

- When do we hear those same words: Jesus took the bread, blessed it, and so forth?

Help the children see the eucharistic theme in this reading.

- What do you think Jesus wants us to learn from this story?

Help the children see that:

- Jesus can do all things.
- Jesus cares about the needs of people.
- Jesus is present in the bread we share at mass.

NINETEENTH SUNDAY IN ORDINARY TIME

YEAR A

PRAYER OF THE DAY:

Lord, you are the God
of power and gentleness.
Open our eyes to find you
in the ordinary things of life:
in the love of our parents,
in the happiness of friends,
in the goodness of this world
in which we live.
And when things
do not go so well,
may we believe
that you are with us always
to support and care for us.
We pray for this
through Christ, our Lord.

FOCUS OF THE READINGS:

The focus of our readings is the presence of God in the calming of the storm.

Elijah finds God, not in the storm, earthquake or fire, but in the quiet, gentle stilling of the storm.

The disciples, frightened by the storm, fail to recognize Jesus walking on the water. It is in the stilling of the storm that they recognize him and praise him.

FIRST READING: *1 Kings 19:9a, 11-13a*

This is a reading from the first book of Kings.

When the prophet Elijah heard
that someone wanted to kill him,
he went to Mount Horeb, the mountain of God,
and stayed in a cave.
God came to Elijah and said,

"Go out and stand
in front of the cave to meet me."

Then there was a powerful, strong wind
that split the mountain
and broke the rocks into little pieces.
But God was not in the wind.
After the wind, there was an earthquake,
but God was not in the earthquake.
And after the earthquake, there was a fire,
but God was not in the fire.
After the fire, there was a gentle breeze
like a quiet whisper.
And when Elijah heard it,
he covered his face with a scarf
and stood at the door of the cave to meet God.

The Word of the Lord.

RESPONSE: *Psalm 40*

RESPONSE:
"Here I am, O my God, I come to do your will."

VERSES:
to Response
1. I have wait - ed pa-tient-ly, you have heard my prayer and so I say:
2. You have shown your ways to me, to pro-claim your Word and so I say:

GOSPEL ACCLAMATION:

Je-sus said: "Don't be a-fraid! Come to me." Al-le-lu - ia! lu - ia!

GOSPEL: *Matthew 14:22-33*

This is a reading from the Gospel of Matthew.

After Jesus had given the bread to the crowd of people,
and everyone had eaten all they wanted,
Jesus told the disciples
to sail the boat to the other side of the lake.
Then he went up into the mountains to pray,
and he stayed there alone until late into the night.

By this time,
the disciples were already out in the middle of the lake,
and their boat was being tossed about by a strong wind.
During the night, Jesus came walking
across the water toward the boat,
but when the disciples saw him walking on the water,
they were terrified, and they screamed,

"It's a ghost!"

Jesus said,

"Don't be afraid! It is I!"

Peter said to Jesus,

"Lord, if it's really you,
tell me to walk to you across the water."

Jesus said,

"Come on, Peter!"

So Peter got out of the boat
and started walking toward Jesus.
But while he was walking on the water,
he saw the waves and the wind,
and he became so frightened
that he started sinking into the water.
And he cried out,

"Lord, save me!"

Jesus reached out, caught hold of Peter's hand,
and said,

"Peter, you have so little faith!
Why didn't you believe?"

When Jesus and Peter got into the boat,
the wind stopped.
The other disciples said to Jesus,

"Truly, you are the Son of God."

The Gospel of the Lord.

REFLECTING ON THE READINGS
WITH CHILDREN:

Help the children visualize and
imagine the Gospel scene:

- the darkness of the night,
- the storm, waves, wind,
- the disciples in a boat being
  tossed about,
- their fear, which is quite natural.

Next help them recall what
happened.

- Where was Jesus before he
  walked on the water?
- What time was it when Jesus
  began to walk toward the boat?
- What do you think the disciples
  were doing in the lake in the
  middle of the night?
- What did the disciples think
  when they saw someone walking
  on the water?
- What did Jesus say? What did
  Peter say?
- Then what happened?
- Why did Peter begin to sink?
- What did Jesus do and say when
  Peter cried out, "Lord, save me"?
- Then what happened?

Something changed between the
beginning of the story and the end.
What changed? Why?

What does this story tell us about
Jesus? What does he want us to
know from this story?

The children should leave knowing that we all have "storms" in life,
we all have fears, and Jesus wants us
to have faith in him; he will always
take us by the hand and help us.

103

TWENTIETH SUNDAY IN ORDINARY TIME

YEAR A

PRAYER OF THE DAY:

Lord,
all people belong to you—
of every race,
color and religion.
Teach us to love them
as you do
and to understand
that their prayers
are precious in your sight.
Let us despise no one
because they are different
from ourselves,
but let us welcome everyone
as Jesus did,
who lives with you,
forever and ever.

FOCUS OF THE READINGS:

Our readings focus mainly on the universality of God's church. The reading from *Isaiah* tells us that the day is coming when people from every nation will come to praise and worship God. For God, this equality, this unity, is a matter of justice. The people are commanded to act in the same way.

This prophecy from Isaiah is clearly realized in Jesus and especially in today's Gospel. The point of the story is that a Canaanite woman—a foreigner, a non-Jew—shows faith in Jesus and is welcomed by him. Her faith is an act of praise, for which Jesus praises her!

FIRST READING: *Isaiah 56:1, 6-7*

This is a reading from the prophet Isaiah.

Our God says:

"Do what is right
and treat everyone with fairness.
For I am coming soon to save all people,
and they will see my justice.
Foreigners will come to me.
If they love my name and serve me,
if they keep my covenant,
I will bring them to my holy mountain,
and I will give them joy
in my house of prayer.
I will accept their sacrifices and their gifts
at my altar.
Yes, my house will be a house of prayer
for everyone, for all people."

The Word of the Lord.

RESPONSE: *Psalm 122*

RESPONSE:
In the House of our God, in the House of our God, we give praise to the Lord in the House of our God.

VERSES:
1. I was glad____ when they said: "Let us go____ to God's house!" And now____ with joy we are stand-ing.
2. Je-ru-sa-lem is built as the cit-y of our God;____ here____ the peo-ple are sing-ing.
3. It is here that we find peace for our fam-i-lies and friends;____ here____ that we find____ jus-tice.

to Response

GOSPEL ACCLAMATION:

Leader: / All: (sing and clap)
1. *Your Word brings us heal-ing.* Al-le-lu-ia, al-le-lu-ia!
2. *Your Word Lord is all we need.* Al-le-lu-ia, al-le-lu-ia!

GOSPEL: *Matthew 15:21-28*

This is a reading from the Gospel of Matthew.

One day a woman from Canaan came to Jesus and cried,

"O Lord, Son of David, help me!
  My daughter is suffering terribly
  because she has an evil spirit in her."

But Jesus didn't say anything.
His disciples were upset with the woman
and said to Jesus,

"Tell that woman to go away.
  She's following us around
  and keeps shouting at us to help her."

But Jesus said to them,

"I came for the people of Israel.
  I am here to save my people who are lost."

But the woman came
and knelt in front of Jesus and said,

"Please, Lord, help me."

Jesus said,

"It isn't fair to take the children's food
  and give it to the dogs."

The woman said,

"Yes, Lord, that's true.
  But even the dogs
  are allowed to eat the scraps
  that fall off their master's table."

Jesus said to her,

"You are a woman with great faith,
  and you will have what you asked for."

At that very moment, her daughter got well.

The Gospel of the Lord.

REFLECTING ON THE READINGS
WITH CHILDREN:

Some points will need clarification for the children. In the course of recalling the story, you will need to explain to the children that many Jews believed that only Jews could be saved. They didn't accept people who weren't Jews and they didn't think God did either.

Jesus seems to deal harshly with the Canaanite woman. Help the children see that Jesus helped the woman make a real act of faith. Sometimes we make our strongest statements of faith when we are "pushed" to it.

Ask the children: What do you think Jesus wants us to know from today's Gospel?

Lead the children in a discussion regarding the acceptance of all people. We too sometimes reject people ("Tell that woman to go away") for various reasons: nationality, race, religion, economic status and so forth. Jesus shows us in today's Gospel (and indeed in all of the Gospels) that he rejects no one. Our relationship with Jesus is based on faith alone—not race, nationality, religion or economic status. That's the Good News!

TWENTY-FIRST SUNDAY IN ORDINARY TIME

YEAR A

PRAYER OF THE DAY:

O God,
in doing your will
Jesus, your Son,
has built the church
on the work and prayers
of men and women
around the world.
Join our work
and prayers to theirs,
serving each other
in any way we can,
so that the church
may be a family of love.
Listen to the prayers of us all
as we make them
through Christ, our Lord.

FOCUS OF THE READINGS:

Our readings focus on the power and fidelity of God made manifest in human ministry.

The prophet Isaiah delivers to Shebna the results of his unfaithful behavior. But God will continue. A new "officer" will be appointed who will be invested with the keys, a symbol of the power and authority of God.

This theme is picked up in the Gospel reading where Peter is given the keys to the kingdom, symbolizing the power and authority of Christ. But the focus is sharpened. Isaiah refers to the wrongful behavior of Shebna. Christ responds to the faith expressed by Peter.

FIRST READING: *Isaiah 22:19-23*

This is a reading from the prophet Isaiah.

God said to Shebna,
the officer in charge of the palace,

"Because you have been so wicked,
  you can no longer be an officer of the palace.
I am taking that away from you,
  and I will make Eliakim
  the officer of the palace.
I will give him all the power and authority
  that you had.
He will be like a father
  to the people of Jerusalem and Judah.
I will give him the keys to the house of David.
He will be able to open and shut the door,
  and no one will stop him.
I will make him strong and secure,
  and he will bring honor to the house of David."

The Word of the Lord.

RESPONSE: *Psalm 89*

RESPONSE: Your love and your prom-is-es are true, O my God, are true!____

VERSES:
1. You made a cov-e-nant____ long a-
2. You keep your prom-is-es for ev-

to Response
1. go, a prom-ise made in love.____
2. er. Your love will nev-er end.____

GOSPEL ACCLAMATION:

Je-sus asked them: "Who am I?"   1. Pe-ter an-swered:
                                 2. Al-le-lu-ia,

1.-2. "You are__ the Christ, you are__ the Son of the Liv-ing God!"

GOSPEL: *Matthew 16:13-19*

This is a reading from the Gospel of Matthew.

When Jesus and his disciples
were in the area of Caesarea Philippi,
he asked his disciples,

  "Who do you think I am?"

They said,

  "Some people say you are John the Baptist,
    and others think you are the prophet Elijah.
    But there are others who say
    you are Jeremiah or some other prophet."

Jesus asked them,

  "And who do you say I am?"

Simon Peter answered,

  "You are the Christ.
    You are the Son of the living God."

Jesus said,

  "Simon, you are blessed.
    You did not learn that
    from any human being.
    No, God told you that.
    And I tell you,
    you will be called Peter, which means rock.
    On this rock I will build my church.
    It will be stronger than the gates of hell,
    and nothing will be able to destroy it.
    I will give you the keys
    to the kingdom of heaven,
    so that what you decide on earth
    will be the same in heaven."

The Gospel of the Lord.

REFLECTING ON THE READINGS
WITH CHILDREN:

  After the Gospel, ask the children:

  • What did Jesus ask the disciples?

  • What did they answer?

  • What did Peter answer?

  • What did Jesus promise Peter?

  Ask the children:

  • If Jesus asked you, "Who do you
    say I am?" what would you say?

  Spend some time with this.
Nothing is more important than each
of us coming to a deep personal faith
in Jesus Christ. For that to be a
reality, we must know who Jesus is.
Jesus constantly revealed himself to
his disciples and continues to reveal
himself to us. But this on-going
revelation centers on this question of
faith—"Who do you say I am?"

  Help the children see that because
of the faith of Peter and the disciples,
we have the church and can know
Jesus in the church. We are not
alone in our faith.

107

TWENTY-SECOND SUNDAY IN ORDINARY TIME

YEAR A

PRAYER OF THE DAY:

All-powerful God,
see how weak we are,
how difficult
for us to live your way.
Make us brave
in following Jesus.
May we never give up
when things become difficult,
never frightened or put off
by those who do not know you
or your Son,
who lives with you,
forever and ever.

FOCUS OF THE READINGS:

Both of our readings focus on the cost of obedience to the will of God.

Jeremiah is constantly ridiculed and persecuted for being the bearer of God's Word to the people. His message, and he, are rejected, yet he remains faithful.

In our Gospel for today, Jesus warns his disciples he himself will suffer and even be killed for being faithful to God's message. The focus then shifts to the disciples: those who want to follow Jesus must accept the same cross, the willingness to be faithful, even if it means giving their lives.

What Jeremiah experienced and Jesus died for, the disciples must accept—the world is opposed to the message of God.

FIRST READING: *Jeremiah 20:7-9*

This is a reading from the prophet Jeremiah.

Jeremiah made this prayer to God:

"O God, you are stronger than I am,
   and I let myself be trapped by you.
Now everyone is making fun of me,
   because I tell the people
   they are going to suffer
   from the way they are living.
And now I am the one who is suffering
   for telling them the truth.
Sometimes I think to myself,

   'I will not talk about God anymore.
   I won't even speak in God's name.'

"But then I feel my heart burning inside me,
   and I know that I must be faithful
   and go on talking about you."

The Word of the Lord.

RESPONSE: *Psalm 63*

RESPONSE: I will praise you, Lord, as long as I live, I will praise you.

VERSES:
1. I trust in you, your hand keeps me safe.
2. I bless your name, for you are my help.
3. Your love for me is bet-ter than life.

GOSPEL ACCLAMATION:

1. "If you would be my dis-ci-ples, ac-cept the cross and fol-low me."
2. Al - le - lu - ia, al - le - lu - ia, "Ac-cept the cross and fol-low me."

GOSPEL: *Matthew 16:21-27*

This is a reading from the Gospel of Matthew.

One day Jesus told his disciples
that he had to go to Jerusalem.
He explained to them that in Jerusalem
the chief priests and the teachers of the law
would make him suffer and then would kill him.
But three days later,
he would be raised from the dead.
Peter took Jesus aside and said to him,

"This will never happen to you!
God will save you."

But Jesus said to Peter,

"Be quiet! Stop talking like Satan!
You are no help to me,
because you are thinking
the way people think,
and not the way God thinks."

Then Jesus turned to his disciples and said,

"If you want to be my disciple,
you must accept your cross and follow me.
If you try to save your own life,
you will lose it.
But if you are willing to give your life for me,
you will live forever."

The Gospel of the Lord.

REFLECTING ON THE READINGS
WITH CHILDREN:

While this Gospel is important in
the on-going formation of children as
well as adults, we must be cautious in
reflecting on it with small children.
*"Accepting one's cross" must be
explained in language and concrete
examples appropriate to the age of the
children.* We want to avoid burdening
them with expectations beyond their
understanding and capacity to fulfill.

After the Gospel, encourage the
children to share their reflections.

- What does Jesus mean when he
  says his disciples must not think
  only about themselves? How
  does this help others?

- What does Jesus mean when he
  says his disciples must live as he
  lives?

- What does Jesus mean when he
  says that if we are willing to give
  up our lives for him we will find
  real life?

Help the children understand
*"giving up our life" means living for
others—living as Jesus wants us to—
no matter what.* This can be a real
"cross" when living the Gospel in fact
requires children to make difficult
choices in their everyday lives.

TWENTY-THIRD SUNDAY IN ORDINARY TIME

YEAR A

PRAYER OF THE DAY:

Loving God,
we have come together
to thank you
for your great goodness,
to beg you
to forgive the things
we have done wrong,
to ask your help
to live as we should.
Remind us always
that Jesus is with us,
joining his prayers with ours.
So it is
that we pray this prayer
through Christ, our Lord.

FOCUS OF THE READINGS:

Both of our readings focus on the obligation we have to help one another grow in goodness. Sometimes this requires us to point out the errors of a brother or sister in the church.

Ezekiel warns the prophets of his day that they have a serious responsibility in the community. They are to guide the people and show them right from wrong. The prophet will be held accountable.

Jesus picks up this theme and applies it to everyone in the church. It is not only the leaders who are responsible, but we are all responsible for one another. This Gospel focuses on the power and authority of the community which has rarely been recognized. The source of that power is Christ: "I am there with them."

FIRST READING: *Ezekiel 33:7-9*

This is a reading from the prophet Ezekiel.

This is what God said to the prophet:

"You must watch over my people.
  Whatever I tell you to say to them,
  you must say.
  When I want you to warn people
  who are doing evil things,
  you must tell them.
  If you don't warn them for me,
  I will blame you for what they do.
  You will be as bad as they are,
  and you, too, will be punished.
  But if you do warn them,
  and they still go on sinning,
  it won't be your fault.
  They will be punished, but you will not."

The Word of the Lord.

RESPONSE: *Psalm 119*

RESPONSE:
Leader: / All:

1. God, our hope is in your Word.
2. Your com-mands are al - ways true.
3. Give us life to do your will.
O - pen our hearts to

lis - ten to you. O - pen our hearts to lis - ten to you.

GOSPEL ACCLAMATION:

1. "Where two or three are gath-ered in my name, I am
2. Al - le - lu - ia, al - le - lu - ia! "I am

1.-2. there with them, __ I am there with them, __ I am there." __

GOSPEL: *Matthew 18:15-20*

This is a reading from the Gospel of Matthew.

Jesus said to his disciples,

"If your brother or sister
does something wrong,
go and talk to that person alone,
just the two of you.
If the person listens to you
and stops doing wrong,
then you have been helpful.
But if the person won't listen to you,
take two or three other people with you
and try again.
If the person won't listen to them either,
tell it to the Christian community.
And if they won't even listen
to the community,
then that person is the kind
who wants to go on sinning."

Then Jesus said,

"I tell you honestly,
whenever two or three of you
agree to pray about something,
God will do it.
For wherever two or three people
are gathered together in my name,
I am there with them."

The Gospel of the Lord.

REFLECTING ON THE READINGS
WITH CHILDREN:

This is not an easy Gospel for
children to contemplate. Most
children have the experience of
being corrected by adults, but few
will have had the experience of
mutuality in correction. This speaks
to adult men and women who can
understand their mutual
responsibility. We might help the
children see in the first part of the
Gospel that Jesus teaches us to talk
over our differences one to one
rather than tattling. But that should
not receive the majority of our time.
Concentrate instead on the last
portion. Help the children to see
that Jesus promises to be with us
when we pray. What is important
here is that we are in community and
that we pray in his name.

TWENTY-FOURTH SUNDAY IN ORDINARY TIME

YEAR A

PRAYER OF THE DAY:

Lord,
sometimes we offend you
by doing wrong
and not loving as we should.
You always forgive us
whenever we turn back to you.
We thank you
for your wonderful love,
for giving us the chance
to begin all over again.
Make us generous in forgiving
those who hurt us
and ready to make friends
with people
whom we have not liked.
We ask you to do this
through Jesus, your Son,
who lives with you,
forever and ever.

FOCUS OF THE READINGS:

Both of our readings focus on forgiveness. Our forgiveness of others is motivated by the forgiveness we have received.

We experience the forgiveness of God in our own act of forgiving. In both readings, we are told that it makes no sense to expect forgiveness if we, ourselves, will not extend forgiveness to others.

FIRST READING: *Sirach 28:2-7.*

This is a reading from the book of Sirach.

Our God says:

"Forgive people when they have hurt you.
Then when you pray,
your sins will be forgiven.
How can you say
you won't forgive someone else
and then ask God to forgive you?
You are a sinner, too,
so have mercy on other people.

"Remember the commandments
and don't hate people.
Remember the promises of God
and forgive others."

The Word of the Lord.

RESPONSE: *Psalm 103*

RESPONSE:

My God, my God, have mer-cy on me, for all my hope is in you, my God, all my hope is in you.

VERSES:
to Response

1. You call us to re-mem-ber the prom-is-es you gave us.
2. As par-ents love their chil-dren, you love your faith-ful peo-ple.
3. You love us and for-give us, you al-ways show us mer-cy.

GOSPEL ACCLAMATION:

Leader/All:

"You must for-give____ with all your heart:

① ②

Sev-en-ty times, sev-en-ty times sev-en."__ says Je-sus.

Leader/All:
(Fine)

Al-le-lu-ia,____ al-le-lu-ia!

112

GOSPEL: *Matthew 18:21-35*

This is a reading from the Gospel of Matthew.

One day Peter asked Jesus,

"How many times do I have to forgive someone
who hurts me? As many as seven times?"

Jesus said to him,

"No, not only seven times, but seventy times seven!"

Then Jesus told the disciples this story:

"Once there was a king
who had many people working for him.
One of the workers owed him a lot of money
but couldn't pay it back.
The king was angry and told the guards
to sell the worker and his wife and children as slaves
to pay what the man owed.
But the man fell on his knees and begged the king,

'Please, be patient with me,
and I will pay you everything I owe you!'

"The king felt sorry for the man and forgave him.
He even said the man didn't have to pay back
the money he owed.
Now, when that same worker was leaving,
he saw another man who owed him
only a little bit of money. He grabbed him and said,

'Pay me what you owe me!'

"The man fell on his knees and said,

'Please be patient with me,
and I will pay you everything I owe you!'

"But the man, who had been forgiven, said, 'No!'
And he had the man put into prison.

"Now when the other workers saw what happened,
they went to the king and told him the whole story.
The king sent for the man he had forgiven
and said to him,

'You wicked man!
I forgave you and even forgot about
what you owed me because you begged me for mercy.
And then you wouldn't do the same for someone else!'

"So the king sent the man to prison to be punished.

"And that's the way it will be with you.
If you want God to forgive you,
you must forgive other people with all your heart."

The Gospel of the Lord.

Jesus insists that our forgiveness should be without limit. Matthew uses the Jewish symbol for absolute perfection or completeness: the number seven. But this symbol is even multiplied here; seventy times seven! The parable illustrates the point and expands the motivation. As we have been forgiven, we must forgive.

REFLECTING ON THE READINGS WITH CHILDREN:

What did Peter ask Jesus? Acknowledge to the children that it can truly and naturally be exasperating when someone hurts or does something wrong over and over again. So Peter's question was quite normal.

What did Jesus answer? What do you think Jesus meant?

Help the children see that Jesus means *always*. We often say things like "I told you a million times," or "I had to wait a hundred years!" We don't mean that literally—we mean a lot or a very long time. Jesus meant always!

Ask the children to recall the story.

- Why was the king angry?
- What did he decide to do?
- What did the king do when the worker begged him not to sell his wife and children?
- How do you think the worker felt?
- What did the worker do when he left the king?
- What did the worker do when his fellow worker begged him to be patient?
- Why were the other workers angry?
- What did the king do then?

What does Jesus want us to know from this story? Help the children see that Jesus teaches us that we must treat others the way we want them and God to treat us.

113

TWENTY-FIFTH SUNDAY IN ORDINARY TIME

YEAR A

PRAYER OF THE DAY:

Lord God,
you give good things
to all people,
even if they
have not earned them.
Show us
how to use your gifts well,
in cheering up the
downhearted,
in helping those who are sick
and are elderly,
and in praying to you
when we need you
and when we think we do not.
We make this prayer to you
through Christ, our Lord.

FOCUS OF THE READINGS:

The ways of God are infinitely different from our ways. God's way of justice is radically different from our literal, juridical concept of justice. Both of our readings focus on that difference.

The reading from *Isaiah* comes from a larger section in which the prophet speaks of God's mercy in the face of the constant infidelity of the people. Justice, in human terms, demands their punishment. But, God's ways are above our ways.

The Gospel provides a parable which makes this point real to us. The story *does not* hold up the norm of human behavior.

FIRST READING: *Isaiah 55:6-9*

This is a reading from the prophet Isaiah.

Isaiah said to the people,

"Look for God.
Pray while God is close to you.
Let people who do evil things
change their lives and come back to God
because God is always ready to forgive.

"For our God says,

'I don't think the way you think,
and I don't do things the way you do.
Just as the heavens
are high above the earth,
so my thoughts
are high above your thoughts,
and my ways are high above your ways.' "

The Word of the Lord.

RESPONSE: *Psalm 145*

RESPONSE:
O God, you are ver-y near. We call to you. You are ver-y near.

VERSES:
1. For ev-'ry-thing you do is kind and lov-ing.
2. For you are al-ways near, and full of mer-cy.

to Response
1. Ev-'ry-thing you do shows us how much you love us.
2. You are al-ways near, we pray that you will hear us.

GOSPEL ACCLAMATION:

"Treat peo-ple as you would like them to treat you." Al-le-lu-ia!

GOSPEL: *Matthew 20:1-16*

This is a reading from the Gospel of Matthew.

One day Jesus told his disciples this parable:

"This is what the reign of God is like.
Once there was a man who owned a grape vineyard.
One morning he hired a group of workers
to pick the grapes in his vineyard.
They all agreed on how much they would be paid
for the day's work.
Later that day, the owner hired a few more workers
and said to them,

'Go into my vineyard to work,
and I will pay you what is fair.'

"Then, later in the day, he found still more workers
and sent them into his vineyard to work.
Finally, about 5:00 in the afternoon,
he saw some others in the town who weren't working
but just standing around. He asked them,

'Why are you wasting your time instead of working?'

"They answered,

'Because no one has hired us to work.'

"So the owner of the vineyard said,

'I will hire you.
Go now to my vineyard and work for me.'

"That evening, the owner called all the workers together
to pay them for their work.
He started with the ones he hired last.
When they came forward,
he paid them for a whole day's work
even though they had worked only one hour.

"Now when the people who had worked all day
came forward, they thought they would be paid more.
But they got exactly the same as everyone else.
They started complaining and said,

'These last people worked only one hour,
and you have paid them the same as you paid us.
But we have worked all day in the hot sun.'

"The owner of the vineyard said,

'My friends, I am not treating you unfairly.
Didn't we agree this morning
on how much you would be paid?
So here, take what you have earned.
I want to pay everyone the same.
Am I not free to do what I want with my own money?
Or are you angry because I am generous and kind?' "

The Gospel of the Lord.

Normal human behavior permits a just pay for a day's work. According to the norm of human behavior, the workers' complaint is understandable and justified. The story is not meant to teach that people should be paid even when they haven't worked. The focus of the Gospel is the radical generosity of God's gift—to the seemingly least deserving. In Matthew's time, these were sinners, social outcasts, Gentiles, and so forth.

REFLECTING ON THE READINGS WITH CHILDREN:

It will be useless to suggest that the owner of the vineyard is a model for employers and still less helpful to suggest that we should be paid for not working. Children know that isn't so.

Help them see that Jesus often used stories that seem farfetched in order to help us think. They sort of surprise us and make us think in a new way. When Jesus tells us a story like this, he wants us to ask ourselves, "What does Jesus want me to know from this story?"

You might explain to the children a little of the culture in which this was written. Many people in Jesus' time thought that only certain people were loved by God. They didn't believe that people who sinned or believed different things were loved by God. They thought only they themselves were worthy of God's love. They are like the people who worked all day. The owner did pay them what they deserved. God will reward people who are always good. But Jesus wants us to know that God also loves those who try to be good. Some people take a long time before they can do what is right. That's okay with God as long as they try. God's love is very big! God loves everyone, even the people who come last and say, "I want to try too!"

TWENTY-SIXTH SUNDAY IN ORDINARY TIME

YEAR A

PRAYER OF THE DAY:

God,
you are always true to us
and keep your promises.
Forgive us
when we do wrong;
help us to see our faults,
and make us quick
to carry out your commands.
We pray this prayer to you
through Jesus, your Son,
who lives with you,
forever and ever.

FOCUS OF THE READINGS:

Both readings focus on the mercy of God for sinners. In their earlier history, the Israelites tended to think almost exclusively in communal terms: communal guilt, communal punishment. Here Ezekiel presents the corrective to that extreme: individual responsibility for individual sin. The truth is in the balance of the two. The major focus, however, when seen with our Gospel reading, is that God always allows the freedom and opportunity to change.

The Gospel presents this in parable form. It is the story of each of us. Sometimes we say yes, and we don't act. Sometimes we rebel and say no—but later have a change of heart and act! God is primarily interested in our final option! God does not hold past sin against us. God hopes and waits for our obedient response.

FIRST READING: *Ezekiel 18:25-28*

This is a reading from the prophet Ezekiel.

Our God says:

"This is how I am:
when people turn away from me and sin,
they are punished for it.
But when people are sorry for their sins,
change their lives, and do what is right,
they are not punished; they are saved."

The Word of the Lord.

RESPONSE: *Psalm 15*

RESPONSE:
We will live with you, O God, we will live for - ev - er.

VERSES: to Response
1. When we do what is right.
2. When we speak the_____ truth.

GOSPEL ACCLAMATION:

"Change your lives and be - lieve in me, "Al - le -
lu - ia, al - le - lu - ia.   lu - ia, al - le - lu - ia!"

GOSPEL: *Matthew 21:28-32*

This is a reading from the Gospel of Matthew.

Jesus said to the chief priests
and the leaders of the people,

"I'm going to tell you a story,
  and you tell me what you think about it.

"There was a man who had two sons.

"One day he said to one of them,

  'Son, I want you to go out
    and work in the vineyard today.'

"The boy said, 'No, I won't go.'

"But, later, the boy was sorry
  that he had said 'no' to his father,
  and so he did go.

"The father then said to his other son,

  'Son, I want you to go out
    and work in the field today.'

"The second son said,

  'Yes, father, I will go and work.'

"But he did not go.

"Now tell me, Jesus asked,
  which boy did what the father
  wanted him to do, the first son or the second?"

The leaders answered,

"The first son."

Jesus said to them,

"I'm telling you the truth.
  People you look down on as sinners
  are going to enter the reign of God before you.
  Because, when John the Baptist came
  and preached the truth,
  you didn't believe him.
  But the people you look down on as sinners
  believed him and changed their lives.
  And even after you saw that they believed
  and changed their lives,
  you still didn't believe and change your lives."

The Gospel of the Lord.

REFLECTING ON THE READINGS
WITH CHILDREN:

What does the Gospel say to you today?

After the Gospel, help the children to see that it is how we act that is important. Sometimes we don't want to act like Jesus—like the first son in the story. But after we think about it, we know we want to. Jesus was telling this story to some people who were like the second son. They *said* they would do what God wanted, but they didn't do it. When God sent John the Baptist to preach to them, they wouldn't listen to him. Instead of listening for God's Word, they were busy judging other people. But Jesus told them that it isn't enough to say something. What's important is that we really do what God wants.

It's hard to escape a "moral" attitude with these readings. We don't want to moralize with the children. But we do need to help them see that there are certain things God wants us to do. They should understand from the Gospel reading that, as good daughters and sons of God, we don't always respond immediately in the best way, but that we can always do better. God always loves us. What Jesus criticized was the attitude of the chief priests and leaders—they thought they were better than others. Jesus praises those who were sinners but believed in him and changed their lives.

You may wish to have three children participate in the reading, as narrator and the two sons. Even this little touch may help the children enter more into the story.

TWENTY-SEVENTH SUNDAY IN ORDINARY TIME

YEAR A

PRAYER OF THE DAY:

O God,
Maker of all things and people,
your greatest gift
is to share your life and love.
Make us worthy of that gift
by our kindness and help
to our family and friends,
always considering their needs
before our own.
With all this,
help us to believe
more and more
that Jesus is your Son
and lives with you,
forever and ever.

FOCUS OF THE READINGS:

Both of our readings focus on the rejection of God's message.

The first reading is a parable of the loving, caring owner of the vineyard who did everything possible for the vineyard. Even after God's constant loving care and grace, there are those who turn away. What more could God have done? God does not force a positive response.

The Gospel parable presents the same theme with more drama. Each time God sent a prophet, he and his message were rejected by God's chosen people. God never gives up. But even the most loving offer, God's own Son, is rejected!

What more could God have done? God does not force a positive response.

FIRST READING: *Isaiah 5:1-7*

This is a reading from the prophet Isaiah.

This is what Isaiah said to the people of God:

"My friend had a grape vineyard on a hillside.
And my friend planted the best vines
and took very good care of them
so that they would give good grapes.
But instead, the vines gave only wild,
bitter grapes that no one could eat."

Then God said,

"Now tell me, is there anything else
I could have done for my vineyard?
When I looked for good grapes,
why did it give me only wild and bitter grapes?

["Now I will tell you what I am going to do.
I am going to destroy that vineyard.
It will be covered with thorns and prickly bushes.
And I will not send any rain on it.]

"My people, you are like that vineyard.
You are the ones I love. I did everything for you.
But when I looked to you for justice and fairness,
I found only evil and killing.
When I looked for goodness,
I found people crying because they are suffering."

The Word of the Lord.

RESPONSE: *Psalm 80*

RESPONSE:
"We are your vine, take care of us. We are your vine, watch o-ver us."

VERSES: to Response

1. We have done wrong, but now we pray:
2. Save us O God, for now we pray:

GOSPEL ACCLAMATION:

Al - le - lu - ia, al-le-lu-ia. Al - le - lu - ia, al-le-lu-ia!

*VERSE:

Plant your Word_ in our hearts._ Let it bear_ fruit in us!_

*Keep singing Alleluia line. Add the verse with a solo or small group.

GOSPEL: *Matthew 21:33-43*

This is a reading from the Gospel of Matthew.

One day Jesus told this story to the chief priests
and the leaders of the people:

"Once there was a man who owned a grape vineyard.
He built a wall around it to protect it,
and he put a tower in the middle of it
so he could watch over it.
Then he hired people to work there
and went to live in another country.
When it was time to pick the grapes,
the owner sent his servants
to collect his share from the workers.
But the workers beat the servants
and killed some of them.
Later, the owner sent more servants,
and they, too, were beaten and killed.
Finally he said,

'I will send my son,
for surely those workers will respect my own son.'

"But the workers said to each other,

'This son will be the owner someday,
and he will have all this property.
Let's kill him and take the property for ourselves.'

"So they took the son,
threw him out of the vineyard, and killed him."

Then Jesus said to the chief priests and leaders,

"Now what do you think the owner will do
when he comes back and finds out
what the workers have done?"

They answered,

"He will punish those wicked people
and give his vineyard to good people."

Jesus said to them,

["Remember what it says in the Psalms,

'The stone which the builders did not want
has become the cornerstone.']

"Now I tell you, the reign of heaven
will be taken away from you who do evil
and will be given to good people who do what is right."

The Gospel of the Lord.

[ ] *Reader may omit text that appears in brackets.*

REFLECTING ON THE READINGS
WITH CHILDREN:

Be sure the children realize that
this parable (story) is being
addressed to those who rejected
Jesus and not to his followers. There
is a call to all of us in every parable,
but the children need not identify
with those who knowingly rejected
Jesus.

Ask the children to recall the
story.

Invite them to allegorize by asking
questions such as:

- Who is the owner?
- Who are the people the owner
  sent to collect the grapes?
- Who are the workers?
- What did they do? Why?
- Who did the owner send last?
- What do you think that means?
- What did the workers do?

If you read the passage in the
brackets, remind the children that
we sang this verse from the Psalm
during Easter.

"The stone which the builders
rejected is the cornerstone."

God invites us to be the "good
people" who do what is right—who
accept Jesus, the Son of God.

TWENTY-EIGHTH SUNDAY IN ORDINARY TIME

YEAR A

PRAYER OF THE DAY:

God our King,
you call us to share your life
and be happy with you forever.
Do not let us be deaf
to your voice
by our selfishness;
guide us along the path of love,
so that one day we will
be worthy to be with you
at heaven's great family meal,
and with Jesus, your Son,
who lives with you,
forever and ever.

FOCUS OF THE READINGS:

Both of our readings focus on the great banquet as the symbolic image of the reign of God.

Isaiah speaks of a time when we will sit at the table and enjoy the richness of God's gifts. There will be no more suffering, no violence, no evil, no tears. All will be joy, and it will last forever.

Matthew takes up this symbol in the parables of today's Gospel but applies it to the reign of God now. The focus of this parable is not the future but the invitation to share in the wedding feast now. The reign is here but not seen or accepted by all who have been invited. We are called by this parable to be ready, not only for the heavenly banquet, but for the banquet now—the reign of God among us with the eucharistic banquet as our celebration of that reality present and to come. Daily we choose to accept the invitation or to be too busy about other affairs.

FIRST READING: *Isaiah 25:6-10a*

This is a reading from the prophet Isaiah.

Isaiah said to the people,

"God is going to give a big banquet,
a feast with all kinds of good food.
This feast will be celebrated here
on God's holy mountain.
And God will destroy all evil
that has hurt people of every nation.
God will destroy the power of death
and wipe away the tears from everyone's eyes.
God will forgive everyone who has sinned.
This will happen
because our God said it would.

"And when it happens, people will say,

'This is the God we have been waiting for,
the God who will save us.
So let us be glad and rejoice in salvation.'

"Yes, the hand of God is here
and will stay on this holy mountain.
God will be with us forever!"

The Word of the Lord.

RESPONSE: *Psalm 23*

RESPONSE:
You are my shep-herd, you are my friend. I want to fol-low you al - ways, _____ just to fol-low my friend.

VERSES:
1. I have all I need. You are my shep-herd, your hand is with me.
2. When path-ways are dark, you are there guid-ing me, keep-ing me safe.
3. You give me to eat. You make me wel-come, you fill me with joy.
4. Your good-ness I know. Your love will be with me all of my life.

GOSPEL ACCLAMATION:

(finger snap)

"Ev-'ry-thing is read-y, __ come to the feast." __

Al - le - lu - ia, "Come to the feast." __ (Fine)

GOSPEL: *Matthew 22: 1-10*

This is a reading from the Gospel of Matthew.

One day, Jesus told this story
to the chief priests and leaders.

"Once there was a king
who gave a big feast for his son's wedding.
But when the servants
went to get all the people who were invited,
they wouldn't come.
So the king said to the servants,

'Go and tell them that the feast is ready,
and I have prepared a wonderful dinner for them.
Everything is ready; come to the feast.'

"But the people who were invited didn't care.
They stayed home
and took care of their farms and businesses.
Some of them hurt and even killed servants
who came to tell them it was time to come.
The king was angry, and he sent his soldiers
to punish those people.
Then he said to some other servants,

'The wedding is ready,
but the people we invited
weren't good enough to come.
Go now into the towns
and invite anyone you see.'

"So the servants went out
and invited everyone, good people and bad people.
And soon the wedding hall was filled with people."

The Gospel of the Lord.

REFLECTING ON THE READINGS WITH CHILDREN:

After the Gospel, invite the children to imagine themselves as one who prepares a big party for a special celebration—a special birthday, maybe.

- What food would you prepare?
- What decorations would you make?
- What games would you have ready?
- Who would you invite?
- Would you enjoy getting your party ready?

Now, suppose on the day of the party, when everything is ready, none of your friends come!

- How would you feel?
- Are those really your friends?

Help the children see the parallels in today's Gospel. Explain to them that this is a story about Jesus inviting people to live with him and celebrate with him. Some people didn't want to be with Jesus, so he invited other people, especially sinners. They are the ones who were happy to come.

Even now Jesus invites us to be with him, to live as sisters and brothers and to share in his banquet at mass. Some people don't want to do that. Do we?

When we go to a wedding or a special party, we wear special clothes, we take a gift, we say special things to the bride and groom or the person who is celebrating a birthday. We do special things; we get ready for the special occasion. How can we show Jesus we are happy he invited us to be with him?

You *may* wish to add: "Every Sunday, just before communion, the priest says, 'Happy are we who are invited to this banquet.' In our hearts we can say, 'Yes, Lord, I am happy. Thank you for inviting me.'"

TWENTY-NINTH SUNDAY IN ORDINARY TIME

YEAR A

PRAYER OF THE DAY:

Lord, by your free gift
you have chosen us
to believe in you.
Increase our believing
and show us how to make
your name great in the world.
Everywhere, people search
for truth and for love;
may they find them in us,
in all that we do
and in all that we say.
We believe
that you listen to our prayer
through Jesus, your Son,
who lives with you,
forever and ever.

FOCUS OF THE READINGS:

Both of our readings focus on the uniqueness of God: there is only one God!

The reading from *Isaiah*, apart from stating this reality again and again, makes its point through the pagan Cyrus. Though he is pagan, he too was named by God. There are no pagan Gods; there is only one God who acts in and through all!

The Gospel makes the distinction between Caesar, thought to be a god, and God, the only true God. The question behind "should we pay taxes to Caesar?" is really, "should we honor him?" Jesus chooses to distinguish between the state and God. The state has its rightful place (of which taxes are a part) but there is only one God—and it's not Caesar!

FIRST READING: *Isaiah 45:1, 4-6*

This is a reading from the prophet Isaiah.

This is what God says to Cyrus, King of Persia,

"Because I love my chosen people of Israel,
I have called you by your name.
I give you a title of honor,
even though you do not know me.
I am God,
and there is no other God besides me.
I am the only God.
Even though you do not know me,
I give you strength.
I do this so that people everywhere
will know that there is no other God but me."

The Word of the Lord.

RESPONSE: *Psalm 96*

RESPONSE: All the nations will praise you, and know that you are God.

VERSES:
1. Give God glo - ry. Give hon - or and praise.
2. Pro-claim sal - va - tion day af - ter day.
3. Tell the na - tions God's won - der - ful deeds.

GOSPEL ACCLAMATION:

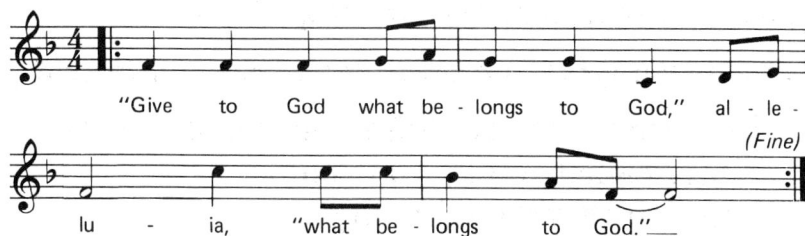

"Give to God what belongs to God," alle- lu - ia, "what belongs to God." *(Fine)*

GOSPEL: *Matthew 22:15-21*

This is a reading from the Gospel of Matthew.

Some Jewish leaders, called Pharisees,
wanted to trick Jesus
into saying something wrong.
So they went to him and said,

"Teacher, we know that you are honest
and that you always teach the truth about God.
We know that you are not afraid
of what other people will say about you.
You treat everyone the same.
So tell us what you think about this:
should we pay taxes to Caesar or not?"

Jesus knew they were trying to trick him,
so he said,

"You phonies!
Why are you trying to trick me?
Show me the money you use
to pay your taxes."

Jesus looked at it and said,

"Whose picture is on this money,
and whose name?"

They answered,

"Caesar's."

So Jesus said,

"Well then, give to Caesar
what belongs to Caesar.
And give to God what belongs to God."

The Gospel of the Lord.

REFLECTING ON THE READINGS WITH CHILDREN:

You may need to explain a little of the background to today's Gospel reading. This should be kept simple not only because of their age, but also because our interest here is not in the historical political situation of the time. It will be helpful if the children know that the Jewish people lived in the Roman Empire. The leader of the empire was Caesar. The Romans believed that Caesar was a god. They worshipped him. His picture was on their money. Explain to them that this is true in many countries today as well. You might show them our coins and, if possible, some from other countries. Explain to them that when the Pharisees asked Jesus, "Should we pay taxes to Caesar?" they were trying to trick Jesus. If Jesus said, "Yes," they could say he worshipped Caesar. If he said, "No," they would tell Caesar Jesus told them not to pay taxes and Jesus would be put in jail.

- How did Jesus answer their question?
- What do you think he meant?

Help the children see that governments are necessary and they help us. You might explain that when their parents pay taxes, that money is used for schools, roads, helping the poor, people who have no jobs, elderly people who can't work anymore, parks, and so forth.

As Christians, we should help with those things. But the Pharisees wanted to know if Jesus would say Caesar was a god. Jesus' answer said that the government is good—but we worship only God.

- What do we give the government?
- How much must we obey the government (the laws?)
- What do we give to God?
- How must we obey God?

Note: the notion that we sometimes must choose between obedience to state or God is unreal for children. Discerning the application of civil disobedience is necessary for adults but not for children of this age.

123

THIRTIETH SUNDAY IN ORDINARY TIME

YEAR A

PRAYER OF THE DAY:

O God, we cannot see you
yet you call on us to love you,
even as we know you love us.
Make us understand
that everybody
without exception
is precious to you,
and that to love them
is to love you.
Let us not be bothered
about what we like
and do not like
but be awake to the needs
of all the people we meet,
just as Jesus did
and who is now
living with you,
forever and ever.

FOCUS OF THE READINGS:

Our readings focus on love of
neighbor. In cycle C the commandment found in today's Gospel is
coupled with a reading from
Deuteronomy which puts the Sunday
focus on love of God and neighbor.
Here in cycle A, our first reading
gives us a list of commandments
relating to the treatment of others.
The list includes foreigners, widows,
orphans, the poor. In short, we are
commanded to love everyone and to
take special care of those in need.

The Gospel is a simple, straight-
forward presentation of the "greatest
commandment." The focus is clear.
Love of God and neighbor is not
merely an option but the definition
of what it means to be Christian.

FIRST READING: *Exodus 22:21-27*

This is a reading from the book of Exodus.

Our God says:

"When there are foreigners
and strangers living among you,
you must never do anything to hurt them.
Remember that you used to be strangers
in the country of Egypt.
And don't do anything
to hurt widows and orphans.
If you do hurt them, and they cry out to me,
I will listen to them, and I will help them.
But I will punish you.

"When you lend money
to people who are poor,
don't make them pay back
more than they owe you.
And if you take their coat
as a promise that they will pay you back,
don't keep it overnight
because they will need it to keep warm.
If they cry out to me, I will help them,
for I love the poor and will take care of them."

The Word of the Lord.

RESPONSE: *Psalm 113*

1. You love the poor, you love the need-y.
2. Teach us to love the poor and need-y,

1. You give them help, you care for them.
2. to give them help, to care for them.

GOSPEL ACCLAMATION:

Leader:
1. Love ___ God with all your heart:
2. Love your neigh-bor as your-self:
All: (sing and clap)
Al - le - lu - ia, al - le - lu - ia!

GOSPEL: *Matthew 22:34-39*

This is a reading from the Gospel of Matthew.

One day, a lawyer,
who belonged to a group called the Pharisees,
asked Jesus this question:

"Teacher, what is the greatest commandment
in the law?"

Jesus said,

"You must love God with all your heart,
and with all your soul,
and with all your mind.
This is the first
and most important commandment.
And the second one is like it:
you must love your neighbor
just as you love yourself."

The Gospel of the Lord.

REFLECTING ON THE READINGS WITH CHILDREN:

At first glance this may seem a simple Gospel to reflect on with children. But, remembering that children take our words very seriously and often literally, we will want to exercise caution. I recall a vivid experience with this very text. After hearing Sister say that we "must love God more than anyone," one little first grade child went home crying. Finally that evening, she told her parents that she thought God didn't love her because she loved them (her parents) more than she loved God. And quite naturally so! Fortunately, the parents were very understanding and had the kindness to tell Sister what happened. When she shared this with the rest of the faculty, it was a learning experience for all of us!

With this caution in mind, let us proceed to our reflection on the Gospel. Rather than dwelling on how much we love God, we might explore with the children ways which we show our love for God:

- in our prayer,
- at mass,
- at home,
- with others, by telling them about the good things that happen (instead of the bad),
- by having a joyful disposition,
- by showing gratitude for God's gifts,
- by showing respect for the things God created and using them respectfully.

We might also explore how we show our love for our neighbor. The children will be able to make many suggestions.

The minister of the Word will want to keep the children focused on ways they can show love of neighbor which are truly possible for them. For example, they *cannot* feed the hungry of the world, but they *can* share their "goodies" generously with others.

They *cannot* make global peace, but they *can* work for peace in their families and with their playmates. What is important is that the children realize that when they show love for others, they are also showing love for God.

THIRTY-FIRST SUNDAY IN ORDINARY TIME

YEAR A

PRAYER OF THE DAY:

God, our Maker, all people
are important to you
and you despise no one.
Do not let us think we are
more important than others,
but make us more like Jesus,
who loved especially those
who were rejected.
May we understand better
that to know
we really need you
is to be filled with your gifts.
We pray this prayer to you
through Christ, our Lord.

FOCUS OF THE READINGS:

The scriptures give us many
images of God: shepherd, king, eagle
with her young, and so forth.
Today's readings suggest the image
of God as creative parent.

The reading from *Malachi* is a
plea for unity, both in what is taught
and in the relationships among the
believers. The motivation for this
unity is we have all been created by
the same God.

Our Gospel for today presents the
same, with a little more expansion.
Malachi rebukes the priests of his
time for not teaching the truth. Jesus
warns against the hypocrisy of the
Pharisees who don't practice what
they teach! His lesson ends with the
same call to unity we find in *Malachi*.
We are to call no one on earth master
because we all have one Master.
That truth motivates our equality.

*If you want to be the greatest,
you must serve everyone else.*

FIRST READING: *Malachi 1:8-10*

This is a reading from the prophet Malachi.

This is what God says to the priests of Israel:

"You have turned away from my ways.
You have led my people away
because of the things you teach.
You have not kept my covenant,
and you teach only what you want to teach
and not the whole truth.
So I will let the people see
how wrong you are,
and they will turn away from you."

The prophet Malachi said to the people:

"We have all been created
by the same God, haven't we?
Then why are we dishonest with each other?
Why do we break the covenant of our family
and hurt one another?"

The Word of the Lord.

RESPONSE: *Psalm 131*

REFRAIN:
Like a child rests in its moth-er's arms, so will I rest in you. Like a child rests in its moth-er's arms, so will I rest in you. *Fine*

VERSES 1-3: *to Refrain*
1. My God, ___ I am not proud. I do not look for things too great.
2. My God, ___ I trust in you. You care for me, you give me peace.
3. O Is-ra-el, ___ trust in God, ___ now and al-ways trust in God.

GOSPEL ACCLAMATION:

1. If you are hum-ble, God will re-ward you.
2. Al-le-lu-ia, al-le-lu-ia!

1.-2. If you are hum-ble, you will be blessed.

GOSPEL: *Matthew 23:1-12*

This is a reading from the Gospel of Matthew.

One day Jesus said to his disciples
and all the people who were there with them,

"The Pharisees and teachers of the law
are important people.
They are teachers of the law of Moses.
So do whatever they tell you.
But don't do what they do,
because they say one thing
and do something else.
They don't do
what they teach other people to do.

"They do everything
so that people will notice them.
They want everyone to see what they do.
For example, when they pray,
they wear clothes
that call attention to themselves,
and they always take the places of honor
at celebrations or in the synagogues.
They love to have people
pay special attention to them
and to call them, 'teacher.'

"I don't want anyone to call you,
'teacher' or 'master,'
because you have only one teacher
and one master—the Christ.
The one who is greatest among you
is the servant.
If you try to make yourself important,
you will stumble.
But if you are humble,
God will make you great."

The Gospel of the Lord.

REFLECTING ON THE READINGS
WITH CHILDREN:

Both points of today's focus should
be discussed. Help the children see
that God is beyond *all* images. We
can't see God. We don't know really
what God is like. But we see what
God does. So we say God is *like* (acts
like) a shepherd because God guides
and cares for us. God is also like a
mother, a king, an eagle, a father, and
so forth. These images help us to
know God better. But God is not
really any of those things. God acts
like those things. This notion of
images for God is extremely
important in order that the children
not be fixated on any one image. The
multiple images of God in scripture
give us a wonderful freedom in
relating to God. Each of us finds in
scripture those images most helpful
to ourselves. We can, by presenting
many images, help children grow in
their relationship with God.

Ask the children:

● How is God like a mother or
father?

Lead the discussion along these
lines (if possible in your situation.)
Children who have the same father or
mother are brothers and sisters.
Malachi and Jesus tell us that
because we all have the same God,
who is like a father or mother, we are
brothers and sisters. Explore that
image (brothers and sisters) with the
children. How do brothers and sisters
act toward one another? Help them
see that this is what Jesus means by
"If you want to be the greatest, you
must serve everyone else." For
Jesus, no one is better than anyone
else. We are all equal and should
serve one another.

THIRTY-SECOND SUNDAY IN ORDINARY TIME

YEAR A

PRAYER OF THE DAY:

Lord God,
you speak to us in our hearts
and one day will call us
to live with you forever.
Do not let us be deaf
to your voice
nor let your final call
take us by surprise.
With your help, may we
keep on praying every day.
And, guided by
your Holy Spirit,
may we learn how to choose
the right things to do
and avoid the bad.
We make this prayer to you
through Jesus, your Son,
who lives with you,
forever and ever.

FOCUS OF THE READINGS:

The focus of both readings is wisdom. It is common in the Old Testament to find wisdom as an expression of God. Here in this reading, we see wisdom praised as the gift which lasts forever. As the presence of God, she is available to all who seek her. She guides their ways to the good.

The Gospel takes this poetic text and puts it into a tangible parable. The focus of the parable is seen in the last line, "Always be ready, for you do not know at what hour the Lord is coming." From the first reading and the parable, we know that being ready comes from wisdom.

FIRST READING: *Wisdom 6:12-16*

This is a reading from the book of Wisdom.

Wisdom is wonderful and everlasting.
Anyone who wants to have wisdom
will find her if they love her and look for her.
Wisdom is always ready to help anyone
who wants her.
People who have wisdom
know what is good and right.
They are free from worry.
Wisdom will lead their thoughts
to what is good,
and she will guide them in all that they do.

The Word of the Lord.

RESPONSE: *Psalm 63*

RESPONSE:
I long for you, I long for you, I long for you my God.

VERSES:
1. O God you are my God, I
2. O God you are my God, you're

to Response
1. give you thanks and praise your name.
2. all I need to guide my way.

GOSPEL ACCLAMATION:

Al-ways be read-y for you do not know when the Lord will come. Al-le-lu-ia, al-le-lu-ia, when the Lord will come, when the Lord will come, when the Lord will come, when the Lord will come.

GOSPEL: *Matthew 25:1-13*

This is a reading from the Gospel of Matthew.

One day Jesus told his disciples this parable:

"This is what the reign of God is like.
One evening there was a wedding,
and ten bridesmaids came to wait
for the bride and bridegroom.
Now five of these bridesmaids were very silly.
They brought their lamps
but didn't bring enough oil to keep them burning.
The other five were very wise.
They brought enough oil to last all night long.

"The groom was late,
and so all ten bridesmaids fell asleep.
But at midnight, someone shouted,

'Wake up! The bridegroom is here!
Come out to meet him!'

"The bridesmaids woke up and got their lamps ready.
The five foolish ones said to the others,

'Give us some of your oil
because our lamps are going out.'

"But the wise bridesmaids said,

'We can't give you any
because there won't be enough
for our lamps and yours, too.
But hurry, go into town and buy some.'

"While the foolish bridesmaids were gone,
the bridegroom came,
and everyone went into the wedding feast.
When the five foolish bridesmaids came back,
they couldn't get in
because the door was already locked.

["They called in, 'Open the door for us!'
But the bridegroom said,
'No, I don't know you!'"]

Then Jesus said,

"Always be ready,
for you do not know when the Lord will come!"

The Gospel of the Lord.

[ ] *Reader may omit text that appears in brackets.*

REFLECTING ON THE READINGS WITH CHILDREN:

Ask the children what they heard.

- What is the story about?
- When did it take place?
- Who was there?
- What were they doing?
- What time did the bridegroom come?

You will need to explain to the children that it was customary for the groom to come to the home of the bride and take her to his home where the feast was usually held. Frequently, the bridesmaids waited for the groom and accompanied him to the home of the bride and back for the feast. Everyone went in the wedding procession with lighted oil lamps. So everyone had to bring enough oil to keep their lamps burning for a long time. It should be explained that locking the doors of the house meant using wooden bars—it was not a simple chore. Once the doors were shut they weren't opened again.

Now to return to the story:

- What do you remember about the ten bridesmaids?
- Why were five of them called "*wise* bridesmaids"?

Help the children see the difference between knowledge and wisdom.

- What did Jesus say after he told this story?
- What does he want us to do now from this story?

THIRTY-THIRD SUNDAY IN ORDINARY TIME

YEAR A

PRAYER OF THE DAY:

Most generous God,
we cannot count
the wonderful gifts you have
poured into our lives.
Above all, you have given us
your Son, Jesus,
who has shown us the way
to our home with you.
Make us wise
in using these gifts
so that they will be
for the benefit of everyone.
Open our hearts to the world
so that we may spread
the Good News about Jesus,
who lives with you,
forever and ever.

FOCUS OF THE READINGS:

Since it is difficult to harmonize our two readings, we will begin with the Gospel.

We are nearing the end of the liturgical year, and the Gospel, like last week's, directs our thoughts to the end of time. Last week the focus was vigilance. This week and next it is "rendering our account." God has given each of us talents, grace, a vocation in life. It is clear from the Gospel that we are meant to use those talents for the good of the reign of God. The importance of the parable is that our reward, "Come be happy with me," is not dependent on the size of our talents, but on our use of what we have been given.

The woman in the first reading is praised because she lived her vocation as wife and mother in a most charitable and noble way. Each of us is called to do that.

FIRST READING:
Proverbs 31:10, 12, 20, 26, 28, 31.

This is a reading from the book of Proverbs.

A woman who is good
is more precious than jewels.
She does not hurt others;
she does good all the days of her life.

She works for the poor
and helps those in need.
She speaks with wisdom
and is kind to everyone.

Her husband and children call her blessed
and tell her how wonderful she is.

May she be rewarded for all that she does,
and may everyone who knows her
sing her praises.

The Word of the Lord.

RESPONSE: *Psalm 63*

GOSPEL ACCLAMATION:

130

GOSPEL: *Matthew 25:14-30*

This is a reading from the Gospel of Matthew.

Jesus told this parable to his disciples:

"Once there was a man going on a long journey.
He called the servants together
and put each one in charge of some money.
One of the servants received $100,
another received $200 and another $500.
The one who received $500 went out quickly
and put the money to good use
and earned another $500 for the owner.

["The one who received $200 earned $200 more.
But the man who had $100, buried it in the ground.]

"When the owner came home from the journey,
the first servant came and said,

'Here is your money.
You gave me $500 to take care of,
but I have earned $500 more for you.'

"The owner said,

'You are a good and faithful servant.
Because you have done so well,
I will put you in charge of even more.
Come, be happy with me.'

["Then the second servant came and said,

'Here is your money.
You gave me $200 to take care of,
but I have earned $200 more for you.'

"The owner said,

'You are a good and faithful servant.
Because you have done so well,
I will put you in charge of even more.
Come, be happy with me.'

"Finally the man who had been given the $100
came and said,

'I know that you are a very strict man
and that you always want more money than you give.
I was afraid of losing your money,
so I buried it in the ground until you came back.
So here is the $100 you gave me.'

"But the owner said,

'You are a lazy man! You knew that I wanted you
to earn more money for me, and, yet,
you only buried it in the ground. You are not
a good servant, and you cannot work for me anymore!'

"Then the owner said to another servant,

'Take the $100 from this man,
and give it to the man who already has earned $500.
Then take this lazy man out to be punished!' "]

The Gospel of the Lord.

REFLECTING ON THE READINGS
WITH CHILDREN:

What did you hear?

Center the discussion on the talents and gifts of the children and people they know. Broaden their understanding of "talents." In the Gospel it meant money. The message of the parable, however, is broader than that. What has God given us? What has God asked us to do? Some people are called to teach, others to cook, others to counsel people, others to preach. People are called to be mothers, sisters, fathers, priests, brothers, single people.

Children too have their gifts and talents. They are filled with God's grace. Center the discussion on the talents and gifts they have and what they can do at their age to use what God has given them.

Help them remember the words that we will hear when we use God's grace wisely.

"Come, be happy with me."

Next week's reading will make this even more understandable.

CHRIST THE KING

YEAR A

PRAYER OF THE DAY:

Lord, you are gentle
and do not ask us
to do more than we are able.
Give us the love
to see Jesus, your Son,
in the hungry and the thirsty,
in strangers and the poor,
in those who are sick
and criminals in prison.
Just as he died for those
who needed him most,
so may we work and pray
for the people
with the most troubles.
We pray this prayer
to you through Jesus
who lives with you,
forever and ever.

FOCUS OF THE READINGS:

The people of Israel saw in their leader the role and function of both shepherd and king. David, for example, is spoken of as both shepherd (which he was) and king (which he became.) The role of the king was not only to rule but to guide, feed, and care for his people. God is also spoken of in shepherd imagery (e.g. Psalm 23.) Here in this passage God says, "I myself will shepherd my flock."

In the Gospel reading, the last judgment, Jesus is both Shepherd and King. He will judge between sheep and goats. The focus is on the *real* manifestation of our faith in acts of charity; on that we will be judged.

REFLECTING ON THE READINGS WITH CHILDREN:

What did you hear? Encourage the children to reflect back on what they heard without comment or question. Throughout the homily, try to bring in the things said by the children.

FIRST READING: *Ezekiel 34:11-12, 15-17*

This is a reading from the prophet Ezekiel.

Our God says:

"I, myself, will take care of my sheep.
As a shepherd watches over the flock,
so will I watch over my sheep.
I, myself, will feed them and give them rest.
I will find those who are lost
and bring them back.
I will heal those who are hurt.
I will be a good shepherd to my sheep.
But remember, I will judge
between one sheep and another,
and I will judge between the sheep
and the goats."

The Word of the Lord.

RESPONSE: *Psalm 23*

You are my shep-herd, you are my friend. I want to fol-low you al - ways, _____ just to fol - low my friend.

VERSES:
1. I have all I need. You are my shep-herd, your hand is with me.
2. When path-ways are dark, you are there guid - ing me, keep-ing me safe.
3. You give me to eat. You make me wel-come, you fill me with joy.
4. Your good-ness I know. Your love will be with me all of my life.

GOSPEL ACCLAMATION:

1. "When you help my broth-ers and sis - ters,
2. Al - le - lu - ia, al - le - lu - ia!

1. ev - 'ry time you do it to me."
2. "Ev - 'ry time you do it to me."

GOSPEL: *Matthew 25:31-40*

This is a reading from the Gospel of Matthew.

Jesus said to his disciples,

"When the King comes in glory,
he will sit on his throne
with all the angels around him.
All the people of the world will come to him,
and he will separate them
just like a shepherd separates the sheep
from the goats.
Then the King will say to the sheep,

'Come and receive your share of the kingdom
which I have prepared for you.
For when I was hungry, you gave me food.
When I was thirsty, you gave me a drink.
When I was a stranger,
you made me feel welcome.
When I had nothing to wear,
you gave me clothes.
When I was sick, you took care of me,
and when I was in prison,
you came and visited me.'

"The people who hear these words will ask,

'When did we see you hungry and give you food?
When did we see you thirsty and give you a drink?
When did we take you in
and make you feel welcome?
When did we give you clothes to wear?
When did we see you sick or in prison
and come to visit you?'

"And the King will answer,

'When you do those things
for any of my brothers and sisters in need,
you do it for me.
And those who do these things
will live with God forever.' "

The Gospel of the Lord.

Who are the people Jesus shows concern for in this Gospel reading?

Help the children to see that all of these people are needy in some way and depend on others.

Can you think of other stories in the Gospel where Jesus showed special love and concern for the poor, the hungry, and so forth?

It is important that the children realize that this text is a summary of all that Jesus taught and did in his life. They should not get the idea that this is a judgment scene which will catch people off guard. Jesus was always identified with the poor, the outcasts, and taught his followers the same. Some people rejected him during his life on earth for this identification. Today's Gospel isn't God's acceptance or rejection of us but *our* acceptance or rejection of what Jesus taught and who he is.

Do we have people in the world, our city or neighborhood, who are hungry, thirsty or who need help?

Help the children to be as specific as possible here. Especially help them to identify those persons in their parish who do things for others.

What do you think Jesus means when he tells us, "When you do those things for any of my brothers and sisters in need, you do it for me"?

This is a difficult concept. The children may not be able to verbalize this truth yet, but reflection on it will nourish the seed.

Jesus invites all people, young and old, to meet him in the poor, the hungry, the lonely, strangers. How can we show our love and our faith in the words of Jesus?

It is most important that children be able to experience themselves responding in action to the Gospel. Children must also be invited to respond according to their capacity. Discourage responses from outside their capacity. For example, sending money to foreign places. Children should be encouraged to help directly and with their own means, e.g. welcoming newcomers to school, helping a child who is hurt or feels rejected. They should not feel guilty for the problems of the world.

What does Jesus say to those who do what they can for others? This is what the children should remember: that Jesus has prepared a place for his followers and wants us to be there.

Holy Days,
Feasts of the Lord,
and
Solemnities

PRESENTATION OF THE LORD

YEAR A

PRAYER OF THE DAY:

O God,
you have shown
such love for us.
You sent
your only Son, Jesus,
to save us.
You have given us great joy.
You have given us light,
through Jesus Christ,
your Son.

FOCUS OF THE READINGS:

The focus of our readings is God's presence in the temple, the one to be adored. In the first reading, the prophet Malachi tells us that God will send a messenger to prepare for the one to come. The Lord of the covenant is coming to the temple and will call all people to change their lives. Christian tradition has seen in this prophecy the persons of John the Baptist and Jesus.

The Gospel recounts the day that Mary and Joseph present Jesus in the temple. There, in the temple, he is recognized by both Simeon and Anna as the fulfillment of God's promise. He is the Savior of the Israelites and the Gentiles as well. But the Gospel also forewarns that this Savior will suffer and will be a sign of contradiction among his own people.

Jesus is the Light and Savior of the world.

FIRST READING: *Malachi 3:1-4*

This is a reading from the prophet Malachi.

Our God says:

"See, I am sending my messenger
to prepare the way for me.
The one you are waiting for is coming.
The Lord of the covenant
is coming to the temple
and will call everyone to change their lives
and do what is right.
Then the people will make offerings
that are pleasing to me,
just as they did long ago."

The Word of the Lord.

RESPONSE: *Psalm 24*

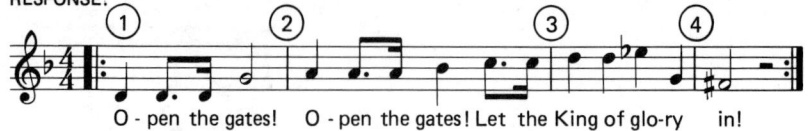

O - pen the gates! O - pen the gates! Let the King of glo-ry in!

GOSPEL ACCLAMATION:

"I have seen the Sav - ior, the light of the world.
I have seen the Sav - ior," Al - le - lu - ia!

GOSPEL: *Luke 2:22, 24-25, 27-36, 38-40*

This is a reading from the Gospel of Luke.

Mary and Joseph brought Jesus
to the temple in Jerusalem
to present him to God
and to make an offering of two turtledoves.
That same day,
a man named Simeon came to the temple.
He was a good and holy man
and was waiting for the Messiah to come.
When Simeon saw the child Jesus,
he took him in his arms and praised God.
He said,

"Now, God, you have kept your promise.
I have seen the Savior.
He is the Light of the Gentiles,
and the glory of your people Israel."

[Jesus' mother and father were amazed
at what Simeon said about him.
Then Simeon blessed them and said to Mary,
Jesus' mother,

"This child will be a sign
for all the people of Israel.
Some people will accept him and be saved.
Others will reject him.
And in your heart
you will suffer because of this."]

There was also a holy woman,
a prophetess named Anna,
who was in the temple.
When she saw the child,
she, too, began to praise God.
And she talked about him to everyone
who was waiting for the Messiah to come.

Mary and Joseph went back to Nazareth.
And the child, Jesus, grew in size and strength.
He was filled with the wisdom and grace of God.

The Gospel of the Lord.

[ ] *Reader may omit text that appears in brackets.*

REFLECTING ON THE READINGS
WITH CHILDREN:

Explain to the children that it was
customary to take the first child (son)
to the temple to be consecrated to
God. Since this rite was specific to
the first male child only, we will not
want to compare it to Christian
baptism. This was a Jewish ceremony
which included a rite of purification
and the offering of a sacrifice. In this
case, the offering was two
turtledoves, the offering of the poor.

Two points might be emphasized
in today's Gospel.

1. Simeon, the holy man,
recognized Jesus as the Light and
Savior of the world. *He is our Light
and our Savior.* Help the children
understand what this means in our
everyday lives.

• How is Jesus our Light?
• How is Jesus our Savior?

Remind the children that we often
use a candle as a symbol of Christ:

• Easter candle,
• a baptism candle,
• an altar candle,
• a sanctuary lamp.

2. Anna, the prophetess, "talked
about him to everyone who was
waiting for the Messiah." Many
people today are waiting for a sign of
hope, for help, for light, for salvation.
Can we talk to them about Jesus?
*Can we, like Anna, tell others the
Good News of Jesus?*

BIRTH OF JOHN THE BAPTIST

YEAR A

PRAYER OF THE DAY:

O God,
you are with us every day.
Each one of us
has been given special gifts.
John the Baptist
was chosen
to preach to the people.
Help each of us
to see our gifts
and to use them
to spread your Good News
through Jesus Christ,
your Son.

FOCUS OF THE READINGS:

Our readings focus on the call of the disciples.

The first reading is one of four passages in *Isaiah* referred to as "songs of the servant." The church has normally seen these passages fulfilled in Christ. Today, this second servant song is applied to John the Baptist. The reasons are obvious. The prophet was called and named before birth. God fills him with strength and honor and his mission is to preach.

The Gospel picks up these themes with the birth of John the Baptist. Even before the child is born, his name, John, has been determined. He lived in the desert where God filled him with strength and holiness to preach to the people, announcing the coming of the Messiah, the Light.

FIRST READING: *Isaiah 49:1, 3, 5-6*

This is a reading from the prophet Isaiah.

This is what the prophet Isaiah said:

"Listen to me, people everywhere!
God chose me even before I was born.
When I was still in my mother's body,
God gave me my name.
God's hand is always upon me,
to give me strength.
And I am honored in God's eyes.

"God said to me,

'You are my servant.
You are the one
who will lead my people back to me.
And I will make you a light to all people
so that they may be saved.' "

The Word of the Lord.

RESPONSE: *Psalm 71*

RESPONSE:
I have been yours since the day of my birth, and you have been my God.___ been my God.___

GOSPEL ACCLAMATION:

You will pre-pare___ the way of the Lord,___ al - le - lu - ia,___ the way of the Lord. You will pre-pare ___ the way of the Lord,___ al - le - lu - ia,___ the way of the Lord.___

GOSPEL: *Luke 1:57-66, 80*

This is a reading from the Gospel of Luke.

When it was time
for Elizabeth to have her child,
she gave birth to a son,
and her neighbors and relatives
rejoiced with her.
When the baby was eight days old,
they came to circumcise him.
The people wanted to call him Zechariah
because that was his father's name.
But Elizabeth, his mother, said,

"No, his name will be John."

The people said,

"But no one in your family is called John."

So they asked his father, Zechariah,
what he wanted to name the baby.
Zechariah asked them
for something to write on, and he wrote,

"His name is John."

And immediately after this,
Zechariah could talk again,
and he began to praise God.
Everyone who heard about this
wondered what it all meant.
They were talking about it
all over the hill country of Judaea
where Elizabeth and Zechariah lived.
The people asked themselves,

"What is this child going to be
when he grows up?"

John grew and became strong and holy.
And he lived in the desert
until it was time for him
to preach to the people.

The Gospel of the Lord.

REFLECTING ON THE READINGS
WITH CHILDREN:

After the Gospel, ask the children
what they heard. If the children
have difficulty verbalizing it, ask
questions that will help them.

- Why do we celebrate the feast of
  John the Baptist?
- What do you know about John
  the Baptist?
- Where did he live?
- What did he preach about?
- What did he do? Where?
- Who is the special person John
  baptized?

God did a very special thing for
Zechariah and Elizabeth. But the
birth of John the Baptist is special
for us too.

- What do you think makes this
  feast so special?
- What do you want to remember
  from today's celebration?

SS PETER AND PAUL, APOSTLES

YEAR A

PRAYER OF THE DAY:

You are our rock,
O God.
We know you are there
when we need you.
Help us to learn
from the strength
of Peter and Paul.
Let us never forget
your love.
We ask this
through your Son,
Jesus Christ.

FOCUS OF THE READINGS:

The readings focus on the special mission of two of the greatest leaders of the church.

The first reading is somewhat of a farewell discourse. Paul seems certain that, having gone the limit, he will be killed for the faith. As he approaches his martyrdom, Paul is confident and even joyful.

The Gospel gives us the beginning of Peter's ministry. Having professed faith in the person of Christ, he is assured of the permanence of the church and his role in it.

FIRST READING: *2 Timothy 4:6-8, 17-18*

*This is a reading
from Paul's second letter to Timothy.*

I am sure that I am going to be killed
because I preach about Jesus.
I have done my best in the race,
and I have stayed faithful.
So I know that the Lord will give me a crown
on that special day when he comes back.
He will reward everyone who loves him
and stays faithful.
The Lord has always been with me
and made me strong
so that I could proclaim the Word of God
to people everywhere.
The Lord has always helped me,
and he will save me from every evil
and keep me safe for heaven.
May everyone give praise and glory to the Lord
forever and ever. Amen.

The Word of the Lord.

RESPONSE: *Psalm 71*

RESPONSE:

I will pro-claim your pow - er! I will pro-claim your won-der-ful deeds! I will pro-claim sal - va - tion, and your faith - ful love!

GOSPEL ACCLAMATION:

Je - sus asked them: "Who am I?" 1. Pe - ter an-swered:
2. Al - le - lu - ia,

1.-2."You are — the Christ, you are — the Son of the Liv - ing God!"

GOSPEL: *Matthew 16:13-19*

This is a reading from the Gospel of Matthew.

When Jesus and his disciples
were in the area of Caesarea Philippi,
he asked his disciples,

"Who do people think I am?"

They said,

"Some people think you are John the Baptist,
and others think you are the prophet Elijah.
But there are others
who say you are Jeremiah
or some other prophet."

Jesus asked them,

"And who do you say I am?"

Simon Peter answered,

"You are the Christ.
You are the Son of the living God."

Jesus said,

"Simon, you are blessed.
You did not learn that
from any human being.
No, God told you that.
From now on you will be called Peter,
which means rock.
I will build my church on this rock,
and it will be strong.
Nothing will be able to destroy it.
I will give you the keys
to the kingdom of heaven,
so that what you decide on earth
will be the same in heaven."

The Gospel of the Lord.

REFLECTING ON THE READINGS
WITH CHILDREN:

Since the Gospel reading appears
elsewhere in the Sunday readings
(Twenty-first Sunday in Ordinary
Time/Year A), it would seem
appropriate today to concentrate on
the two men themselves. Peter and
Paul stand out among the saints, and
even the apostles, as two giants of
the early church. Their common
feast has been celebrated in the
church since the year 258.

There are several books for
children which contain the lives of
Peter and Paul which may be useful
for presenting the highlights of their
lives. We will want to avoid,
however, pictures and stories which
do not correspond to the Biblical
presentation. For example, many
books for both children and adults
show pictures of Paul falling from a
horse on the road to Damascus.
There is no indication in any of the
several accounts of Paul's conversion
which suggests that. The accounts of
their lives should focus on reality and
the great contribution of these two
men.

141

THE TRANSFIGURATION OF THE LORD

YEAR A

PRAYER OF THE DAY:

O God in heaven,
you have given us
the greatest gift of all.
You sent Jesus
to live with us
and to show us how to love.
We will listen, God.
We will do our best for you
and your Son, Jesus,
our Lord.

FIRST READING: *2 Peter 1:16-19*

This is a reading from the second letter of Peter.

Brothers and sisters,

When we told you about the power of the Lord,
Jesus Christ, and how he would come again,
we were not just telling you interesting stories
that someone made up.
No, we saw the majesty of Jesus.
We were with Jesus on the holy mountain
when God showed how special Jesus is,
and we heard the voice of God saying,

  "This is my beloved Son.
   I am very pleased with him."

We are sure now
that what the prophets said a long time ago
is true.
You should listen very carefully
to what they said,
because it is like a lamp shining in a dark place
until the daylight comes.

The Word of the Lord.

RESPONSE/ GOSPEL ACCLAMATION: *2 Peter 1:17*

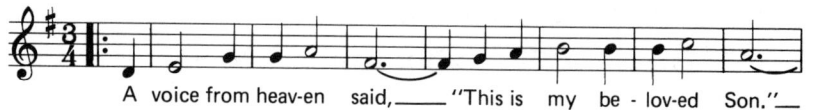

A voice from heav-en said,____ "This is my be-lov-ed Son."____
____ Al - le - lu - ia. Al - le - lu - ia.____ Al - le - lu - ia. Al - le - lu-
ia.____ Al - le - lu - ia. Al - le - lu - ia. Al - le - lu - ia.

FOCUS OF THE READINGS:

In each cycle, the Gospel account of the Transfiguration is the same as the Gospel reading for the Second Sunday of Lent. We suggest you use the reflections for that Sunday. We reprint them here for your convenience.

GOSPEL: *Matthew 17:1-9*

This is a reading from the Gospel of Matthew.

One day Jesus took Peter, James, and
James' brother John up on a high mountain,
away from everyone.
While they were there,
his face changed and shone like the sun,
and his clothes became white as light.
Suddenly, the disciples
saw Moses and Elijah there,
talking with Jesus. Peter said,

"Lord, it's good for us to be here!
If you want me to, I will make three tents—
one for you, one for Moses,
and one for Elijah."

While Peter was still talking,
the shadow of a cloud came over them,
and a voice came from the cloud saying,

"This is my Son, whom I love very much.
Listen to him."

When the disciples heard this,
they fell to the ground and covered their faces
because they were afraid.
But Jesus came and touched them and said,

"Get up. Don't be afraid."

And when they looked up,
they saw only Jesus standing there.
When they were coming down
from the mountain, Jesus told them,

"Don't tell anyone what you have seen
until I am raised from the dead."

The Gospel of the Lord.

REFLECTING ON THE READINGS
WITH CHILDREN:

While heeding the call of God can
be understood by children, the
notion of being killed for the faith
may not serve as a suitable model of
response.

Ask the children what they heard.
If they have difficulty recalling, you
may wish to help them with
questions such as:

- Who did Jesus take with him to
  the mountain?

- What happened while they were
  there?

- Who did Peter, James and John
  see with Jesus?

- What did Peter say? What did
  Peter, James and John hear
  God say?

Ask the children if they have ever
seen previews of coming attractions
on television or in a theatre. Help
them understand that previews tell
us about the coming attraction and
help us look forward to it.

At the Transfiguration, Jesus was
giving a preview of what he will be
like after the Resurrection. He was
also showing us that we will be like
him. We will live with him in glory.
As Jesus was showing this to Peter,
James and John, God told them what
we must do to live with Jesus forever.

Do you remember what God said
to Peter, James and John? God tells
us, too, "This is my beloved Son,
listen to him."

How do we listen to Jesus today:

- in the Bible?

- in our parents and others who
  teach us?

- in the good thoughts we have
  that encourage us to do the
  right thing?

THE ASSUMPTION OF MARY

YEAR A

PRAYER OF THE DAY:

O God in heaven,
you sent your only Son, Jesus,
to live among us.
You made Mary his mother.
How happy she must have been
to share in Jesus' life.
Let us learn from Mary, O God,
and from Jesus Christ,
your Son, our Lord,
forever and ever.

FOCUS OF THE READINGS:

Both of our readings, as they are chosen and placed together for this feast, tell us something about the place of Mary in the church. The reading from *Revelation*, rich in symbolism, presents Mary in various aspects of her role in the church. She is the Mother of the Son, born to be the Messiah. She is the image of the church with the twelve stars (twelve tribes of Israel, twelve apostles) around her head. And the crown seems to indicate her entrance into heaven where she received the reward of those who remain faithful (*2 Tim.* 4:8).

The Gospel reading, usually called "The Visitation," indicates the real meaning of today's feast. Mary is the Mother of the Lord, and all generations will call her blessed because she believed. The feast of the Assumption places Mary among the blessed, and indeed the model of the blessed.

REFLECTING ON THE READINGS WITH CHILDREN:

Rather than reflecting on the readings specifically, it may be appropriate to reflect on the meaning of the feast.

FIRST READING: *Revelation 12:1-2, 5-6, 10b*

This is a reading from the book of Revelation.

I, John, had a vision.
I saw a woman with the sun shining on her,
and the moon was under her feet.
She was wearing a crown on her head,
and it was made of twelve stars.
The woman was expecting a child,
and she was crying in pain.
She had a baby boy,
and he immediately
was taken up to God's throne,
because this child
was to become the ruler of the world.
And the woman went to the desert,
where God had prepared a place for her.

Then I heard a voice in heaven say,

"Christ has come with all the power
and authority of God's kingdom.
Now salvation is here."

The Word of the Lord.

RESPONSE: *Psalm 24*

RESPONSE:

O-pen the gates! O-pen the gates! Let the King of glo-ry in!

GOSPEL ACCLAMATION:

You are blessed a-mong wo-men. Ma-ry you are blessed. You be-lieved God's prom-ise. You are blessed a-mong wo-men, the moth-er of my Lord. Al-le-lu-ia, al-le-lu-ia! "The Moth-er of my Lord."

GOSPEL: *Luke 1:39-56*

This is a reading from the Gospel of Luke.

When the angel Gabriel told Mary
that her cousin, Elizabeth,
was also going to have a baby,
Mary went as quickly as she could to the town
where Zechariah and Elizabeth lived,
up in the hill country of Judah.
As soon as Elizabeth heard Mary's voice,
the baby inside her began to move.
Elizabeth was filled with the Holy Spirit,
and she said to Mary,

"Of all the women on earth,
you are most blessed.
And the baby in your womb is also blessed.
I am so honored because you,
the mother of my Lord,
have come to visit me!
You are blessed, Mary,
because you believed in the promise
that God made to you."

And Mary said,

"I sing with praise the greatness of the Lord,
and my heart finds joy in my Savior.
The Lord has chosen me, a humble servant;
now all people will say I am blessed.
The Lord, who is mighty,
has done great things for me.
Holy is God's name.
God has destroyed the power
of people who are proud
and honored those who are poor and humble.
God has given good food to hungry people
and sent the rich away with nothing.
God has come to help the people of Israel
because of the promise
made to Abraham and Sarah
and their family forever."

Mary stayed with Elizabeth about three months
and then returned to her home in Nazareth.

The Gospel of the Lord.

The feast celebrates Mary's entrance into heaven. It tells us that human beings are destined to live, like Mary, in heaven, in the presence of God. But why was Mary taken to heaven? Why has the church celebrated this feast centuries before it was proclaimed as dogma in 1950? This would be a good time to help the children see the "blessedness" of Mary as she is presented in scripture.

Ask the children what they remember about Mary. The obvious is that she gave birth to Jesus. Help the children recall the main features of Luke's story of the Annunciation.

- What does this tell us about Mary? *She was a woman of faith.*

Mary at Bethlehem:

- What does this tell us about Mary? *She was a wife and mother.*

Mary at the temple:

- What does this tell us about Mary? *She was a woman who followed her religion.*

Mary at Cana:

- What does this tell us about Mary? *She was a woman who cared for the needs of others.*

Mary at the foot of the cross:

- What does this tell us about Mary? *She remained faithful to the end.*

Mary at Pentecost:

- What does this tell us about Mary? *She was a woman of prayer.*

Help the children see that these qualities are what makes Mary special and why we know she is in heaven. Mary is a human being, a woman of great faith to be imitated by all believers. And we too, when we live that way, will be in heaven.

Note: This may be an occasion to give the children a small picture or holy card of Mary.

TRIUMPH OF THE CROSS

YEAR A

PRAYER OF THE DAY:

Praise you, O God,
for loving us enough
to send your only Son
among us.
Your love is never ending.
Your love lives on
with Jesus Christ,
your Son,
forever and ever.

FOCUS OF THE READINGS:

Our readings focus on the entire life of Christ. It would be a mistake to see the cross, the death and Resurrection as the only message of today. Both of our readings put the Triumph of the Cross as the climax of a total life given for us, beginning with the Incarnation.

The first stanza of the first reading tells us that Jesus was always God. At a point in history he became a human being and lived in every way like us. As a human being, he obeyed God in everything, even though it meant he would be killed, God raised him to a new life. Because of this, death on a cross has become the sign of God's power over death.

The Gospel gives us the reason for Jesus' coming to earth. "God loved the world so much." Jesus is the visible expression of God's unconditional love for us. Everyone who believes that Jesus came, lived and died for us, and was raised to new life, will live forever.

FIRST READING: *Philippians 2:6-11*

*This is a reading
from Paul's letter to the Philippians.*

You must think and live like Christ.
Even though he was always God,
Jesus did not try to hold onto that.
Instead, he became a human being just like us.

As a human being, he lived a humble life.
He obeyed God in everything,
even though it meant he would die on a cross.
Because he obeyed God in everything,
God raised him up and gave him the name
which is above every other name,
so that at the name of Jesus,
everyone should kneel and worship him.
Everyone in heaven,
on earth and everywhere
should give glory to God
by proclaiming, "Jesus Christ is Lord!"

The Word of the Lord.

RESPONSE: *Psalm 34*

Glo-ri-fy God, glo-ri-fy God, glo-ri-fy God with me. Let us praise God's ho-ly name. Glo-ri-fy God glo-ri-fy God's ho-ly name!

GOSPEL ACCLAMATION:

1. Ev - 'ry-one who be-lieves in him, they will live for ev-er,
2. Ev - 'ry-one who be-lieves in him, Al - le - lu - ia,

1. they will live for ev-er, they will live for ev-er as the Lord has said.
2. al - le - lu - ia, they will live for ev-er as the Lord has said.

GOSPEL: *John 3:14-18a*

This is a reading from the Gospel of John.

Jesus said to Nicodemus,

"God's Chosen One must be lifted up
so that everyone who believes in him
will live forever.

"Yes, God loved the world so much
that God sent the only Son into the world,
so that everyone who believes in him
will live forever.

"God did not send the Son
to judge the world,
but to save it.
And everyone who believes in him
will live forever."

The Gospel of the Lord.

REFLECTING ON THE READINGS WITH CHILDREN:

Neither of our readings has a "story line" which will be easy for children to follow, understand and retain.

You might ask the children to recall what they heard in the first reading. It might be helpful to read the text slowly, stopping after each stanza. Ask the children what they think is the most important line in each stanza. Perhaps you could help them arrive at the following and write these on a large poster.

- He became a human being just like us.
- He obeyed God in everything.
- God raised him up.
- Jesus Christ is Lord.

We, like Jesus, want to obey God in everything. And we, like Jesus, will be raised up after we die.

- Why do you think God sent Jesus?

Let's listen to the Gospel and hear what St. John tells us.

After the Gospel, give the children a chance to reflect on what they heard.

Ask the children what sentence was repeated three times. Add this to the large poster.

- Everyone who believes in him will live forever.

Note: As there are no leaflets for the feasts, you may wish to have the important lines of the first reading already prepared on a paper which the children can take home, decorate and put in their room. (You might change the pronoun he to Jesus.)

ALL SAINTS
YEAR A

PRAYER OF THE DAY:

We love you, God.
As members
of your family,
we want to show you
our love by living
as Jesus did,
in your name,
forever and ever.

FOCUS OF THE READINGS:

The feast of All Saints focuses attention on two of our fundamental beliefs as Christians: we are baptized into a community and we will live forever. We celebrate today our union with all those believers, children of God, who have been "rewarded in heaven," and now see God.

The first reading focuses on our life as Christians here and now. *We are children of God now!* As such, we must try to be good and pure as we wait for the day when Jesus will come again and we will see him as he is and be like him. And so, the reading also pulls us into the future. We live a life of "already/not yet." We are *already* children of God, but we are *not yet* perfect as Jesus is.

The Gospel too focuses on the already/not yet, but with an emphasis on the future. We are assured of reward in heaven, the blessing to come, when we live the life of Jesus. It is this assurance of seeing God and eternal life of blessing that motivates us to live the beatitudes here and now. Combined, these readings present the Christian view of both present and future.

The saints are those children of God who have lived the beatitudes.

FIRST READING: *1 John 3:1-3*

This is a reading from the first letter of John.

Brothers and sisters,

See how much God loves us!
We are called children of God.
And we really are God's children.
We know that when Jesus comes again,
we will be like him
because we will see him as he really is.
Everyone who believes this
tries to be good and pure,
just as Jesus is good and pure.

The Word of the Lord.

RESPONSE: *Psalm 15*

RESPONSE:

Those who seek your face, Lord, with a pure heart

shall stand in your Ho - ly Place!

GOSPEL ACCLAMATION:

```
1. You are bless-ed, all you who hear me;
2. Al-le-lu-ia, al-le-lu-ia,

1. you are blessed if you live by my Word.
2. al-le-lu-ia,____ live by my Word.
```

GOSPEL: *Matthew 5:1-12*

This is a reading from the Gospel of Matthew.

Jesus and his disciples went up on a mountain, and they sat down so Jesus could teach them. Jesus said to his disciples,

"Blessed are people who know they need God,
for the kingdom of heaven belongs to them.
Blessed are people who are sad now,
for later God will comfort them.
Blessed are people who are humble,
for God will give them everything.
Blessed are people who work for justice,
for God will give them all they need.
Blessed are people who give mercy to others,
for God will have mercy on them.
Blessed are people
who have hearts that are pure,
for they will see God.
Blessed are people who make peace,
for they will be called children of God.
Blessed are people who suffer
for doing what is right,
for the kingdom of heaven belongs to them.

"And you are blessed when people hurt you
and say bad things about you
because you believe in me.
Be happy and glad,
for God will reward you in heaven."

The Gospel of the Lord.

REFLECTING ON THE READINGS
WITH CHILDREN:

We want to emphasize with the children that we live the beatitudes because we are children of God. The beatitudes are, for Christians, a way of life. We do not need to earn our relationship with God by living the beatitudes, we are already children of God.

You might compare this to family relationships. Members of a loving family do not need to earn the love of one another by being good and kind. They are good and kind because they already love one another.

We belong to the family of God. We are truly God's children and so we live as children of God. We know that we are not perfect, but one day we will see Jesus, our brother, as he really is and we will be like him. The beatitudes tell us how we should live until that day.

The saints are people who did that. They live forever with God. Today would be an ideal time to share the lives of some saints who are special to your parish or city.

ALL SOULS

YEAR A

PRAYER OF THE DAY:

Your love is strong,
O God.
Nothing can stop you
from loving us.
Help us be strong too,
O God,
strong enough to live
as Jesus lived,
in your name.
Amen.

Note: In keeping with the Directory for Masses With Children *(Paragraph 43), the authors have elected to use readings from selections offered for Masses for the Dead instead of All Souls readings because they seem best suited "to the capacity of children."*

FOCUS OF THE READINGS:

Our readings focus on death and eternal life. The first reading assures us that nothing, not even death, can separate us from the love of God. God intended us to live forever and revealed that explicitly in Jesus Christ. We have God's promise and nothing can take that from us.

The Gospel gives us the image of the seed which must "die" in order to bear fruit. The grain of wheat, when buried, becomes hidden. Only this burial will allow it to grow into what God intended it to become. Jesus himself was the example of this for us. Only by dying could he rise to new life. Death, then, becomes the process through which we become the person God intended us to become, to be lifted up by Christ and to live with him forever. We come to this new life not only through physical death, but by being willing in our daily lives to give up our lives for others.

FIRST READING: *Romans 8:31-34, 38-39*

*This is a reading
from Paul's letter to the Romans.*

If God is on our side,
who will be against us?
Surely not God,
who was willing to give up even Jesus
for our sake.
God has saved us through Jesus.
No one can take that away from us.

If God is on our side,
who will reject us?
Surely not Christ Jesus,
who died and was raised to life
and is now with God to help us.
I am sure that nothing
will ever take us away
from the love of God.
Not death, not anything in life,
nothing now or in the future—
nothing will ever take us away from God's love,
which is in Christ Jesus, our Lord!

The Word of the Lord.

RESPONSE: *Psalm 27*

RESPONSE: *Gently*

O God, noth-ing can take us from your love, _____

noth-ing can take us from your love. _____

VERSES:

to Response

1. I be-lieve that I will see you. __ Keep my heart strong. __
2. And when e-vil is a-round me, __ I have no fear. __

GOSPEL ACCLAMATION:

1. "Those who give up their lives for me, they will live for ever,
2. "Those who give up their lives for me," Al - le - lu - ia,

1. they will live for ev-er, they will live for ev-er," as the Lord has said.
2. al - le - lu ia, "they will live for ev-er," as the Lord has said.

GOSPEL: *John 12:24-25, 32-33*

This is a reading from the Gospel of John.

Jesus said to Philip and Andrew,

"You know that if you do not bury
a grain of wheat,
it stays just one grain of wheat.
But if you do bury it in the ground,
it grows and becomes many grains.

"In the same way,
those who try to hold onto their lives
will lose them.
But those who are willing
to give up their lives
will live forever.
And when I am lifted up,
I will bring all people to me."

When he said this,
Jesus was telling them how he was going to die.

The Gospel of the Lord.

REFLECTING ON THE READINGS
WITH CHILDREN:

Let the sung response be the
reflection on the first reading.
Through the gentleness and
memorable quality of the refrain, the
children will internalize that nothing
can take us from God's love.

After the Gospel, show the
children a seed. Ask them what a
seed will become if it stays on the
table or in an envelope. Most
children will know that a seed must
be planted in order to grow. It must
be buried in the earth. Discuss this
process with them. After it is buried,
we no longer see it. It seems like
nothing is happening to it. Then one
day, we see a sprout. It's growing.
That means it's really alive. Now it
doesn't look like a grain, but wheat.

Jesus tells us that our death is
like that. When people die, it looks
like the end. But, like the grain of
wheat, they are alive and one day will
be raised to a new kind of life. We
don't know what we will look like or
be like, but we will be alive. Jesus
showed us that this is true because
he died and was raised to a new life,
and he is now alive and with us.

DEDICATION OF ST. JOHN LATERAN

YEAR A

PRAYER OF THE DAY:

Loving God,
you have given each of us
a place to call our own—
a home in your own house.
Thank you, God,
for the love
you share with us,
forever and ever.

Note: In keeping with the Directory for Masses With Children *(Paragraph 43), the authors have elected to use the Gospel from the 31st Sunday in Ordinary Time, Year C because it seems best suited "to the capacity of children."*

FOCUS OF THE READINGS:

Today's feast focuses on the church. The particular church, St. John Lateran in Rome, is the cathedral church of the Bishop of Rome and is also therefore the symbol of the universal church. Several choices for readings are permissible for this feast, all of which point to the true nature of the church.

In the first reading, Paul tells us that we are the temple of God. Since the word "you" is in the plural in Greek, it is clear that Paul speaks of the Christian community as the church.

The Gospel is good news for sinners! The church, the presence of Christ, is for sinners! Christ is the church and he says to Zacchaeus, "I want to stay at your house." The church is the gathering of sinners—those who are lost—around the Lord.

REFLECTING ON THE READINGS WITH CHILDREN:

The concept of church as Body of Christ or Presence of Christ will be too abstract for most children. Children will naturally associate church with the building. However we can at least plant the seeds.

After the first reading, ask the children to recall the image Paul used. A building is a place where people live or work.

• What special "building" are we?

FIRST READING: *1 Corinthians 3:9b-11, 16-17*

*This is a reading
from Paul's first letter to the Corinthians.*

You are like a building that belongs to God.
God asked me to begin forming you,
and I used all my talent
to build a good foundation for you.
And that foundation is Jesus Christ.
So, really, you are God's temple,
and God's Spirit lives in you.
God will punish anyone
who tries to destroy that temple.
For God's temple is holy,
and you are God's temple!

The Word of the Lord.

RESPONSE: *Psalm 122*

GOSPEL ACCLAMATION:

GOSPEL: *Luke 19:1-10*

This is a reading from the Gospel of Luke.

Jesus was going through the city of Jericho,
and lots of people came out to see him.
There was a man there, named Zacchaeus,
who was the head of all the tax collectors
and was very rich.
Zacchaeus also wanted to see Jesus
and find out who he was.
But Zacchaeus was a very short man
and couldn't see Jesus through the crowd.
So he ran ahead
and climbed up into a sycamore tree
and waited for Jesus to pass by.

When Jesus came to that place,
he looked up and said,

"Zacchaeus, come down! Hurry!
I want to stay at your house today!"

Zacchaeus was so excited that he hurried down
and welcomed Jesus into his home.
The people who saw this were angry and said,

"Look, this man Jesus
is staying in the home of a sinner!"

But Zacchaeus said to Jesus,

"Lord, I am going to give
half of everything I have to the poor.
And if I have ever cheated anyone
out of money, I am going to pay them back
four times as much."

Then Jesus said to Zacchaeus,

"Now you are truly living
like the family of Abraham.
And so, today, you have been saved,
for I came to find and to save
people who are lost."

The Gospel of the Lord.

Try to help the children see that we use the word "church" in two ways. It is the building, but also the group of Christians who go there. You might suggest this as a comparison. If we have a Christian gathering—for example a mass in the park—that is also the church. If a group of Christians gather to prepare food for the poor, that is also the church. Whenever we do things in the name of Christ, that's the church. When we say we belong to the church, we don't mean the building, we mean the Christian community.

The children will relate much more easily to the story of Zacchaeus. If you feel it appropriate, reflect only on the Gospel. The encounter between Jesus and Zacchaeus is joyful and easy to enter into. Perhaps there is a little Zacchaeus in all of us!

We suggest you follow the same reflections given for the Thirty-first Sunday in Ordinary Time, year C. They are reprinted here for your convenience.

This Gospel story will almost always appeal to children. There is a light-heartedness to it that makes of the encounter between Zacchaeus and Jesus an event we naturally want to applaud to show our joy.

Ask the children, "What did you hear?" Help them to imagine the scene:

- The crowds,
- Jesus and those with him,
- Zacchaeus scurrying along, looking for an open space, and finally running to climb the sycamore tree.
- What might the crowd have been like?
- Why did everyone want to see Jesus?
- Who was Zacchaeus?
- Why did he want to see Jesus?
- How did Jesus and Zacchaeus meet? (It is important that the children see that Jesus spoke first to a sinner. Jesus sought him out.)
- What did Jesus say to Zacchaeus? (Emphasize that he *ate* in Zacchaeus' house.)
- How did Zacchaeus respond?

Two points should be emphasized:

1. Jesus came to look for sinners so he could save them.

2. When we truly meet Jesus, we change our lives.

Background
to the
Sunday Readings
and
Liturgical Seasons

1. Introduction to the Sunday Readings

"What we have heard, and what we have seen with our own eyes; what we have watched and touched with our own hands, we proclaim to you so that you may be in union with us, as we are in union with God and with the Son, Jesus Christ. And we are writing this to you so that our joy may be complete" (1 John 1:1, 3, 4).

The first disciples, filled with the joy of the Resurrection, were consumed with the desire to proclaim the Good News! This Good News of God's faithful and unconditional love continues to be proclaimed in the church today, especially in the liturgy. In a special way, this saving Word is embodied in the sacred scriptures. The Second Vatican Council reminds us that God is truly present to us in the scriptures, and that this Word reveals God's saving love and also nourishes us on our journey of faith. For this reason, the church teaches that all the Christian faithful should have easy access to the sacred scriptures and that translations and versions should be prepared which could more easily be read and understood by the people of God. (Paragraphs 22 and 25, *Constitution on Divine Revelation.)*

The church is also concerned with the availability and understanding of the scriptures for children, who, as members of God's family, have their rightful place in the church.

"Jesus said, 'Let the little children come to me; do not stop them; for it is to such as these that the kingdom of God belongs.' Then he put his arms around them, laid his hands on them, and gave them his blessing" (Mark 10:14, 16).

Jesus made a special point of welcoming children. In his great love for them, he put his arms around them and gave them his blessing. The scripture readings in SUNDAY have been adapted so that children may more easily understand the Word of God, and through that

Word, be touched and blessed by this same Jesus who is ever present in his Word.

These children have the right to hear God's Word, and God wants them to hear it. We are all aware, however, of the difficulty they have in understanding the Word since the scriptures were written in a language for adults which is beyond the capacity of little children.

Happily, the Congregation for Divine Worship recognized this difficulty and provided a means for solving it. The *Directory for Masses With Children*, issued on November 1, 1973 opens the door for realizing the dream of parents, catechists and priests to make the Word of God accessible and understood by children. This challenging document calls us to use *"words and signs"* in our liturgies which are *"sufficiently adapted to the capacity of children"* (Par. 2). The challenge to provide such adaptation, especially of the scripture readings, is aided by the prudent and useful guidelines provided within the document itself where ministers of the Word with children are encouraged to make selections and adaptations of texts guided primarily by the *"spiritual advantage which the readings can offer children"* (Par. 44).

All those who minister to children in a formal capacity, as well as parents who long to share their faith with their own children, are aware of the necessity for such adaptation. It is to assist in this important ministry that we have prepared scripture readings for each Sunday. Our selection and adaptation of these readings has been guided by four principles.

1. Retain the Sunday Readings of the Liturgical Year.

The Bible, a collection of seventy-three books, was written over a period of some 1800 years, in various places by a myriad of authors. Through

156

these books, we come to see that each human being neither receives nor transmits God's revelation in exactly the same way. The various authors wrote on different topics using a variety of literary forms such as poetry, prose, narration, epic story, letter, etc. By recognizing the variety of the readings, we are open to more of God's revelation to us.

The church has spread these readings over the course of a three-year cycle during which we hear selections from both the Old and New Testaments, including nearly every book in the Bible. Through them we are in touch with the faith community throughout the ages and we hear God's call for a response in our own time.

In the Liturgy of the Word, children, too, receive God's wonderful revelation through the readings and are invited to respond in their daily lives. In almost all circumstances, therefore, the choice of readings already assigned for each Sunday has been preserved. In this way, the children may experience the mystery of God's love for them as it is unfolded during the liturgical year.

There are, however, some readings which are particularly problematic for children. In these instances, an alternative reading has been selected in accordance with the *Directory for Masses With Children.*

"If all the readings assigned to the day seem to be unsuited to the capacity of children, it is permissible to choose readings or a reading from the Lectionary for Mass or directly from the Bible, taking into account the liturgical seasons" (Par. 43).

Young children often have difficulty being attentive to three readings within one liturgical celebration. With this in mind, we have presented two readings for each Sunday.

Because of the harmony which usually exists between the first reading, from the Old Testament, and the reading from the Gospel, we have generally adapted these two. On occasion, however, when deemed more suitable for children, the second reading replaces the Old Testament reading. It remains for the minister of the Word to determine the suitability of reading only the Gospel or using the two readings presented.

"If three or even two readings on Sundays and weekdays can be understood by children only with difficulty, it is permissible to read two or one of them, but the reading of the gospel should never be omitted" (Par. 42).

2. *Remain Faithful to the Meaning of the Text.*

Since Christ himself is present in his Word and in the assembly of the faithful, the scriptures, as the inspired Word of God, always speak to us on some level. While not all of the meaning of each text is clear to adults, and certainly not to children, it is true for both adults and children that frequent reading of the scriptures reveals more and more of the meaning of that which was received initially as a seed to be nurtured. It is often through unfamiliar parables and images that God's message is revealed, and it is our prayerful meditation of these parables and images that cultivates in us a profound sense of the mystery of God's presence and unconditional love for us.

Children, who are especially open to wonder and mystery, are often easily led to a deeper level of faith and a desire to respond to God through the proclamation of the Word. Any adaptation of the readings must, therefore, remain faithful to the rich images and literary forms used by the sacred writers to reveal God's love and saving power. In order that this fidelity be safeguarded, the *Directory* insists that adaptations *"should be done cautiously and in such a way that the meaning of the texts or the sense and, as it were, style of the scriptures are not mutilated"* (Par. 43). And further: *"Paraphrases of scripture should, therefore, be avoided"* (Par. 45).

In all cases, the authentic meaning of the text has clearly been preserved, even when this meaning will not be immediately evident to all children.

3. Use Language That is Intelligible to Children.

It is evident that children sometimes fail to understand the Word simply because it is couched in words beyond their learning. If children are to understand the scriptures and be nourished by them, every effort must be made to make adaptations using a language appropriate to their capacity of comprehension. There is no question here of watering down the Word of God or of rendering it in current colloquialisms. It is, rather, a question of being familiar with the vocabulary level and language structure of the age range for which the adaptation is being made. Often the meaning of an entire passage will be made clear to children by reducing multisyllabic words to a simpler vocabulary or by rearranging the order of the words in a sentence. In instances where sentences are unusually long or contain a number of clauses, we have separated these into shorter, more direct sentences.

Some exceptions to the principle of simpler vocabulary have been made. Frequently the names of cities, the use of words or phrases in Hebrew or Aramaic have been retained. For example, in *Mark* 5:21-43 (Thirteenth Sunday of Ordinary Time, Year B*),* we have kept the phrase *"Talitha kum"* which means "Little girl, get up, I tell you." And in *Mark* 7:31-37 (Twenty-third Sunday of Ordinary Time, Year B*),* we retain the word *"Ephphatha"* which means "be opened." These words and phrases are as foreign to adults as they are to children, yet they have become part of our scriptural heritage and do not pose a problem for us. In fact, these bits and pieces of the original language seem to make a particular passage come alive for us. By retaining these, we hope to enlarge the biblical vocabulary of the children and at the same time expose them to some of the flavor of the time in which the scriptures were written.

Apart from these few exceptions, there has been a consistent effort to present the readings in a simple, direct language which should be easily understood by children between the ages of seven and twelve. Recognizing that children's comprehension levels may vary greatly, even within a two year span, we have concentrated on the vocabulary level of the seven- and eight-year-old. In this way, the readings will be easily understood by older children and by some younger children. Many catechists and ministers of the Word will have children much younger, perhaps three to six years old. Until such time when readings are prepared specifically for these children, we encourage ministers of the Word to freely adapt these readings still further. Again, we call upon the guideline given in the *Directory for Masses With Children* which tells us that the primary goal is *"the spiritual advantage the readings can offer the children."*

4. Use a Language Which is Inclusive of All God's People.

Since the renewal of the liturgy, which made possible the use of the vernacular, the Christian community has become more aware of the language used in liturgical celebrations, especially the Eucharist. While this language has been almost exclusively masculine, many now recognize that whatever the origins of this practice, both historical and grammatical, the use of exclusive language does not represent the true meaning of the sacred scriptures or the true nature of the church and should, therefore, be avoided in revisions of liturgical texts and translations of the Bible.

Because children relate more easily with concrete terms than with abstract concepts, the need for inclusive language is particularly important. The use of exclusively masculine or feminine language at liturgical celebrations may develop for them a limited image of God, God's people and ministry in the church. The readings in liturgical celebrations proclaim God's saving Word for all people and it is important that children hear and understand this. We have, therefore, adapted the readings using a language which is inclusive of both men and women when this is clearly the intention of the sacred writer.

In presenting these Sunday readings adapted for children, we wish to encourage all ministers of the Word, the professionals, the volunteers, and especially the newcomers, to continue in their important ministry in the church. As a further aid, we have included this background information on the Sunday readings and liturgical seasons. This weekly Leader Guide includes suggestions for reflecting on the Word with the children, background materials for the minister of the Word, dramatizations, music, responses, Gospel acclamations, seasonal reflections and a prayer for each Sunday.

With SUNDAY, we wish to affirm and support those who desire to share the Word of God with children, of whom Jesus said, *"The Kingdom of God belongs to such as these"* (Mark 10:14).

2. Introduction to the Liturgical Seasons

Most people enjoy celebrations. Birthdays, weddings, graduations, football victories, centennials, ship launchings are just a few of the occasions people celebrate, sometimes quietly and intimately, sometimes loudly and with great gusto.

The church, for all its seriousness of purpose, is no laggard when it comes to celebrating. Indeed, the liturgy, the heartbeat of the church, is celebration. We do not say or read the liturgy, we celebrate it. Every time we come together for the liturgy we celebrate an event, a happening in the long history of God's dealings with men and women down the ages. Liturgy is the unfolding of the story of our salvation through, with, and in Jesus Christ.

This celebration takes place within two inter-linked cycles: one which we call the seasons and the other, the saints. The cycle of seasonal liturgies (Advent, Christmas, Lent, Easter and Ordinary Time) commemorates the principal events of our redemption, while the sanctoral cycle, as it is called, commemorates particular men and women who have lived out that redemption in a special way.

Liturgical celebrations are important because the church assembles not just to look back to long-past events, but to participate fully in those same saving events. Through the liturgy, the full effects of the work of our salvation are made present: we become part of them, they become part of us. The unfolding in the liturgical seasons of the life and times of Jesus Christ is at the same time an invitation to us to actively participate in that life. Each liturgy presents us not with a faded memory or a lesson from the past, but with the grace-filled effects of that event, made present in the proclamation of God's Word and the celebration of the sacrament by a people called by God. To celebrate the liturgy is as effective for our redemption as if we had been personally present on the historical occasion commemorated. So, celebrating Christmas is more than a pleasant memory; it is involvement with the incarnation of our Savior, Jesus Christ.

Sunday is central to the church's annual cycle of celebrations. It is a journey on which we follow in the path of Christ, fully and really. By so doing we are caught up in his great journey, the victory over sin and death, which we call the paschal mystery.

A final word. The events of our salvation in Christ were, on his part, acts of worship of the God who sent him. Our participation in the unfolding history of our redemption—celebrated in the church's year and in the power of the Spirit—is, therefore, a participation in the greatest possible act of worship. What could be more important than the church's liturgy?

3. Season of Advent

Advent is a time of expectation, a time of preparing for the coming of the Lord. Expectation and preparation are part of the Christian way of life. We are on a journey of faith, pressing forward with greater or lesser zeal, toward the kingdom. In one breath we can say, "The Lord has come," and in the next, "He will come again." To celebrate the future hope of Christians is to celebrate that element which makes faith complete.

The Advent liturgy keeps this expectation alive. The Gospel readings in all three cycles of the lectionary begin the season on the First Sunday of Advent with Jesus' warning about the unexpectedness of the end of all things and our need to be prepared for it, at whatever time it should come. The Second and Third Sundays of Advent throw a spotlight on the person and teaching of John the Baptist. This emphasis might appear at first sight to place John in the role of prophet of the imminent birth of the Savior at Bethlehem, until we remember that, according to the Gospels, John exercised his ministry long after Jesus' birth, directly before his public ministry.

It is only on the Fourth Sunday of Advent that the Gospel readings unequivocally turn their attention to the events leading up to Jesus' birth to Mary. It would help our understanding of the full meaning of Advent if we were to remain more faithful to the pattern laid down by the season's Gospels. Commercial pressures and pre-Christmas Nativity plays, not to mention Christmas parties in early December, diminish the meaning of the preparation of Advent.

Consequently, long before the season begins, children will have been looking forward to the actual celebration of Christmas and the gifts which will accompany it. This is a pity. Such early anticipation of the climax diminishes the force and meaning of the time of preparation.

We should perhaps recognize more clearly other liturgical signs of the season and point them out to the children. First, there is the omission of the *Glory to God*, a hymn of joy, at all eucharistic celebrations of the season, though it is doubtful that a young child will notice this anyway. More noticeable is the use of liturgical colors for vestments and, in some churches, the absence of flowers. Once upon a time, Advent was invested with many more signs of penance, and perhaps the attempt to make it into a mini-Lent was going too far, but at least we should not treat Christmas as if it were already here.

What the liturgy of Advent does, and what we should help the children to begin to understand, is fill us with expectation and an attitude of hope. The readings tell us that we should be on the watch, always ready, not only for the celebration of the birthday of Jesus, but also for his second coming, which puts the first one into perspective. Christianity is a faith for the future.

4. Introduction to the Prophet Isaiah

During cycle A, all of the Old Testament readings for the liturgy come from the book of *Isaiah*, and in cycle B three come from *Isaiah*; cycle C presents passages from four different prophets. Throughout the Advent season, even the Gospel readings are heavily laced with quotations from the book of *Isaiah*. Because this book plays such an important part in our Advent readings, we will give a brief, general introduction to it as a backdrop for the more specific, liturgical introductions for the individual Sundays.

It is generally agreed by biblical scholars today that the sixty-six chapters of the book of *Isaiah* are not the work of a single prophet, but rather the work of two, or possibly three writers. While many theories about this have been presented by various scholars, it is commonly thought that the book can be divided into two major sections: chapters 1-39 being the work of the eighth century prophet, Isaiah, and chapters 40-66 the work of a prophet who lived after the Babylonian exile, perhaps in the fourth century B.C. The major reason for dividing the book into these two sections is that the content, style of writing, and audience are clearly different after chapter 39. Accordingly, chapters 1-39 are called *First Isaiah*, and chapters 40-66 are called *Second Isaiah*. (You may also find them called "Proto-Isaiah" and "Deutero-Isaiah.") The readings for cycle A come from *First Isaiah* and in cycle B from *Second Isaiah*.

First Isaiah (Chapters 1-39)

Isaiah identifies himself in the opening verse of the book, and throughout the early chapters, gives us some of the details of his life. He speaks of his call and his fear of responding to that call. In chapter six he tells of his conversion from this fear to a willingness to be the spokesperson of God. From his writing we know also that Isaiah was married to a prophetess and that they had at least two children. He was an educated man who had easy access to the kings of his time, and to other members of the royalty. He tells us that he prophesied during the reigns of "Uzziah, Jotham, Ahaz, and Hezekiah, kings of Judah" (1:1). This places Isaiah in Jerusalem during the eighth century B.C.

Isaiah's task was to guide his nation through a critical period. The people were rooted in the tradition of King David and longed for a return to that golden period in their history. During the eighth century, God's promise of a "lasting dynasty in the House of David" seemed doomed. The prosperity and glory of Judah as a leading nation were fading, and the Assyrians were a constant threat to their security and independence.

From Isaiah's prophecies, it seems that God's people responded to these events by yielding to the temptation of compromising with foreign nations and, as it were, bargaining for their security rather than trusting in God. Coupled with this was the arrogant attitude that if God were truly on their side, they could do as they pleased and God would come through in the end. For Isaiah, both of these attitudes were sins of pride against the very holiness of God.

At this same time, the nation was changing from an agricultural society to a more stratified society with a class structure. Isaiah witnessed the increasing gap between the rich and the poor and the injustices that resulted from it. Those who were prosperous soon forgot the communal nature of God's chosen people!

These sins of pride and blatant injustices reflected the neglect of the moral standards expected in the covenant and resulted in a breakdown of national strength and security. Isaiah preached that God, who is holy and faithful, would surely save Israel, but would also surely punish them for their sins. Hence, Isaiah consistently proclaimed that the fall of Israel and Judah would be the punishment of their infidelity, and at the same time, he gives a constant call to return to the covenant, to live justly and to trust in the God who would forgive and redeem them.

Second Isaiah (Chapters 40-66)

Whereas the prophet of *First Isaiah* clearly identifies himself, the prophet of *Second Isaiah* remains anonymous. From his writing, however, we can say that he lived during the time of the Babylonian exile. Throughout his prophecy, the destruction of the city of Jerusalem and the temple, the suffering of the people in exile are presumed. His is a message of comfort and hope (40:1). He assures the people that God will restore Israel through Cyrus, the King of Persia.

Second Isaiah's writing is highly liturgical, using psalms and hymns as a primary literary form. His attention is focused on the restoration of Jerusalem and the temple, the place of worship. God's people will be brought back from the desert (40:3) and will be made secure in Jerusalem.

Second Isaiah speaks of God in a language that seems to take on a more personal dimension. He speaks of God's intimate relationship with the people of Israel and describes God's fidelity and salvation in personal, relational images of mother, father and shepherd. The time of redemption also seems to take a more personal shape. Primarily, redemption or salvation meant freedom from oppression and a time when Israel would again be a secure, powerful nation. It was a time when God would restore strength and power to Israel. This time was called messianic time which means "the time of anointing." From this we have our word, "Messiah" which means "the anointed one."

During the time of *Second Isaiah*, this messianic hope became focused on a person who would be God's anointed one. This Messiah is described as the servant of God who will proclaim truth and will atone for the sins of the people. Though he will suffer greatly, God will vindicate him. Quite obviously, Christianity has seen in these passages the foreshadowing of Jesus. These passages which describe the servant are called the "songs of the suffering servant." The notion of a person being the redeemer, the savior, and who embodies the suffering of the people distinguishes *Second Isaiah* from all former prophecy, including *First Isaiah*.

Above all, *Second Isaiah*, while exposing again the sins of Israel, proclaims the message that salvation is sure. God is our Redeemer.

5. *Introduction to Jeremiah, Baruch, Zephania & Micah*

The prophets of the Old Testament provide us with the backdrop for the New Testament and prepare us for the coming of Christ. As we read the prophets in the context of liturgy, we must always remember the nature of their ministry. They worked in and through the political and social order of their day, challenging and exhorting the people, especially the leaders, to return to the covenant and remain faithful to the ways of God.

During cycles A and B, we hear from the prophet Isaiah. In cycle C, we hear the message of four different prophets from the 7th and 8th century BC.

Jeremiah

Jeremiah appears as perhaps the most human of the prophets. Often reluctant to fulfill his role, his writing reveals the pain and agony he experienced in being faithful. Yet, as a public figure, Jeremiah maintained uncompromising fidelity, though he was often commanded to present God's message through rather strange signs. For example, he was commanded not to marry or have children as a sign to the people that they were not living in harmony with God and that a complete restoration was in order. Jeremiah lived a life of hope and despair; he was loved and hated, ridiculed and respected. Through it all, his message was consistent: return to the covenant. Live in justice and God will save you.

Baruch

Baruch is best known as the secretary to Jeremiah. What we know of him is gleaned from the book of *Jeremiah* rather than from the book which bears his name. Much of the book of *Jeremiah* was either dictated to Baruch or written by him, and he sometimes delivered the messages to the people in Jeremiah's name. The last ten chapters contain a lengthy biography of Jeremiah, written by his faithful servant, Baruch.

Zephania

Zephania was a man of great conviction who spoke out fearlessly against the infidelities of his people. Though he issues strong warnings, he speaks of the "Anawim," the faithful remnant who will enjoy salvation. Of his personal life, we know almost nothing, except that he was decended from Hezekiah, who may be the King Hezekiah so often mentioned in the Old Testament.

Micah

Micah came from the small village of Morsheth in Southwest Judah. Coming from a peasant background, he was familiar with the injustices suffered by the poor at the hands of the rich. In unpolished and often blunt language, he spoke out against every kind of injustice; those of the leaders, the priests and prophets, as well as the common people. Because of his constant demand for justice as the true worship of God, Micah is known as the prophet of social justice.

6. The Season of Christmas

That the Son of God should have taken upon himself our human nature is the most astounding and incomprehensible truth we can imagine. Indeed, it is beyond all imagining: for we know the truth only because it has been revealed to us by the power of the Holy Spirit. The joy and excitement which permeates this season is not misplaced.

The exchange of gifts which marks this entire season is thoroughly appropriate as an active symbol of God's gift to us, sinners as we are. But should we be carried away by emotion and excitement, the liturgy firmly stresses the seriousness and, if you will, the practicality of the gift. *". . . The child born today is the Savior of the world"* (prayer after communion), *". . . all the ends of the earth shall see the salvation of our God"* (first reading). *"Today in the town of David, a Savior has been born to you"* (Gospel). The child born in the stable has come not just to be among us, but to save us from our sins.

Soon after Christmas Day, we celebrate the feast of the Holy Family. Less than helpful artistic representations of what the life of Jesus, Mary and Joseph was thought to be like, and moralizing meditations of Christian family life, have tended to obscure the truth of this feast. As the Gospel for cycle B tells us: *"Meanwhile, the child grew to maturity, and he was filled with wisdom; and God's favor was with him."* Jesus was truly a human being, like us in all things but sin. He lived, learned, loved and laughed like any other child of his time. He was one of us. Yet, even in the midst of the joys of Christmas, a more sombre note is struck. All three Gospels of the lectionary cycle for the Holy Family speak of tension, threat, perplexity, like distant thunder announcing an impending storm. The flight from Herod's persecution, Simon's prophecy of the piercing sword, and the loss of the child in Jerusalem warn us of a mission to be accomplished.

The epiphany sheds a sharper light on that aspect of the season. *"Today you revealed in Christ your eternal plan of salvation and showed him as the light of all peoples"* (Preface of the Epiphany). He is not a passive Emmanuel, a God-among-us with no function. On the contrary, he is the Savior of all, sent by God to proclaim the Good News and lead all peoples to the peace and joy of the Kingdom. That this is God's will is made abundantly clear at the very end of the Christmas season when, at the baptism of the Lord, we hear a voice from heaven, *"This is my Son, the Beloved; my favor rests on him."*

Savior, Son, beloved though he is, Jesus seeks our free cooperation. For his mission to succeed, we must respond with a constant "yes!" The first and most complete "yes" was uttered by Mary. The solemnity of Mary is celebrated on January 1st and is a reminder of the humility and love with which we must match—that of Jesus himself. *"Let it be done to me according to your word!"* is echoed by *"your will be done"* as Jesus prayed in Gethsemane.

7. Introduction to the Infancy Narratives

All of our Gospel readings for the Christmas season, as well as the last Sunday of Advent, come from the Infancy Narratives of Matthew and Luke. These wonderful stories tell us, in vivid images, of the unique Son of God who was born of a young virgin, and the virgin's name was Mary. They present Jesus as the One of whom the prophets spoke, the One who fulfills the expectations and desires of the people of Israel. He is Messiah and Savior, Light to the Gentiles and Lord of all.

The Infancy Narratives are a witness to all that the early Christians believed about Christ. But, in reading, praying and proclaiming the Infancy Narratives, we need to guard against two extremes. The first is to assume that these events were meant to be presented literally and are, therefore, historically accurate in every detail. On the other hand, we want to avoid rejecting the narratives as not historical

163

and, therefore, regard them as pure legend. The purpose of the Infancy Narratives, in the view of most scripture scholars, may best be summarized in the words of the Jerome Biblical Commentary: *"The details of the narratives are symbolic and Biblical. They communicate the mystery of redemption, not a diary of early events."*

We have, perhaps, become accustomed to the Christmas story with all the details of the shepherds, the star, magi, angels, manger, etc. seen together. Yet, when we look at the two narratives separately, we find two stories that are entirely different in their presentation, both in the telling of events and in mood. For example, Matthew speaks of the star guiding the magi to Bethlehem where they adore the newborn King. Luke, on the other hand, tells us of the shepherds who, at the word of the angels, came to Bethlehem to find the child, lying in a manger.

Matthew, a Jew writing for Jewish converts, presents Jesus as one who experiences the struggles of his people, even from his birth. Throughout the narrative, we read of fear, suspicion, danger and concern for the survival of the infant. In Matthew's narrative, Jesus shares in the struggles of his Jewish ancestors and, at the same time, fulfills their hopes for salvation.

Matthew uses the language and images familiar to his Jewish audience. His narrative is written within a patriarchal context. The annunciation is made to Joseph. Joseph is to name the child. Joseph leads the family to safety, and when they return from Egypt, he settles in Nazareth.

Luke, too, used the language and images which would speak to his people. But he and his Christian community were not primarily Jewish, but Gentile in origin, with a variety of backgrounds. So his narrative is one which appeals to a more universal audience. His narrative is written around a whole host of characters, Jewish and non-Jewish, rich and poor, men and women. His audience was not part of the struggle common to Matthew's community; so his narrative is filled not with struggle but with songs of joy, sung by Zachariah, Mary, the angels, and Simeon.

Nor is Luke's community a patriarchal society. In his Gospel, the annunciation is made to Mary. Mary is to name the child. Mary takes the good news to the hill country of Judea. Mary is addressed by Simeon and Anna in the temple, and Mary treasures all these things in her heart.

Whatever the differences in detail, both Matthew and Luke present the central mystery: Jesus was conceived by the power of the Holy Spirit and was born of the Virgin Mary. We are invited through their vivid and varied images to read the story of the birth of this child and, in faith, to see "more than meets the eye."

8. *Season of Lent*

Lent is the season with the strongest liturgy. Ashes, palms, purple vestments, omission of alleluia—all intertwined with finely tuned texts—contribute to a liturgy which makes a deep impression on all who take part in it.

Lent is a time of preparation. First and foremost, the church is concerned with the preparation of the catechumens who are to be initiated into the Christian community at the Easter Vigil services. On the First Sunday of Lent they appear before the community which gives its assent to them becoming elect, and so may embark on the final period of prayer and purification.

Lent is a time of reflection and celebration in which, especially on the third, fourth and fifth Sundays, the community prays with the men and women who are soon to become their brothers and sisters in the Lord. As the Gospel stories of Jesus' encounter with the Samaritan woman at the well (third Sunday), of the healing of the man born blind (fourth Sunday) and the raising of Lazarus (fifth Sunday) unfold, all those assembled for worship are plunged once again into a renewed understanding of what it is that happens to us when we are initiated into the community which is Christ.

Lent is also a time of renewal. If the baptismal waters beckon the initiates onward, the ashes are a spur to those who have long since been members of the Christian community but have lost something of their first innocence. As the baptized accompany the soon-to-be-baptized on their journey of faith, they enter a period of prayer and fasting which must be a constant feature of the Christian way of life.

This is brought home to us graphically on the first Sunday in all three cycles when we hear the account of Jesus' time of prayer, fasting, and temptation in the desert. As he sets out on his journey to Jerusalem and his Passover, we are reminded that our own journey will not reach its destination if it is not accompanied by the rejection of sin and a renewed adherence to the will of God.

That there is a destination of glory is emphasized in the account of the Transfiguration of Jesus, presented in the Gospel of the second Sunday in all three cycles. Thereafter, cycle B continues the theme of dying and rising, particularly exemplified in Jesus' words that: *"unless a grain of wheat falls on the ground and dies, it remains a single grain; but if it dies, it yields a rich harvest"* (fifth Sunday).

Cycle C is more concerned with repentance and forgiveness. The moving and mysterious story of the adulterous woman (fifth Sunday) underlines the truth that if we turn from sin, the Lord will more than match our conversion with his loving forgiveness. On the preceding Sunday, we listen to the parable of the Prodigal Son, which perhaps best sums up our relationship with God. While we witness the catechumenal journey, we are reminded that we, too, share fully in a loving relationship with God. We have fallen away. But still, like the father of the Prodigal Son, God anxiously awaits our return so that we can be restored to our true home.

Passion Sunday, with its blessing and procession of Palms and the reading of the accounts of the Passion by Matthew, Mark and Luke, launches us into the final period of Lent. Paradox, as always, is there: a triumphal entry into Jerusalem, only to end in Jesus' ignominious death. But, of course, we know that death is not really the end.

9. Introduction to the Gospel of John

Who is John?

The disciple who wrote the fourth Gospel tells in the last verses: *"This is the disciple who is bearing witness to these things, and who has written these things. And we know that his testimony is true."* This eyewitness to the life of Jesus is the "beloved disciple," the apostle John. He is one of the first to be called by Jesus. While fishing with his brother, James, and his father, Zebedee, he *"left everything and followed him."* John, unlike the other three evangelists, was with Jesus on some rather privileged occasions: the wedding feast at Cana, the healing of Peter's mother-in-law, the healing of Jairus' daughter, the Transfiguration, and he was seated next to Jesus at the Last Supper. His Gospel reveals the closeness of their relationship.

When and why did John write and for whom?

John's Gospel, composed near the end of the first century (90-100), was written for Christians who had never known the earthly Jesus. For John, Christians living in the second century and beyond have the same intimacy with the Lord as did those who were privileged to walk with him on earth. He sees Jesus as living among us in a sacramental way.

As a Palestinian Jew, John explains for his audience many of the things that would not be understood either by non-Jews or by those who lived after the events had taken place. For example, he explains why it would be unusual for Jesus to be speaking with the Samaritan woman (*John 4*) and why the parents of the blind man refused to speak (*John 9*).

What are the special characteristics of John's Gospel?

There are many unique characteristics of the fourth Gospel that make it quite different from the other three: his emphasis on the sacramental life of the church, his highly symbolic language and his emphasis on discipleship rather than a hierarchical church based on the apostles.

John presents the divinity of Christ through the signs that Jesus gives. Rather than concentrating on the miracles themselves, John sees in them the signs of who Jesus is. So, for example, at the wedding feast of Cana, John concludes by saying, *"this was the first of his signs, and his disciples believed in him."*

There are seven such signs in John's Gospel. There are seven *"I am"* sayings: *"I am the bread, the light, the door, the shepherd, the Resurrection, the way, the vine."* When we recall that *"I am"* is the name of God revealed to Moses, we see in these *"I am"* sayings the revelation of Christ's divinity. This revelation reaches its climax in the confession of Thomas, *"My Lord and my God."* John's sacramental presentation is climaxed in the response of Jesus, *"Blessed are those who do not see (me) and have believed."*

It is for us, those who have not seen Jesus with our eyes, that John has written about the *"signs Jesus did in the presence of the disciples,"* that we *"might believe that Jesus is the Christ, the Son of God, and that believing, we may have life in his name."*

10. Easter Season

For fifty days, up to the celebration of the Spirit at Pentecost, the church rejoices in a special way in the risen Lord and in the life which he gave to his people. Yet the Resurrection is incomprehensible without the dying which goes before it. So Easter season begins with what we call the Easter Triduum. This starts with the celebration of the evening mass of the Lord's Supper, continues through the Good Friday Passion celebration, and so to the excitement of the Easter Vigil—three celebrations making the summit of the church's year.

Yet, not three celebrations, but one. The Triduum celebrates in word, song, silence and ritual the paschal mystery of Jesus Christ, his passing over from death to life, from this world to the reign of God. The entire life of Jesus may be seen as a journey, and it is in the last three days of Holy Week that we see and experience the journey reaching its conclusion. At the evening mass on Holy Thursday, we commemorate the passover meal which Jesus had longed to eat with his disciples (*Luke* 22:15). On Friday, we contemplate the moment when Jesus gave himself as the sacrificial victim of the new passover. Then, at the vigil service, Jesus' passover journey is completed, and we celebrate the Resurrection.

Others have also been on a journey, a passover. For some time past, the catechumens have been journeying in faith, and the Easter Vigil is that moment when, through the initiation sacraments of baptism, confirmation and Eucharist, their journey is united with Christ's. They participate in his dying and rising and become fully one with the Christian community. Thereafter, Easter season is the welcoming of the new members into the community and a continuing celebration of the Resurrection event.

With the feast of the Ascension of the Lord, we focus more sharply on the fact that Jesus' mission must become ours. We are to be his witnesses to the world. Even as Jesus is taken up into heaven "to sit at the right hand of God," where he reigns in glory, he promises that he will send his Spirit to be with us in carrying out this mission.

The Easter season is completed at Pentecost as we celebrate the coming of the Holy Spirit upon the church, which, transformed and empowered, proclaims God's Word to the nations.

11. Introduction to the Acts of the Apostles

In all three cycles, the first reading throughout the Easter season comes from the *Acts of the Apostles*. It might be helpful, therefore, to have a short introduction to this exciting book.

Who wrote the Acts of the Apostles?

The introductions to the third Gospel and the *Acts of the Apostles* indicate that they were written by the same author. From earliest times, it has been accepted that both were written by Luke as a single, two-volume work and were later separated in the canon of the New Testament.

Luke was a companion of St. Paul on at least one of his missionary journeys. In his letters, Paul refers to Luke as the beloved physician and twice mentions that Luke is with him as a co-worker. Luke describes himself as a careful writer who researches well before committing his story to writing.

What is the purpose of the Acts of the Apostles?

Luke tells us that in his first book, the Gospel, he *"dealt with all that Jesus did and taught before he was taken up."* His purpose in *Acts* is to show the development of the church after Pentecost. *"When the Holy Spirit comes upon you, you are to be my witnesses in Jerusalem, throughout Judea and Samaria and to the ends of the earth"* (*Acts* 1:8). The rest of the book unfolds this mission, beginning with the speech of Peter on Pentecost in Jerusalem and concluding with the arrival of Paul in Rome, the city which symbolized *"the end of the earth."*

Through the speeches and activities of the disciples, but principally those of Peter and Paul, Luke stresses two main ideas. First, Jerusalem is the mother church, the place of its birth and the seat of its teaching. Second, through the power of the Holy Spirit, the church reaches out from Jerusalem to embrace the entire Gentile world. Luke recounts in vivid detail the missionary journeys of Paul which take him all over the known world. Throughout these journeys, Paul looks to the twelve apostles in Jerusalem for approval of his teaching. After telling us that Paul was taken to Rome and put under house arrest, Luke abruptly ends his book. His mission has been accomplished. Peter had proclaimed the Good News in Jerusalem and Paul had carried it to the ends of the earth.

Why is this book so appropriate for the Easter season?

Through the activities of the early disciples, we learn of the struggles and persecutions as well as the joys and successes of the early church. Under the guidance of the Holy Spirit, the first Christians lived in community, witnessed to the risen Lord, taught his message, preached his Word, healed in his name, baptized converts and endured persecutions. From Jerusalem, the disciples proclaimed, in word and deed, the Good News of the Easter message: He is risen!

12. Sundays of the Year

Advent, Christmas season, Lent, and Easter season are the times of calling. In those seasons we celebrate the Incarnation and all the other events which made up Jesus' life on earth. It is a time of calling because it broadly commemorates the calling together of the community. "Come, follow me" is the key phrase.

A call is no use without a response. The Spirit has been sent upon the church so that we may make that response. The Sundays which follow Pentecost (the "green" Sundays) are, in a certain sense, the time of the Spirit in which the church sets forth to proclaim the living Word of God. There is no imposed thematic structure for the 33 Sundays. They follow a pattern whereby the Gospel of Matthew is proclaimed in cycle A, Mark in cycle B, and Luke in cycle C. The first reading from the Old Testament is selected to match some particular truth contained in the Gospel of the day.

The season is concluded by the celebration of Christ the King. It is as if we are saying, *"The humble infant who grew to adulthood, preached the good news of reconciliation, brought it about in his death on the cross and rising from the dead, who sent his Spirit upon the church to complete his work, he is the King of all creation. Glory to him forevermore. Alleluia! Amen!"*

13. Formation of the Gospels

Over the course of the three-year cycle, we hear from each of the four evangelists and so receive the Good News of Jesus Christ from four united, yet quite distinct, sources. During cycle A, the Gospel of Matthew is read; during cycle B, we have the Gospel of Mark; cycle C presents the Gospel of Luke. The Gospel of John is read for most of the Sundays of the Easter season in all three cycles.

Each of these evangelists has a unique portrait of Jesus to present. As we prepare to enter into their Gospels during the liturgy, we might ask ourselves what factors might account for four different portraits of the same person, Jesus the Christ?

In searching for our answer, it is important to realize that the Gospel, the Good News, was handed on orally for over thirty years before it was written down in any organized way. Thus, the four written Gospels, as we have them today, represent not the beginning but the final step in their formation. In a document issued by the Pontifical Biblical Commission in 1964, the three stages in the formation of the Gospels are clearly outlined.

The *first stage* of the Gospels is, of course, the actual ministry of Jesus. The Good News, from which we get our word "gospel," was first proclaimed by the life, death and resurrection of Jesus himself. In his preaching, his miracles, his encounters with others, he proclaimed the Good News of salvation. It is, therefore, the words and deeds of Jesus during his earthly ministry that are the source for all Christian tradition, both oral and written and, hence, the first stage in the formation of the Gospels.

Traditionally, we say that this first stage lasted about three years, that is, from the baptism of Jesus until his crucifixion.

The *second stage* in the formation of the Gospels is the ministry of Jesus as it was understood and preached orally by the disciples between the Resurrection of Jesus and the actual writing of the Gospels. This stage is very important in the formation of the Gospels, because it is here that the various portraits of Jesus begin to emerge. The early disciples had only one goal in preaching the Good News: to bring all people to the saving power of Jesus Christ, the Lord.

Obviously, Jesus did and said more than we find in the written Gospels. And so, even as we do today, the early preachers recounted those stories, deeds and words of Jesus which they found most appropriate for their local community in a particular time and in a particular place. Also, as is true today, no two preachers had the same style. Hence, the Gospel came to take a slightly different shape in the various communities where the disciples went to preach. Some stories, deeds and words took on prominence in one area, others in another area. This second stage, which we might call "the oral Gospel," became the substance for the Gospels as we have them today.

The *third stage* in the process of the formation of the Gospels spans a great number of years, perhaps from 65 to 110 AD. After years of handing on the Gospel through oral preaching, disciples of those earlier eyewitnesses, the apostles, began the process of putting it into writing. Mark was the first to undertake this task sometime between 65 and 70 AD. The Gospels of Matthew and Luke were written between 80 and 90 AD, using much of Mark's Gospel as well as material from other sources, including the oral tradition in their local areas. The Gospel of John, written between 90 and 110 AD, seems to be dependent on entirely separate sources. His Gospel departs radically from the style and content of the first three. The individual style and content of each of the four will be discussed in separate introductions to each of the Gospels.

All four, however, gathered their primary material from the oral tradition known to them. Each evangelist sought to bring the Good News to his contemporary community and so selected the material needed for his purpose and arranged it in the order and style best suited to his audience.

Some stories or incidents in the life of Jesus appear in only one of the four Gospels. For example, the "Pearl of Great Price" appears only in *Matthew*, the parable of the Good Samaritan is found only in *Luke*, the story of the woman at the well is told only by John. Sometimes the same story will be found in two or more of the Gospels but in a different order of events, with different details, and perhaps even a different meaning. In other words, the evangelists used the deeds and sayings of Jesus differently according to their audiences and their own understandings of the meaning of Jesus. The result of this is that we now have four accounts of the Gospel, each with its unique presentation of the life, death and resurrection of Christ.

In reading the four Gospels separately, allowing for the intention of each evangelist, we experience the richness of the early church as it sought to live and proclaim the meaning of the risen Lord. This is precisely why the church presents them separately in the three-year cycle.

14. Introduction to the Gospel of Matthew

"*As Jesus was walking, he saw a man named Matthew sitting by the customs house, and he said to him, 'Follow me.' And he got up and followed him*" (Matthew, 9:9).

Who is Matthew?

In the list of apostles, he is identified as "Matthew, the tax collector" (*Matthew* 10:3). Is Matthew, the tax collector and apostle, the author of the Gospel which bears his name?

Given the situation of the Gospel, which dates it near the end of the first century, around 80-90 AD, this seems unlikely. However, we may say that the author of this Gospel is a disciple of the apostle and that he relies on the oral tradition that comes from Matthew's eyewitness account.

It was not at all unusual at that time to attach the name of an important person to one's work, either to give it prominence or to honor the person so named. It would seem that the author of this Gospel has done so here. As is traditional, however, we continue to refer to the author as Matthew. Of all four evangelists, Matthew is the most clearly Jewish.

Why and when did Matthew write?

The Gospel of Matthew was written near the end of the first century. His community had experienced a separation from the synagogue, the center of their relationship with God. The Jewish authorities had agreed that anyone who acknowledged Jesus as the Christ should be expelled (*John* 9:22). Accustomed to the rituals and ways of the synagogue, these Jewish Christians needed the assurance that Jesus himself was the Messiah and was now the center of their relationship with God. The primary purpose of Matthew's Gospel, therefore, is to show Jesus as the Messiah.

What are the specific characteristics of Matthew's Gospel?

Writing for a community of Jewish converts, he uses images, stories, references and literary techniques that are well-known to Jewish people. Matthew uses more Old Testament passages than the other three Gospels combined. He frequently frames the teachings of Jesus in a dialogue with the Jewish teaching authorities, to whom he is superior.

Matthew appeals to the background of his audience. He does this by comparing Jesus to the figures of Jewish history who represented all that was ideal, all that looked forward to salvation. Jesus is the new Moses, the liberator par excellence. As Moses led the people from slavery in Egypt, so Jesus liberates us from the slavery of sin. As Moses gave the Ten

Commandments on Mt. Sinai, so Jesus gives the fulfillment of this law in his sermon on the Mount. Jesus is the new David. Just as David, the ideal king, was promised an everlasting kingdom, so Jesus is the Son of David, the king who inaugurates the kingdom of heaven here among us. This identification between Jesus and the Old Testament figures is seen clearly in Matthew's presentation of Jesus' family tree (*Matthew* 1:1-17). Whereas Luke traces the genealogy to *"Adam, son of God"* (*Luke* 3:23-38), Matthew begins with *"Jesus Christ, son of David, son of Abraham."*

At the same time, this Jewish community was faced with an influx of Gentile converts. How does a people, who thought of themselves as the sole inheritors of God's salvation, come to accept the possibility of universal salvation? Matthew's Jesus reveals the fulfillment of God's promise to the Jews and the unfolding of a more universal plan of the same God. He insists that Jesus could be recognized as Messiah but was rejected by the Jews. This rejection has turned the mission of Jesus to the Gentiles. Matthew, at the end of the first century, wants his contemporary Jewish Christian community to avoid the blindness of earlier Jews. He calls them to faith in Jesus—the new Moses, the Son of David—who brings the old law to fulfillment in the reign of heaven, a reign which includes the Gentiles as well as the chosen people.

The portrait of Jesus that emerges from Matthew's Gospel is Messiah, in the person of Emmanuel—God with us.

15. Introduction to the Gospel of Mark

Who is Mark?

While we know very little about the actual person of Mark, some hints within his Gospel allow us to make at least some attempt at a description. His careful attention to details and his vivid accounts may indicate that he was an eyewitness to the life of Jesus. Traditionally, it has been thought that Mark was a disciple and secretary to Peter. Some have suggested that he is the young man described in 14:51-52. Here, Mark tells us that during the arrest of Jesus, a young man, wearing only a linen cloth, followed him at a distance. Fearful that he, too, might be arrested, the young man ran off naked, leaving the linen cloth in their grasping hands. Still others have suggested that he is the John Mark who traveled with Paul during his first missionary journey (*Acts* 13:14). Having deserted Paul, the two were later reconciled (*2 Timothy* 3:11-12).

Why and when did Mark write and for whom?

It is generally agreed by scholars that Mark's Gospel was the first to be written. Perhaps the most consistent opinion is that Mark, a Jew, wrote for Gentile Christians in Rome, sometime in the late 60s or early 70s. It seems clear from his emphasis on the suffering of Jesus that Mark is writing for people who themselves are undergoing persecution and who need to be encouraged by the example of the suffering Christ. During this time of persecution, they may have been tempted to doubt the viability of Christianity or to abandon it altogether out of fear of suffering or even death.

What are the special characteristics of Mark's Gospel?

As the first of the evangelists, Mark has truly invented a unique literary form, which has come to be known as "gospel." Certainly, before the writing of the first Gospel, there existed the oral preaching of the disciples and the letters of St. Paul. But here, for the first time, the deeds and sayings of Jesus were collected in a single narrative in an attempt to present the meaning of Christ in the lives of believers at the time of the writing. Mark, taking into account the needs of his audience, selected the events and sayings from the life of Jesus and arranged them in such a way that this audience would understand their meaning in their own lives. Later, Matthew and Luke organized their Gospels around the material found in *Mark*.

Mark's Gospel is clearly divided into two parts. In the first half of the Gospel, Jesus reveals great power and authority, both in action (miracles) and in teaching. Great emphasis is placed on the "authority" of Jesus—a constant source of misunderstanding. Often it is the demons who recognize him rather than those who should be his disciples. This leads to his frequent command to keep silent about his miracles. This messianic secret, so characteristic in *Mark*, is the evangelist's way of insisting that the authority and power of Jesus are not to be identified only in his miracles, but also in his death and resurrection. Until he is recognized for who he truly is, he does not want his name or his actions revealed.

The second part begins with the focal point of the Gospel. This comes in 8:29 when Jesus asks the disciples, *"Who do you say that I am?"* The answer to his question (*"the Son of man who must suffer many things, and be rejected by the elders and the chief priests and the scribes, and be killed, and after three days rise again"*) leads us into the second part of the Gospel. From this point on, Mark will insist that fidelity to this Christ is the hallmark of discipleship. The disciple is one who, like Jesus, suffers what is necessary for the mission. Only if one truly understands the cross will one understand resurrection. Mark's is a message of victory through suffering.

The portrait of Jesus that emerges in Mark's Gospel is Jesus—Son of God, Son of Man—who suffered the human condition and invites us to follow him. We are called to resurrection. But the journey there is by way of the cross.

16. Introduction to the Gospel of Luke

Who is Luke?

The New Testament tells us more about Luke than any other evangelist. He was the companion to St. Paul on his missionary journeys and remained his "dear friend," "co-worker," and "beloved physician." He himself tells us that he was a careful writer (*Luke* 1:1-4) who wrote both the life of Jesus and the early life of the church (*Luke* 1:1). Luke was a convert from paganism who was familiar with both Jewish and Gentile customs.

When and why did Luke write and for whom?

The Gospel of Luke, written perhaps between 75 and 90 AD, emphasizes the universal salvation of all people, Jew and Gentile alike. Luke's primary purpose in writing seems to be to renew the faith and fidelity of Christian converts living outside of Palestine who had lost some of their earlier zeal. They had allowed community factions to occupy their attention and Luke reminds them that true discipleship means responding to the Gospel in concrete, daily situations within the community. Their very community life is to be a witness.

What are the specific characteristics of Luke's Gospel?

Luke presents the story of Jesus within the framework of a long journey. As Jesus presses on toward Jerusalem to his death, resurrection and ascension, he teaches, exhorts, and manifests his power as Lord. To those who follow him on this journey, he reveals his mission, a mission which, for Luke, has four specific characteristics: the prominence of the Holy Spirit, the importance of prayer, an attitude of joy and a special concern for marginal people such as foreigners, women and social outcasts.

He recounts stories of such people which are found only in his Gospel: the Good Samaritan, the sinful woman, the ten lepers, the widow at Nain, the good thief, the pharisee and the publican, and the prodigal son. And Luke includes more women in his Gospel than the other three combined. To all people, and especially to those without status, Luke gives the assurance of the tender mercy of God.

More than either Matthew or Mark, Luke presents the Holy Spirit as the creative power of God: in the Incarnation, in the mission of Jesus, and in the lives of the disciples. Jesus announces his mission on earth with a quotation from the prophet Isaiah, *"The Spirit of God is upon me"* (*Luke* 4:18). It is this same Spirit that works in and through the disciples as a sign of God's saving power on earth.

God's saving power is cause for joy and Luke's Gospel abounds with this attitude. His Infancy Narrative contains four songs of joy sung by Zachariah, the angels, Mary and Simeon. And Luke tells us that there will be great joy in heaven over each sinner who repents.

The mission of Jesus and, therefore, of his disciples, is accomplished through prayer. Unlike the accounts of Matthew and Mark, Luke tells us specifically that Jesus was at prayer when he was baptized, at the Transfiguration, before choosing the twelve apostles, and before teaching the Lord's prayer. Frequently, Luke introduces a teaching or a healing story with the phrase, "while he was at prayer."

The portrait of Jesus that emerges from Luke's Gospel is the Lord of all, whose Spirit enlivens the disciples, and who calls us to live out his mission in daily, real-life situations within the Christian community.

"And the Word was made flesh and dwells among us . . ."
John 1:14

172

PLANNING AND EVALUATION

Centering song or music _____

Welcome: *(Inspired by focus of readings)*

Readings:

First _____ Reader _____

Responsorial Psalm _____ Singer _____

Gospel Acclamation _____ Reader _____

Gospel _____ Reader _____

Reflections on Readings: *(Personal notes)*

Special Activities: *(Dramatization, reading in parts, environment, etc.)*

Symbolic Actions: *(Including special rites, gestures, banner, etc.)*

Prayers: *(Creed, prayer of the faithful)*

Evaluation of the Celebration of the Word:

What went well:

What needs improvement:

Please duplicate this form for your leaders. Use it every week.

Appendix

Supporting the vital role of parents . . .
BRINGING GOD'S WORD INTO THE HOME

The celebration of the Word with children offers parishes a natural way of involving parents in the Christian initiation and formation of their children at home. The vision of the "Directory for Masses With Children" and the "Order for the Christian Initiation of Adults" as it applies to children brings a new focus on parents and significant adults in the lives of children. This involvement of parents means more than simply organizing religious education programs to which parents bring their children. It means adults (parents) are responsible for personally sharing their faith with those children who are part of their lives.

We can support adults in this Christian duty by the kind of material we give them to use at home. Something as simple as a weekly children's leaflet with the Sunday scriptures adapted in language children understand can make the difference in whether or not this sharing of Christian faith actually happens.

Don't misunderstand. The medium, as the expression goes, is still the message. This is not to say that children's leaflets are the message. *God's Word made flesh in us is the message.* The way we live and how we respond to God's Word is a primary source of influence on children. That is why we need to reflect with children on what God is saying to us when we gather each week to celebrate God's presence in the Word.

Children's leaflets help make this happen. Sending leaflets home with God's Word illustrated for children to see and reflect upon through the week is a vital part of the SUNDAY celebration series. So often, parishes invest only in materials for leaders to use when children gather—and fail to provide parents with the help they need to nurture the faith of their children at home. Parents and children need this simple support. The SUNDAY leaflets for parents and children have been carefully thought out and designed to keep in focus on God's Word—not on what someone else tells parents and children to hear *about* God's Word.

Should children's leaflets have lots of activities?

The function of children's leaflets is to put into the hands of parents and children God's Word in language and illustrations children understand. No more and no less. Attempts are often made by publishers to give children things to do— crossword puzzles and fill-in-the-blanks kind of "learning" activities. Often these activities distract children from focusing on God's Word and responding in prayer or quiet reflection.

Leaflets filled with "learning" activities and "gospel applications" often reveal a lack of faith in the power of God's Word to initiate in children their own original and creative response. Children's leaflets, such as those in the SUNDAY series, can successfully focus the child on God's Word by providing illustrations—conceived to embrace the message of the scriptures—that the child can color or paint as a reflective activity. Or, the child might be invited to create a prayer in response to the readings. We facilitate. God's Word creates.

Should children's leaflets be graded?

There is a notion carried over from the sacramental preparation (or classroom) model that raises this question about grading children's leaflets, liturgies and the scripture readings. The Christian initiation model sees older children as "companions" on the journey; their interaction with younger children is formative of the entire community. In other words, Christian initiation has less to do with age than it does with disposition of the heart. Also, in the home, parents do not relate to their children as a "graded system" but as a family sharing common experiences.

Furthermore, the lectionary is not a textbook of God's Word. Though we learn from the readings, the lectionary is not a book for education but for celebration—designed to facilitate children's participation in the liturgical experience of God's presence in the Word. While some parishes may feel a need to gather the very young children (3 to 5 years old) for a greatly simplified celebration, older children can gather in a mixed age group and be enriched by their varied responses to God's Word. Children's leaflets that include picture-story illustrations, such as those in the SUNDAY series, help even very young children grasp enough understanding of the scriptures to feel they are part of the celebration.

Do families really use the leaflets at home?

This question often masks another concern, parish finances, for good reason—parish budgets are usually tight. We want to be sure money is well spent. We get uneasy when we can't see someone using something for which we have paid good money. A leaflet blowing across the empty parking lot makes one wonder, not only about what's happening at home, but also about what support we give parents from the pulpit and the quality of our liturgies.

Experience has shown that the children's leaflets are not only used, but families have complained when they didn't get theirs. Experience has also shown that when the use of leaflets is encouraged from the pulpit, parents respond positively. Admonitions may reduce parking lot litter but will accomplish little toward an intelligent use of the leaflets at home.

We need to keep focused on what we're about—enriching the community's response to God's Word. If our liturgies provide adults and children with a rich experience of God's presence in the celebration of the Word, families will value God's Word and carry that sense of presence into the home. Although we may not see to verify and measure it, the adapted readings carried home in the children's leaflets will help families sustain the spirit of God's presence in the Word at home. This happens in simple ways: at mealtime conversations, at bedtime prayer, when the children are coloring or painting the scripture illustrations.

Even in the best of parish worlds, we cannot be certain that families will not occasionally leave leaflets behind. We can be certain, however, that if we do *not* provide parents with leaflets, then *none* of the families will take them home. That may give us control, but it does not give families the support for which they hunger.

When is the best time
to distribute the children's leaflets?

The best time is after mass. It seems obvious, but some communities give leaflets to the children during their celebration of the Word. Children's leaflets that contain the readings adapted for children are not to be used as some parishes use missalettes. (Nor should children's leaflets that contain activities and paraphrases of the readings be used at the celebration.) A basic liturgical principle is involved here: God's Word is to be proclaimed and heard in a dramatic ritual style. (Those who cannot hear may want to read from a book.) Also, the celebration of the Word is not the time for "learning" activities. It is the time to celebrate God's presence in song and prayer and shared reflections.

Other parishes distribute children's leaflets at the end of their celebration when they return to the adult assembly. Such use invites distractions during the celebration of the eucharist. Again, this practice should be avoided.

The most suitable time to distribute leaflets is after mass. Then the leaders of the celebration of the Word have a chance to make contact with the families. The children are excited about receiving the leaflets and begin to look at them during the ride (walk) home. Their interest provides an opportunity for family members to share their responses to God's Word.

There is no more natural way in which to involve parents in the Christian initiation of their children than through sharing the celebration of the Word throughout the liturgical year. Such sharing draws children into the heart of the Christian community and invites us all to grow up in Christ.

Gerard A. Pottebaum

Resources

Note: This listing of publications includes both basic documents and materials that will help you implement the celebration of the word with children. While these materials come from a variety of publishers, they are available through a single source (prices subject to change):

Treehaus Communications, Inc.
P.O. Box 249
Loveland, Ohio 45140
(800) 638-4287
Fax: (513) 683-2882

A Child Shall Lead Them:
A Guide to Celebrating the Word With Children

Anyone who celebrates the Word with children should follow *A Child Shall Lead Them*. It places celebrating with children within the context of the spiritual life of children. Moreover, it captures the vision and sensitively applies the guidelines of *The Directory for Masses With Children*. Highly recommended for inservice training, the Guide follows the celebration step-by-step, giving detailed reflections and ideas on each step as the ritual unfolds. An indispensable resource for anyone who celebrates the Word with children.

Editor/Contributing Author: Gerard A. Pottebaum
Contributing Authors: Sister Paule Freeburg, D.C. & Joyce M. Kelleher.
144 pp. Treehaus/1992 ISBN 0-929496-65-5
$9.95

To Walk With A Child:
Homiletics for Children/A Guide

As the practice of celebrating the Word with children spreads, the need for training homilists becomes more crucial. This is not a book of a hundred-and-one sermon ideas. Rather, it helps homilists and children to see life from inside the Word, drawing upon their rich imagination, as well as this sense of awe and celebration in the presence of God. By Gerard A. Pottebaum.

170 pp. Treehaus/1993 ISBN 0-929496-95-7
$9.95

Sing God A Simple Song

Sing God A Simple Song does more than the ear may hear. Our children need to feel they belong. Singing together provides this experience of belonging as profoundly as does sharing food. So does our parish music serve to initiate our children into the ritual life of our parish assembly, even when our children meet in separate Liturgies of the Word. For this purpose, *Sing God A Simple Song* provides a selection of music children can sing—music drawn from the parish assembly's repertoire.

The accompanying CD recording provides the melody of each song, sung by children, to help those who cannot play an instrument learn or recall the tune. We hope that this practical aid will help more and more children and leaders to . . . sing God a simple song.

128 pp. Treehaus/1995 ISBN 1-886510-03-2 Bk
ISBN 1-886510-02-4 Bk/CD Set
Set: $29.95 Additional Books $14.95

Jesus and the Children

Author/scholar Hans-Ruedi Weber explores the often quoted—and often misunderstood—references to children in the Gospel. Just what was Jesus' relationship with children? What was the place of children in Jewish culture and Graeco-Roman society? While focusing on key references to children in the Gospel, *Jesus and the Children* explores what Jesus teaches us adults through children. Complete with study outlines, helpful comparisons of texts from four Gospel accounts. For catechists, parents, and anyone who wants to gain a new insight into the Gospel through the metaphor of children.

164 pp. Treehaus/1995 ISBN 0-929496-96-5
$12.95

CIC UPDATE
The Christian Initiation of Children Newsletter

The CIC UPDATE Newsletter is published four times a year. Its purpose is to keep readers informed of developments in the Christian initiation of children, particularly as envisioned by the RCIA and the *Directory for Masses With Children*. You can receive CIC UPDATE through individual or bulk subscriptions. For complete information contact Treehaus Communications, Inc. (800) 638-4287.

The Rite of Christian Initiation of Adults
Study Edition

The complete text of the rite together with additional rites approved for use in the dioceses of the United States of America. The order for the Christian initiation of children is an integral part of the RCIA and the context within which the Christian initiation of children is to function.

396 pp. LTP/1988 ISBN 0-930467-94-9 $8.00

The Directory for Masses With Children

This document provides the official guidelines for eucharistic celebrations with children as well as for celebrations of the word with children at gatherings attended largely by adults. The *Directory* is essential reading for those who want to enrich children's worship. It is concerned with all the ways of initiating children into full and active participation in the liturgical life of the church. Its perspective is broad and its guidelines practical.

24 pp. USCC/1973 ISBN 1-55586-291-8 $1.95

The Church Speaks About Sacraments
With Children

This brief volume contains excerpts from basic church documents related to the Christian initiation of children. Mark Searle provides an illuminating commentary that will help pastoral leaders formulate guidelines for the initiation of children.

66 pp. LTP/1990 $4.50

Sharing our Biblical Story
Revised Edition

Joseph P. Russell has written an idea book for religious educators and parents that shows how to base Christian education on the Bible stories that occur in the context of worship. This book focuses on biblical stories from each of the three cycles (with variations in readings as they appear in the lectionaries of different denominations), provides background material and offers suggestions for emphasis.

346 pp. Morehouse-Barlow/1988
ISBN 0-8192-1425-6 $19.95

The Spiritual Life of Children

Robert Coles, professor of psychiatry and medical humanities at Harvard University, has spent 30 years listening to children around the world and is one of the most respected contributors of our time to our understanding of the culture of children. In this book, Dr. Coles shows us children face to face with the idea of God, in whose presence they seem to be fearless. Children discourse on the nature of God's wishes, on the devil, heaven and hell, faith and skepticism. Recommended for parents as well as parish leaders.

378 pp. Houghton Mifflin/1991
ISBN 0-395-55999-5 $10.95

The Children's God

David Heller, a clinical psychologist, interviewed forty children of four different religious backgrounds (Jewish, Catholic, Baptist, and Hindu) about God. Though he finds some differing views attributable to age, gender, and religious background, he discovers to a surprising degree a common vision of God that cuts across ethnic and religious differences.

151 pp. Univ. of Chicago Press/1986
ISBN 0-226-32636-5 $8.95

The Religious Potential of the Child
Second English Edition

This book describes an experience with children from ages three to six, an experience of adults and children dwelling together in the mystery of God. Author Sofia Cavalletti offers a glimpse into the religious life of the atrium, a specially prepared place for children to live out their silent request: "Help me come closer to God by myself." Preface by Mark Searle.

248 pp. LTP/1992 ISBN 0-929650-67-0 $12.95

The Christian Initiation of Children:
Hope for the Future

Robert D. Duggan and Maureen A. Kelly provide a challenging vision and practical suggestions for restructuring parish religious education practices to complement the implementation of the *Rite of Christian Initiation of Adults.* An excellent description of the convergence of liturgy and catechetics and its ramifications for shaping the future church.

138 pp. Paulist Press/1991 ISBN 0-8091-3258-3 $6.95

The SUNDAY Handbook for Ministers of the Word

A practical resource for every minister of the word—provides methodology a well as an over-view of biblical texts and liturgical seasons. Developed under the direction of Christiane Brusselmans.

32 pp. w/pocket cover Treehaus/1989 ISBN 0-929496-06-X $7.95

SUNDAY Lectionary for Children

The Sunday lectionary adapted for children, endorsed for liturgical use by the Canadian Conference of Catholic Bishops, features: inclusive language, large type, lines of text end to complement natural speaking breaks, adapted in keeping with the *Directory for Masses With Children*, handsomely bound for use in celebrations of the word. Year A, B, and C in separate volumes. Developed under the direction of Christiane Brusselmans with Sr. Paule Freeburg, D.C., Rev. Edward Matthews, Christopher Walker.

172 pp. Treehaus/1991-92 ISBN 0-929496-38-8 (Year A); ISBN 0- 929496-57-4 (Year B); ISBN 0-929496-91-4 (Year C) $29.95 each when purchased in a set ($49.95 individually)

SUNDAY Leader's Weekly Guide

Each volume covers 52 Sundays and special feasts. Each celebration features: 1) Focus of the Readings; 2) Ideas for Reflecting on the Readings with Children; 3) the Sunday readings adapted for children; 4) Music for Responses and Gospel Acclamations; 5) Prayer of the Day.

Also features Background to the Sunday Readings and Liturgical Seasons as well as Planning & Evaluation Form. Developed under the direction of Christiane Brusselmans with Sr. Paule Freeburg, D.C., Rev. Edward Matthews, Christopher Walker.

178 pp. Treehaus/1990-93 ISBN 0-929496-93-0 (Year A); ISBN 0- 929496-58-2 (Year B); ISBN 929496-92-2 (Year C) $29.95 each when purchased in set of 3. ($49.95 individually.) Contact Treehaus for bulk discounts.

The SUNDAY Liturgy of the Word &
Catechetical Planning Guides

These are the only guides available that carefully relate the formative character of liturgy and catechetics while keeping the two distinct. A significant addition to the SUNDAY family of Christian initiation materials, these Guides feature a process for reflecting on the word with children in both liturgical and catechetical settings. The Guides also provide comprehensive plans with suggested musical resources, accom-panying gestures and ritual activities, biblical and liturgical background notes, as well as Creeds and Prayers of the Faithful based on the readings and appropriate for children. Published and mailed quarterly (148-160 pp. per quarter).

Treehaus/1995 $24.95 per quarter

SUNDAY Family Leaflets

These four-page and six-page weekly leaflets are for use at home or school after the Sunday celebration. They feature: the Sunday readings adapted for children ages 5 to 12 years; picture-story illustrations of the readings; prayers; and description of biblical people and places. Essential for family involvement and continued reflection on the word at home.

Weekly / Treehaus / Call (800) 638-4287 for bulk rates & discounts.

MY SUNDAY SHEPHERD
Family Leaflets

These full-color seasonal leaflets are for families with children 3 to 5 years old. Designed to help the young child take those first steps—

hand-in-hand with parents—in celebrating the gospel story on Sunday and responding in praise throughout the week. *My Sunday Shepherd* initiates the young child gradually into the liturgical life of the church through a prayerful family life. Each leaflet features a story-picture of the Sunday gospel on one side and, on the other side, a prayer guide that helps parents pray in a way that enables their children to pray with them and to respond to God's word throughout the week. Set of 8 leaflets and 1 Parent Guide for each of the following seasons: Advent/Christmas; Lent/Easter Sunday; Eastertide/Pentecost.

Weekly during these seasons / Treehaus / Call (800) 638-4287 for subscription information and bulk discounts.

SUNDAY Scripture Response Posters

A complete series of 53 beautiful posters (17 x 22 inches), designed to be decorated or colored by leaders, helpers, or parents, for use during the celebration of the word. Each poster features the enlarged text of Responses and Gospel Acclamations and a large picture-story illustration of the Sunday scriptures. Especially helpful for younger children. Available for all three cycles, Year A, B, and C.

Weekly / Treehaus / Call (800) 638-4287 for prices and discounts.

How to Celebrate the Word With Children . . . and Why
Video

Features a demonstration celebration with commentary by Father Edward Matthews, one of the primary authors of the *Directory for Masses With Children.*

30 minutes with guide / Treehaus /1990 $49.95

SUNDAY: A Basic Celebration Resource
Video

A video "dictionary" for the SUNDAY Celebration of the Word material, hosted by Christiane Brusselmans and Gerard A. Pottebaum. Each element of the SUNDAY Celebration of the Word

material is defined, along with its uses. An important tool for any parish developing liturgies that respect the spiritual life of children.

21 Minutes / Treehaus /1990 $19.95

How Parishes Are Celebrating The Word With Children
Video

A TRAINING AID / FOUR ILLUSTRATIONS

This video serves a critical need: training ministers of the Word. Observe and learn from four parishes including Anglo, Hispanic, and African-American where children celebrate the Word together. A study guide aids identifying and discussing what is and is not appropriate practice. Running time: 10, 19, 13, and 9 minutes. Includes guide.

Treehaus/1993 Rental: $15.00 Purchase: $49.95

The Children's Lectionary for Sunday Masses

In 1993 the U.S. Catholic Bishops released for publication the texts of the Sunday readings adapted for children and approved for liturgical use. Several publishers are releasing various editions of these adapted readings. We have chosen to co-distribute a handsomely bound edition with The Liturgical Press. While maintaining the flavor of biblical language, this lectionary is suited for older children (above primary grades) and is not comprehensive in the use of inclusive language. You can order the Sunday readings in separate volumes or in combination with the weekday readings.

Ritual Edition: Year A, B, C / Sunday with Weekday - $29.95 ea.
Ritual Edition: Year A, B, C / Sunday only - $19.95 ea.
Study Edition: Year A, B, C / Sunday only - $9.95 ea.

Index of Scripture Readings